A

MEMOIR

OF

THE LIFE AND TIMES

OF THE

REV. ISAAC BACKUS, A.M.

BY

ALVAH HOVEY, D.D.,

PROFESSOR OF CHRISTIAN THEOLOGY IN NEWTON THEOLOGICAL INSTITUTION.

BOSTON:
GOULD AND LINCOLN,
59 WASHINGTON STREET.
NEW YORK: SHELDON, BLAKEMAN & CO.
CINCINNATI: GEORGE S. BLANCHARD.
1859.

ELECTROTYPED AND PRINTED
BY W. F. DRAPER, ANDOVER, MASS.

TO THE

REV. BARNAS SEARS, D.D., LL.D.

WHOSE

INSTRUCTIONS IN THE DEPARTMENT OF ECCLESIASTICAL HISTORY,

AND WHOSE WORDS OF ENCOURAGEMENT WHEN MOST

NEEDED, WILL NEVER BE FORGOTTEN;

AND

TO THE REV. SILAS HALL,

THE

RESULTS OF WHOSE CAREFUL EXAMINATION AND ARRANGEMENT OF

THE BACKUS PAPERS, AS WELL AS OF MUCH ADDITIONAL LABOR,

HAVE BEEN GENEROUSLY BESTOWED;

This Work

IS GRATEFULLY INSCRIBED.

BY

THE AUTHOR.

PREFACE.

MORE than four years have passed since the writer was requested, by the councillors of the Backus Historical Society, to prepare for the press a new edition of the Ecclesiastical History of New England, by the Rev. Isaac Backus. Several considerations, some of which may be specified, led him to attempt a compliance with this request.

It seemed quite possible for one who was entrusted with the department of Church History in this Institution, to perform such a task, not only without detriment to his special work, but even with some prospect of advantage, as it would prepare him, partially at least, to satisfy a desire which had been expressed by friends of Newton, that the history of baptized Christians in modern times might enter more largely into the course of instruction.

And further, it seemed desirable that a new edition of the history mentioned above should be published with all convenient despatch, inasmuch as it had become very rare and almost inaccessible, while at the same time it was of great value, both as a storehouse of important facts not elsewhere preserved, and as a record of sentiments worthy of attention at the present day. It was felt that it would be a great oversight in the Baptist denomination to suffer this memorial of their New England fathers to perish, and that the time which might be consumed in preparing a new edition would be wisely spent in the Master's service.

It also seemed reasonable to expect that the publication of this valuable history would serve to awaken a deeper and more general interest in the society which had given it afresh to the public. And the coöperation of a large number was looked upon as indispensable to success in carrying out the purposes of the society, and thus securing the objects for which it was formed. These objects, it is generally known, were two; first, to collect, so far as possible, and preserve at some accessible point, the materials which still exist for a history of the Baptist denomination, especially in New England; and, secondly, to secure from time to time the publication of such monographs or more general works as might be deemed of present interest and permanent value.

The object first named was understood to be of paramount importance and to demand immediate attention. Many documents were believed to be still in existence, which are necessary to elucidate the history of the denomination, and which, unless systematic efforts were made to collect and preserve them, must speedily and inevitably perish. Pamphlets, addresses and periodicals, centennial, semi-centennial and funeral discourses, minutes of conventions, associations and councils, manuscript sermons, journals, and records of extinct churches, in short a great variety of papers, unpublished as well as published, which were written by Christians of a former age, are still preserved in the older Baptist dwellings, which, if brought together and properly arranged, would be invaluable to every student of the past. It is only, however, by gathering them together and thus uniting and blending their scattered rays of light, that they can avail to illuminate the darkness of an earlier period. Separately their light is too feeble and uncertain to guide the explorer's steps. Hence the wisdom of immediate and systematic efforts to obtain and deposit in a suitable place these frail and diminishing but precious records. To secure the coöperation of their brethren throughout New England in accomplishing this primary object of the society, it was deemed advisable by the Board of Councillors to undertake at once a new edition of Backus's History. It was at the same time proposed that this new edition be introduced by some account of the Life and Times of Isaac Backus; and the fruit of this proposal is the present volume.

By way of apology for the late appearance of this volume, the writer desires to say that the preparation of it has involved a much larger amount of historical investigation than was anticipated at the outset; and that a change in his sphere of labor in the Institution, made soon after he undertook the present work, has diminished very greatly the amount of time which he could devote to it.

If the following pages do not give so favorable an account of churches of the standing order, during the last century, as might have been expected from the high character of Congregationalists as a body at the present day, it should be borne in mind that the regular churches of that period comprised certain heterogeneous elements which have since parted asunder and become two very distinct if not antagonistic bodies. It should also be remembered that the presence in the community of a growing denomination which insists upon a credible profession of faith as prerequisite to church membership, must have had a powerful tendency to bring every other evangelical denomination to insist upon the same thing. And, finally, it should be noted, that, owing to peculiar circumstances, Mr. Backus was led to expose the errors and defects of the standing order more frequently, perhaps, than to commend the right principles maintained or illustrated by it.

Should it be thought that undue prominence has been given in this volume to the question of religious liberty, or that it is unwise to perpetuate the remembrance of wrongs which have passed away forever, it may be answered that no more prominence has been given to the subject specified than was necessary in order to afford the reader a true idea of Mr. Backus and his life; and that the spirit of religious oppression is not so thoroughly eradicated from the hearts of men as to relieve thoughtful observers of all apprehension as to the future. Is it not customary even now to excuse or justify the fathers of Massachusetts by saying: "they simply expelled from their commonwealth those who stubbornly refused to comply with requisitions which they deemed essential?" and by adding: "they were a voluntary association, and had certainly a right to prescribe the rules of their own society?" Just as if men have a right to bind themselves under civil pains and penalties not to receive any more light from the Word of God! and not to relinquish any error which they now ignorantly hold! Or as if they have a right to bind their own children, under pain of banishment, to believe just what they believe! or to dispossess their neighbor of his property and home because his conscience will no longer permit him to endorse their views of God's truth! While such opinions are advocated by intelligent and influential men, liberty of conscience, and the relation of civil government to the Church of Christ, cannot be properly understood.

It remains for the writer to express his gratitude to those who have assisted him in this work; and in particular to the Rev. Frederick Denison, of Norwich, Connecticut, for examining and transcribing important records preserved in that place, both at the Backus homestead and elsewhere; to the Rev. Silas Hall, who generously placed in the writer's hands the results of his protracted study of the Backus papers, and at the same time communicated his early impressions and recollections of the subject of this narrative; and to one whose name he is not permitted to mention, but without whose aid in transcribing nearly the whole work, its publication must have been indefinitely postponed.

May the Head of the Church accept this memorial of one who recognized His authority and loved His service, and make it a blessing to Zion!

A. H.

NEWTON THEOLOGICAL INSTITUTION,
October 18, 1858.

CONTENTS.

CHAPTER I.

MOULDING INFLUENCES.

CHAPTER II.

CONVERSION.

CHAPTER III.

BACKUS A SEPARATIST.

CHAPTER IV.

CALL TO THE MINISTRY.

CHAPTER V.

ITINERANT PREACHING AND SETTLEMENT.

CHAPTER VI.

EARLY PASTORSHIP AND MARRIAGE.

CHAPTER VII.

CHANGE OF BELIEF RESPECTING BAPTISM.

CHAPTER VIII.

COUNCIL UPON COUNCIL.

CHAPTER IX.

BACKUS BECOMES A REGULAR BAPTIST.

CHAPTER X.

JOY IN SERVICE.

CHAPTER XI.

LEGISLATION FOR THE CHURCH.

CHAPTER XII.

WIDER INFLUENCE.

CHAPTER XIII.

EFFORTS FOR RELIGIOUS LIBERTY.

CHAPTER XIV.

BACKUS AS AGENT.

CHAPTER XV.

VISIT TO PHILADELPHIA.

CHAPTER XVI.

SHARP CONTROVERSY.

CHAPTER XVII.

THE BILL OF RIGHTS.

CHAPTER XVIII.

LIBERTY SECURED AT LAST.

CHAPTER XIX.

MINISTERIAL AND HISTORICAL LABORS.

CHAPTER XX.

LETTERS FROM CORRESPONDENTS.

CHAPTER XXI.

CHARACTER OF BACKUS.

APPENDIXES.

LIFE AND TIMES OF ISAAC BACKUS.

CHAPTER I.

MOULDING INFLUENCES.

SILENCE OF CHRISTIANS AS TO THEIR LIFE BEFORE CONVERSION. — NO ACCOUNT OF THE EARLY LIFE OF MR. BACKUS. — BEST SUBSTITUTE FOR SUCH AN ACCOUNT. — CONGREGATIONALISM OF THE PLANTERS OF CONNECTICUT. — CAMBRIDGE PLATFORM. — CONNECTION OF CHURCH AND STATE — TENDENCY TO PRESBYTERIANISM. — SAYBROOK PLATFORM. — GENERAL ADOPTION OF IT. — REJECTION OF IT IN NORWICH. — CHARACTER OF MR. BACKUS'S GRANDFATHER. — OF HIS GRANDMOTHER. — OF HIS FATHER. — OF HIS MOTHER. — EXTRACTS FROM HER LETTERS. — HIS LITERARY EDUCATION IN YOUTH.

MANY of the early Christians looked upon their existence prior to conversion as unworthy of being called life, and spoke of the time which brought them into fellowship with Christ by His Spirit as the day of their birth. When therefore for any reason they gave a biographical account of themselves or of others, very little attention was paid to that which preceded their reception of Christ. "Whence shall I begin," inquires *Pontius*, in his life of *Cyprian*, "but from the dawn of his faith and from his celestial life?" The Confessions of Augustine are an important exception to our statement; and the flood of light which they pour upon his own character and upon the age in which he lived awakens deep regret at the mistake of others in consigning their early history to oblivion.

But this mistake was not confined to the primitive Christians. Not a few servants of Jesus since that period have pursued the same course. They have been led by a sense of the sovereign mercy of God to leave behind them some memorial of His grace to their souls, but they have forborne, for wise reasons it may be, to magnify the riches of that grace, as did Bunyan, by recounting the sins of their youth. An illustration is before us. *John Leland* begins a sketch of his own life in the following words: " *Volumes* might be written upon the wanderings, darkness and errors of my life, which would afford no pleasure to others in hearing thereof, and to relate which would be of no advantage to me; therefore, I shall pass them by, and attend only to a few of God's gracious and notable dealings with me, a great sinner, in my ministerial labors."

Unfortunately for the interest of our present work, Isaac Backus treated his early life with almost equal neglect. It will therefore be impossible for us to give any particular account of his childhood and youth. But in place of this, and as the best substitute for it, we shall endeavor to describe the community and family in which this formative period of his life was passed. It will be evident, we think, from this description, that the influences of friends and home in the morning of life were so ordered by the God of providence as to aid in preparing him for the work of later years. The social and domestic atmosphere which surrounded him in youth, conspired, with the natural gifts which he possessed, and with the renewing grace of God, to qualify him for the arduous and peculiar labors which he rendered to the cause of truth.

The churches of Connecticut were originally congregational in their polity. "They maintained that the right of choosing and settling their ministers, of exercising discipline and performing all judicial acts, was in the church, when properly organized; and they denied all external or foreign power of presbyteries, synods, general councils or assemblies."[1] Ordination was regarded "as no more than putting the pastor elect into office, or a solemn recommending of him and his labors to the blessing of God. * * * It was the general opinion, that elders ought to lay on hands in ordination, if there were a presbytery in the church, but if there were not, the church might appoint some other elders or a number of the brethren to that service.[2] Moreover the earliest ministers of Connecticut "at first maintained, that all the pastor's office-power was confined to his own church and congregation, and that the administering of baptism and the Lord's Supper in other churches was irregular."[3] So careful were they at first to guard against the introduction of presbyterianism or prelacy, against any proper dependence of one church upon another!

Accordingly, when Mr. James Fitch was ordained at Saybrook in 1646, "although Mr. Hooker was present, hands were imposed by two or three of the principal brethren, whom the church had appointed to that service."[4] This account is given by Trumbull as "the tradition." It is however confirmed by the recorded action of the church when his successor was ordained. "A council of ministers and churches assisted at his ordination, but the imposition of hands was performed by the

1 Trumbull, History of Conn. I., p. 284.

2 Trumbull, I., p. 283, compare Cambridge Platform, c. 9.

3 Trumbull, I., p. 283, compare Cambridge Platform, c. 9.

4 Trumbull, I., p. 286.

brethren, as it had been before in the ordination of Mr. Fitch. The council considered it an irregular proceeding, but the brethren were so tenacious of what they esteemed their right, that it could not be prevented without much inconvenience."[1] This occurred in 1660, when Mr. Fitch, with a majority of his church and congregation, removed from Saybrook and planted the town of Norwich. "Three or four planters joined them from New London, and two or three from the towns of Plymouth and Mansfield in Massachusetts."

The first settlers of Norwich were, therefore, beyond a doubt, zealous advocates of the Cambridge Platform and of the congregational polity. They believed every true church to be of right an independent body; and during the ministry of Mr. Fitch their convictions on this point were undisturbed.

But even in the Cambridge Platform principles were laid down inconsistent with the independence of the churches. For this document affirms, that "the end of the magistrate's office is not only the quiet and peaceable life of the subject in matters of righteousness and honesty, but also in matters of godliness, yea, of *all godliness;*" and again, "neither is their power to be exercised in commanding such acts of the outward man, and punishing the neglect thereof, as are but mere inventions and devices of men; but such acts as are commanded and forbidden in the Word; yea, such as the Word doth clearly determine, though not always clearly to the judgment of the magistrate or others, yet clearly in itself. In these he of right ought to put forth his authority, though ofttimes actually he doth it not." Idolatry, blasphemy, *heresy*, and the like, are then specified as things to be

[1] Trumbull, I., p. 286.

restrained and punished by civil authority, and it is said: "If any church, one or more, shall grow *schismatical, rending itself from the communion of other churches*, or shall walk incorrigibly or obstinately in any corrupt way of their own, contrary to the rule of the Word; in such case the magistrate is to put forth his *coercive* power, as the matter shall require." This language evidently claims for the standing order of churches in New England the same support from the civil power which in other lands is claimed for the papal church by the Romish hierarchy. It assigns the duty of preventing any important deviation from the faith or practice of the established churches to the civil power, and calls upon this power to bring heretics back into the fold even by coercion. This was in reality, though not formally and directly, subjecting every particular church to the authority and control of other churches; and it was doing this, not with spiritual but with carnal weapons.

To the control of other churches, we say; because, in Massachusetts, when this Platform was adopted, none but church members were allowed to participate in the civil government; and hence it must be presumed that the majority of electors, being at the same time the majority of church members, were able to put men in office whose views of ecclesiastical orthodoxy were identical with their own. Thus each particular church was liable to coercion from a power originated by the great body of churches and representing their judgment. *Vox populi vox Dei;* the voice of the people of God, or rather of the major part of them, was to be enforced by pains and penalties as the voice of God.

A similar connection between Church and State existed in Connecticut. In their original constitution the citizens of this Commonwealth say: "We * * * do, for ourselves and our successors, and such as shall be adjoined to us at any time hereafter, enter into combination and confederation together, to maintain and preserve the liberty and purity of the Gospel of *our* LORD JESUS, which we now profess, as also *the discipline of the churches, which, according to the truth of said Gospel, is now practised amongst us*," etc.; and they inserted a provision, "that the governor be always a member of some approved congregation," or, according to the interpretation of Trumbull, "a member of some regular church," and a "regular church," it is well known, was a church of the "standing order." Moreover, it was early enacted, "that no persons within this colony, shall in any wise embody themselves into church estate, without consent of the General Court, and approbation of neighboring elders," and we are told by the historian of Connecticut that "the General Court would not suffer any plantation to be made, which would not support an able, orthodox preacher."[1]

But the spirit and determination with which a people will assert their own religious freedom cannot always be measured by the degree of freedom which they possess, much less by the degree of freedom which they concede to differing consciences. This statement is illustrated by the ecclesiastical history of Norwich. In 1699, John Woodward succeeded Mr. Fitch as pastor of the church and people of this town. For several years harmony prevailed between the new pastor and his flock. But in 1708, the Legislature of Connecticut passed an act, requiring the ministers of the several counties in that colony to meet together at their respective county towns, with such messengers as their churches should see cause to send with

[1] Trumbull, I., p. 387.

them, to consider and agree upon a form of ecclesiastical discipline; also, to appoint two or more of their number as delegates to meet at Saybrook, and by comparing the results of the county meetings draw up a form of discipline for the churches, to be presented to the General Court and confirmed by the same. This was accordingly done; and Mr. Woodward was appointed one of the delegates from New London county. He appears to have been a hearty friend and supporter of the scheme.

Sixteen delegates—twelve ministers and four laymen—met at the place designated on the 9th of September 1708, and adopted the articles of discipline commonly known as the Saybrook Platform. These articles were promptly communicated to the Legislature, and in October 1708, were approved and established by the same; yet with the following proviso, "that nothing herein shall be intended or construed to hinder or prevent any society or church that is or shall be allowed by the laws of this government, who soberly differ or dissent from the united churches hereby established, from exercising worship and discipline, in their own way according to their consciences." "Mr. John Woodward, then minister of Norwich," says Isaac Backus, "soon got and read off to his congregation the first part of this act, but without the proviso. Richard Bushnel and Joseph Backus, esquires, who had opposed that scheme in the assembly, informed their church of the liberty they had to dissent from it; but the minister carried a major vote against them; therefore, those representatives, and other fathers of the town, withdrew * * * * and held worship by themselves for three months. For this the minister and his party censured them; an account of which being sent to the next meeting of the assembly, they were expelled therefrom. * * * * But not long after the Norwich minister had censured their representatives, he consented to refer the matter to a council; and they followed it with council after council for about six years. Governor Saltonstall came there himself upon one of those occasions, and Mr. Stoddard of Northampton was moderator of the last but one of those councils. * * * * At last, by advice of a council that met August 31st 1716, said minister was dismissed; and the church in Norwich determined to abide upon its ancient foundation. * * * * The church in East Windsor, under the care of Mr. Timothy Edwards, father of Mr. Jonathan, also refused to receive the Saybrook Platform."

It appears from the events just recited that the inhabitants of Norwich were distinguished for their adhesion to pure Congregationalism. While the churches generally accepted without hesitation the Saybrook Platform, the leading members of the church in Norwich resisted its acceptance with a persistent and successful resolution. By a formal agreement, Mr. Lord, the successor of Mr. Woodward, pledged himself at the time of his settlement to adhere to the Cambridge Platform, and peace was thereby restored to the church. And it is reasonable to presume that the long and serious contest between Mr. Woodward and some of his people made the whole community familiar with questions of church polity, and filled the social atmosphere with the spirit of ecclesiastical independence.

Having ascertained the ecclesiastical views and spirit of the people generally with whom Isaac Backus spent the early years of his life, we may now approach the narrower circle composed of his relatives, and examine the principles of those who had a more direct and controlling influence over his youthful mind. It will be found that his course in manhood was in no small degree the result of his training in boyhood, that his character through life was the ever ripening fruit of seed planted in his mind when a child. From the atmosphere of piety and freedom which pervaded the home of his youth he inhaled the spirit which animated him to the hour of death.

Joseph Backus, the grandfather of Isaac, was a leading man in the town. Besides being a Justice of the Peace, an officer of much dignity at that time, he was for several years a representative of Norwich in the Legislature of Connecticut. We have already mentioned his opposition to the Saybrook Platform in that body, and likewise his expulsion from it, because he had withdrawn with others from the church in Norwich when it accepted the Platform. This, however, did not abate his zeal. So anxious was he to have the church resume its former position and maintain the principles of Congregationalism, that he made a journey to Ipswich in Massachusetts, for the purpose of consulting with Mr. John Wise, minister of that place; for not long before Mr. Wise had written a keen and convincing answer to proposals for an ecclesiastical constitution in Massachusetts somewhat similar to that which had now been established in Connecticut. He desired Mr. Wise to publish a new edition of his answer, but the latter did not at that time see fit to comply with the request. Mr. Backus also visited the two Mathers in Boston, whose views upon the question at issue agreed with his own. He seems, indeed, from the brief notices which remain of him, to have been a genuine lover of "the old paths," an able and energetic defender of the congregational polity, a man of deep, radical convictions which governed his action and made him willing to suffer loss for the sake of Christ and His truth. The tone and spirit of such a man are a legacy to his offspring, and not unfrequently do they transmit themselves to the third or fourth generation.

His wife, the grandmother of Isaac, was altogether worthy of her companion. A woman of truly Puritanic energy and devotion, she survived her husband many years, living to a very advanced age, and is often mentioned in the journals of Isaac Backus, sometimes with admiration and always with great respect. A few of these references will be cited in the progress of our narrative.

Mr. John Tracy, grandfather of Isaac on his mother's side, "was a man eminent for vital and practical religion. He was strict in the religious education of his family; for which, we are told, his daughter was ever thankful as long as she lived." Indirectly through her he may be said to have participated in the early training of Isaac; but only thus, for in 1726, when the latter was but two years of age, he died, "with such comfortable views of another world, it is said, that he charged his friends to give him up and not hold him any longer by their prayers."[1]

Samuel Backus, the father of Isaac, was a quiet, enterprising farmer, prosperous in his own business, but having little to do with public affairs. He was an affectionate husband and kind father; but he made no profession of religion until 1736, four years previous to his death. It must therefore be presumed that his influence as a Christian upon the minds of his children was limited to this brief period. We find no evident allusions to it, in distinction from that of his wife, in the writings of his son.

The mother of Isaac Backus was, in the truest and highest sense of the expression, an excellent woman. Often does he speak of her in terms of deep respect and love. With special satisfaction does he dwell upon the fruits of

1 Backus. Gospel Comfort for Mourners. p. 19.

genuine piety which appeared in her life. In a sermon occasioned by her death he calls her "my dear *godly* mother;" and there is ample reason for the belief that she was worthy of such a designation. In order therefore to understand the christian influences pervading the domestic circle in which the early years of Isaac were passed, it will be necessary for us to exhibit more fully the character of his mother. This shall be done, for the most part, in her own language or in that of her son.

She was received into the regular church of Norwich in 1720, and sometime in the following year was, by the grace of God, made a living member of the household of faith.[1]

"She has often," says her son, "mentioned to her children a work of conviction and conversion which she experienced in the year 1721." From this time forward she manifested a tender solicitude for the spiritual welfare of her family, and illustrated in some good degree by her life the power of vital godliness. After the death of her husband in 1740, her christian character seems to have matured very rapidly. By the blessing of God, affliction bore fruit in sanctification. The following words which she wrote some time after the death of Mr. Backus will confirm the statement just made. "And now some months after this, having examined my case often, and comparing the case of my soul now with what it had been in months past, I could freely say from my heart, I could not be willing to be again in that sleepy state of soul towards God and the things that concern my everlasting peace, no, not to be in the most prosperous condition in temporal things that ever I was in, all my life. Now I can say, I hunger and thirst after the Word, it is

1 Denison. Historical Notes, p. 44. Compare Gospel Comfort, etc. p. 19.

the delight of my soul." The subjoined extracts from her correspondence with the subject of this work after his settlement in Middleboro' will reveal the exercises of her mind and the depth of her religious experience.

"Jan. 11, 1748. The Lord hath sweetly comforted and quickened my soul from time to time; I have had many sweet love-feasts. The Lord hath brought me into his banqueting house, and His banner over me was love."

"Oct. 21, 1748. The last Sabbath was a day much to be remembered. Your grandmother almost left the body. As to my own case, I have had a more abiding sense of the uncertainty of visible things and of the certainty of invisible things."

"March 26, 1750. My dear Son: I long you should hear of and rejoice with us in the work of God amongst us. It began the fore part of February, and for three weeks or more it was as great a time of conviction as I ever saw. Great flocking to hear the Gospel; meetings every day, especially among the children at our end of the town; sundry of them converted, some backsliders came home, and such adoring free grace, such calls and invitations to sinners, as make the town shake. * * * I remember my love in Jesus to the saints in the house where you live, and to all that little flock."

The following letter has been often published, but the present sketch would be imperfect without it.

"Norwich, Nov. 4, 1752. My dear Son; I have heard something of the trials amongst you of late, and I was grieved till I had strength to give up the case to God, and leave my burden there. And now I would tell you something of our trials. Your brother Samuel lay in prison twenty days. October 15th, the collectors came to our house, and took me away to prison, about nine o'clock, in a dark, rainy night. Brothers Hill and Sabins were brought there the next night. We lay in prison thirteen days, and were then set at liberty, by what means I know not. Whilst I was there a great many people came to see me, and some said one thing and some said another. Oh the innumerable snares and temptations that beset me! more than I ever thought of before. But oh, the condescension of Heaven! though I was bound when I was cast into this furnace, yet I was loosed and found Jesus in the midst of a furnace with me. Oh, then I could give up my name, estate, family, life and breath freely to God. Now the prison looked like a palace to me. I could bless God for all the laughs and scoffs made at me. Oh the love that flowed out to all mankind; then I could forgive as I would desire to be forgiven, and love my neighbor as myself. Deacon Griswold was put in prison the 8th of October; and yesterday old brother Grover, and [they] are in pursuit of others, all which calls for humiliation. This church has appointed the 13th of November to be spent in prayer and fasting on that account. I do remember my love to you and your wife, and the dear children of God with you, begging your prayers for us in such a day of trial. We are all in tolerable health, expecting to see you. These from your loving mother,

ELIZABETH BACKUS."

The Rev. F. Denison, of Norwich, mentions the following particulars respecting Mrs. Backus, when she was taken by the collectors for rates due to Mr. Lord, pastor of the regular church.[1] "She was sick, and, thickly wrapped

1 A fuller account of this matter will be found further on.

in clothes to produce perspiration, sat near the fire by her stand, reading the family Bible. The officer thought that, under the circumstances, she would yield and pay the rates. But Mrs. Backus was not the woman to abandon her religious principles."[1]

"March 20, 1754. Last Friday I was brought to a stand and made to see the awfulness of trifling away time. * * * And now I saw that a Christian cannot enjoy God and live in conformity to the world. * * * Oh that I might improve my time well!"

"June 15, 1754. I am still in the furnace, wave after wave rolling over me; and my God is graciously supporting, teaching and comforting my soul from time to time in the midst of my various trials. Blessed be his name! The cause of Zion lies near my heart, but there is hope in God, that is able to deliver."

"March 6, 1757. I am waiting for my great and last change. Scarce one day hath past for some months without some realizing sense of death and eternity. And though I am so full of sin, Jesus hath come over the mountains and spake peace to my soul."

"March 24, 1754. I tell you I am quite sick of myself, the more I am acquainted with my heart. But oh, how good is my Lord to me, who does many a time speak a word to my soul that gives it a lift with a view of the stability of the covenant of His faithfulness and loving kindness, and the sweetness of His kingly power in subduing us to himself. Praised be his name!"

And Isaac Backus says of his mother: "When He (Christ) granted a glorious visitation of his spiritual presence to this land, in the year 1741, it was as welcome and

[1] Historical Notes, p. 28. Compare Backus's "A Fish caught in his own Net," p. 21.

joyful a season to her as His personal company was to Elizabeth of old. Oh, how freely did she speak of the wonders of redeeming grace to her children and others around. And I believe very few have lived with more constant devotedness to God than she has ever since." In his sermon occasioned by her death, he remarks: "Did I say *loss?* Must I not retract the expression? For we are not wont to call our weary friends lost, when they are got to rest in a quiet sleep; and none sleep so quietly as those who sleep in Jesus. They have done their work and are receiving their reward, have fought the good fight and are shouting the glorious victory. And shall we begrudge them their happiness? Rather let us congratulate their safe arrival to the realms of peace."

Our account of the family in which the childhood and youth of Isaac Backus were spent, may be fitly closed by the following passage from an imperfect sketch of his life, written by himself, when more than eighty years old. "My mother sprang from the family of Mr. Winslow, who came over to Plymouth in 1620, and my father from one of the first planters in Norwich in Connecticut in 1660. My father, Samuel Backus, was born in Norwich, Jan. 6, 1693, and Elizabeth Tracy, my mother, on April 6, 1698; and they were married, January 18, 1716. Both they and their parents were members of the first church in Norwich, and trained up their children in the nurture and admonition of the Lord. I was born there January 9, 1724, and was well educated in the christian religion and also in the principles of civil liberty."

The literary advantages of Mr. Backus in early life were limited to the public schools of his native place. In these he learned the use of figures, became a ready penman, and acquired some knowledge of his native language.

Without brilliant parts, he possessed a good understanding, and became an accurate scholar in the branches of study which engaged his attention. Whether he acquired a taste for reading at this period we have not been able to ascertain, but even in youth, it is manifest he formed his mind to habits of careful observation and reflection, which were of great service to him in later years.

It is, however, for many reasons, to be regretted that his literary culture was so defective, since he possessed a natural taste for composition and was called, by Divine Providence, not only to take part in the ministry of reconciliation, but also to put on record a portion of the history of God's people. He was fully aware of this defect and made persevering efforts to remedy it. These efforts were in part successful; and if nevertheless in his best productions, there are few graces of style to attract the reader, the simplicity, perspicuity, integrity and manliness, which reveal themselves in every line, more than compensate for the lack of lighter attractions.

CHAPTER II.

CONVERSION.

DECLENSION OF RELIGION PREVIOUS TO THE GREAT AWAKENING. — REVIVAL AT NORTHAMPTON UNDER THE PREACHING OF EDWARDS. — FIRST LABORS OF WHITEFIELD IN NEW ENGLAND. — EXTENT OF THE GREAT AWAKENING. — KIND OF PREACHING BLESSED. — GENUINENESS OF THE WORK NOTWITHSTANDING IMPRUDENCES. — MR. BACKUS'S ACCOUNT OF HIS OWN CONVICTION AND CONVERSION.

MR. BACKUS refers the most important event of his life to a very interesting period in the history of New England, the time of the Great Awakening. Previous to this Awakening there had been a sad declension. Many persons had been educated for the ministry and had undertaken to perform its sacred duties while strangers to renewing grace, and therefore in many places the peculiar and efficacious truths of Christianity had been imperfectly taught or entirely overlooked. "We have long," says Jonathan Edwards, "been in a strange stupor; the influences of the Spirit of God upon the heart have been but little felt, and the nature of them but little taught." "No serious Christian," writes another, "could behold it without a heavy heart, and scarce without a weeping eye, — to see the solid, substantial piety, for which our ancestors were justly renowned, having long languished under sore decays, brought so low, and seemingly just ready to expire and give up the ghost."

It must, however, be remarked, as an evidence of remaining life, that Christians were deeply conscious of the stupor and coldness complained of. There were, moreover, during this period, several local revivals which served to awaken a general desire in the hearts of believers for a "time of refreshing from the presence of the Lord." The "Narrative of Surprising Conversions," prepared by Jonathan Edwards, and giving an account of the glorious work of God at Northampton, in 1734, did much to spread and strengthen this desire. In the spring of 1735, before the publication of this narrative, two ministers of Connecticut, namely, Mr. Lord of Norwich, and Mr. Owen of Groton, had visited that place, "that they might see, and hear, and form a judgment for themselves. They conversed with Mr. Edwards, and with many of the people, to their great satisfaction. They declared that the work exceeded all which had been told, or that could be told. On their return, they reported what they had heard and seen, to their own people, on whom it had a great effect. It appeared to be a means of beginning a similar work in Norwich, which in a short time became general."[1] In many other places the people of God were refreshed by his presence, and throughout New England there seems to have been a growing desire on the part of Christians for a genuine revival.

It is not therefore strange that good men in Boston, "where religion was at a very low ebb," heard with peculiar interest of Whitefield's success as a preacher of the Gospel in the southern colonies and in his native land, and sent him earnest invitations to visit New England. Sailing from Charleston, South Carolina, in answer to their call, he landed at Newport, Rhode Island, on the fourteenth day of September, 1740, and at once began his labors. Thousands

[1] Trumbull, II. 141.

hung upon his words; and these words were accompanied by "the demonstration of the Spirit and of power." From Newport he proceeded to Boston, where he remained about ten days, and preached the truth to multitudes with astonishing effect. From that city he extended his journey eastward to York, Maine, finding everywhere on his way eager listeners to the word of life. Retracing his steps, he labored once more a short time in Boston, and then directing his course toward the west, he visited Edwards in Northampton. Passing thence through Connecticut, he preached in a large number of towns, and the power of God was signally manifested in turning sinners unto Himself. Meanwhile, revivals commenced in many places which he was unable to visit. Religion became the principal topic of conversation. Faithful pastors redoubled their efforts and urged upon the attention of their hearers with unwonted zeal the most affecting and pungent truths of revelation. Godly persons were encouraged by the remarkable success of the Gospel, to pray with more confidence for the outpouring of the Holy Ghost upon themselves and their friends. Many, too, of the ungodly were led to believe that the present was their only day of grace.

Trumbull, in his history of Connecticut, after describing at length the peculiarities of this religious awakening, thus proceeds: "Notwithstanding the unreasonable and powerful opposition made to the work of God at this time, and all the clamor which was made about errors and disorders, it was the most glorious and extensive revival of religion, and reformation of manners, which this country ever experienced. It is estimated that in the term of two or three years thirty or forty thousand souls were born into the family of heaven in New England."[1] There has never,

[1] Trumbull, II., p. 263.

probably, been a time since the settlement of New England, when the minds of her people were so generally and so intensely directed to the characteristic doctrines of Christianity. The preaching of such men as Edwards and Bellamy and Whitefield and Tennant and Wheelock and Pomeroy, was in the main Calvinistic and highly discriminating. It led to self-examination and deep conviction of sin. The law was exhibited in all its breadth and spirituality, until the unconverted hearer felt himself to be a guilty "sinner in the hands of an angry God." Salvation was declared to be a free gift, an effect of sovereign, electing, infinite love.

These doctrines are very repugnant to the natural heart, and can be received by those only who understand the exceeding sinfulness of sin. Yet they take strong hold of the awakened mind, and when applied by the Holy Spirit, lead it into the presence of God and fill it with peace and strength indescribable. Under the influence of such preaching the transition from death to life was often strongly marked. "As their convictions were powerful, and their distress, in some instances, almost intolerable; so their light and joys, on a change of heart, were unusually great. They appeared to rejoice with joy unspeakable and full of glory."[1] Sometimes the overpowering emotions of the soul produced strange agitations in the body. Yet these bodily changes were not regarded as proofs of inward grace; they were deprecated rather than desired. Still, by the friends of the revival they were neither ascribed to Satanic agency nor thought to be inconsistent with the gracious operations of God's Spirit. Jonathan Edwards refers to imprudences and sinful irregularities, to transports and ecstasies, to errors in judgment and indis-

[1] Trumbull, II., p. 142.

creet zeal, to outcries and faintings and agitations of body, but he nevertheless finds the clearest indications of a work of God, even in the hearts of some who were thus carried away by the strength of their emotions. And after a careful examination of the evidence, few will dissent from his opinion.

In the great awakening which we have briefly noticed, Backus was brought to a saving knowledge of the truth. He had no opportunity to hear either Whitefield or Tennent, but the revival which attended their labors, "reached Norwich in 1741, under the preaching of Dr. Wheelock and others." "This work," says Mr. Backus, "was so powerful, and people in general were so ignorant, that they had little government of their passions. Many cried out and fell down in meetings. But I had so much doctrinal knowledge, that I never was overcome in that manner. Neither could I put off my concern, as I had done before, for a more convenient season. No, though I was in good health, I saw that life was forfeited by sin, and that God had a right to take it away in a moment. I saw also that He had now given me an opportunity to repent and turn to Him, and that, if it was neglected, I was lost for eternity. Time was then taken out of the way, and a vast eternity was directly before me, without any hope of ever having another day of grace, should this be neglected. This moved me to the earnest use of all the means, public or private, within my reach, that I might get a good heart to come to Christ with. For all the sound teaching with which I had been favored had given me no higher ideas than that a good disposition of mind was necessary in order to come to Christ for salvation. But all the awakening preaching that I now heard, and all the books which I read, were so far from producing any such disposition, that my heart seemed to grow worse and worse daily; and I saw seeds of all the evils of the world in me. While others were crying out and falling down in distress, I felt like a stupid beast before God; and nothing was more terrible to me than the fear of losing my convictions and being left of God to a hard heart and reprobate mind; for I fully believed that now was my only time to obtain salvation, that I should never have another day of grace. Neither could I bear to be deceived with a false hope. When a minister once stated a case like mine, and then said to his hearers: "If this be your case, be not discouraged, but see if God does not appear speedily for your help," I was powerfully tempted to cast off my concern and to hope for help hereafter. But this appeared plainly to come from the adversary, and it increased my distress. Again, one morning these words came into my mind like an audible voice, "Thou art not far from the kingdom of heaven." But my soul was alarmed thereby, through fear of being settled down in something short of a union with Christ, and this alarm made me cry out to Him for help.

"In the beginning of August, Mr. James Davenport came to Norwich, where he was met by Doctors Wheelock and Pomeroy, and meetings were held incessantly for three days. People were greatly affected and many hopefully converted, while I grew worse and worse in my own view. Powerful preaching, and the sight of many in distress or joy, while I remained a hardened sinner, caused such anguish as words cannot express. Yet hereby God laid open to me the plague of my own heart and the folly of seeking life by my own doings. My tears were dried up, and I could find no good in me. Instead of this I felt inclined to quarrel with the sovereignty and justice of God, and the freeness of his grace, a grace so free that he was not obliged to have mercy upon me after all my doings. A sight of these corruptions increased my distress and filled me with confusion before God. And as I believed this to be my last opportunity, and my convictions seemed to be going off, and the work of God to be abating among us, how awful did my case appear! But God's thoughts are as high above our thoughts as the heavens are above the earth; for He thus drew me off from all trust in myself or any creature, and led me to embrace salvation in His own way.

"As I was mowing alone in the field, August 24th, 1741, all my past life was opened plainly before me, and I saw clearly that it had been filled up with sin. I went and sat down in the shade of a tree, where my prayers and tears, my hearing the Word of God and striving for a better heart, with all my other doings, were set before me in such a light that I perceived I could never make myself better, should I live ever so long. Divine justice appeared clear in my condemnation, and I saw that God had a right to do with me as he would. My soul yielded all into His hands, fell at His feet, and was silent and calm before Him. And while I sat there, I was enabled by divine light to see the perfect righteousness of Christ and the freeness and riches of His grace, with such clearness, that my soul was drawn forth to trust in Him for salvation. And I wondered that others did not also come to Him who had enough for all. The Word of God and the promises of His grace appeared firmer than a rock, and I was astonished at my previous unbelief. My heavy burden was gone, tormenting fears were fled, and my joy was unspeakable.

"Yet this change was so different from my former ideas of conversion, that for above two days I had no thought of having experienced it. Then I heard a sermon read which gave the characters of the children of God, and I had an inward witness that those characters were wrought in me; such as a spirit of prayer, a hatred of sin, an overcoming of the world, love to the brethren, and love to enemies; and I conclude that I then had the sealings of the Spirit of God, that I was a child of His. New ideas and dispositions were given me; the worship and service of God and obedience to His will were the delight of my soul. I found such happiness therein as I never had in all the vanities of the world; and this I have often experienced since."

Mr. Backus then proceeds to speak of those alternations of spiritual joy and despondency, to which every Christian is peculiarly subject in the beginning of his course. H^ observes, that although darkness at times overspread h mind, he was unable to revive his former terrors; although doubts in respect to his piety were experienced, he sought in vain to recover his previous state of conviction. He attributes his depression and distress to a want of watchfulness and to a neglect of known duty.

CHAPTER III.

BACKUS A SEPARATIST.

STATE OF THE "REGULAR CHURCH" OF NORWICH.—MR. BACKUS RELUCTANTLY JOINS IT.—SEPARATES FROM IT WITH OTHERS.—REASONS FOR SO DOING AND FOR THE SEPARATE MOVEMENT GENERALLY: 1. RECEPTION OF UNCONVERTED PERSONS INTO THE REGULAR CHURCHES; 2. NEGLECT OF DISCIPLINE; 3. ADOPTION OF THE SAYBROOK PLATFORM; 4. UNSATISFACTORY PREACHING.—COURSE OF DR. LORD.—ANECDOTE OF DR. BALDWIN AND DR. LORD.—INTERVIEW BETWEEN REV. IVORY HOVEY AND MR. BACKUS.—LETTER OF MR. HILL TO DR. LORD.

MR. BACKUS early thought of uniting with the church in his native place, but was prevented for a time by observing that neither due care was exercised in receiving members nor proper faithfulness to those who were in the church. The same laxity had been common and was still far too prevalent. Referring to the period between 1735 and 1740, Trumbull remarks: "It does not appear that ministers in general, at that time, made any particular inquiry of those whom they admitted to communion, with respect to their internal feelings and exercises. The *Stoddardean* opinion generally prevailed, that unregenerate men could consistently covenant with God, and when moral in their lives, had a right to sealing ordinances."[1] It is plain that Mr. Lord, pastor of the church in Norwich, agreed with the majority of his brethren; for in 1744 he "obtained a major vote to admit members into

[1] Trumb. II. p. 143.

the church without so much as a written account of any change of heart."[1] The scruples and delay of Backus were not therefore unreasonable. But at length, after ten months, wishing to "enjoy the precious ordinance of the supper," and finding no better way to secure this privilege, he "joined the First Congregational Church in Norwich, July 11, 1742; concluding to bear those things as a burden and to hope for a reformation."

But his connection with this church did not long continue. If there was at first any prospect of the reformation for which he hoped, it grew fainter and fainter. The burden which he undertook to bear was gradually increased; and therefore in the beginning of 1745, soon after the vote, to which allusion has been made, was passed, Mr. Backus and many other persons[2] withdrew

1 This vote was as follows: "Though it is esteemed a desirable thing that persons who come into full communion offer some public relation of their experience; yet we do not judge nor hold it a term of communion." (Records of the First Congregationalist church in Norwich.) In his reply to Mr. Fish, written in 1768, Mr. Backus says: "I never knew an instance in my day, of any who were admitted into those churches (of the standing order), by declaring *personally the faith wrought* in their souls; and a great part of them have now dropt even giving *written relations.*" (p. 18.)

2 "A large part of the first church in Norwich drew off from said minister and met for worship in another place." — *Backus.* "Thirty male members, including one deacon, and a large number of females, left the Old Standing Church at about the same time. Others soon followed. Among these were some of the most wealthy and influential men in the town. The Separatists and their friends finally out-voted the Old Church in the Town Meetings, and declared that they would no longer pay the minister's rates, as they were conscientiously opposed to the union of Church and State. But, upon a complaint entered, the General Court interfered, and they were taxed, by a special act, to support Dr. Lord and his society. Refusing to pay the tax they were imprisoned. For this cause as many as forty persons, men and women, were imprisoned in a single year." — *Historical Notices*, by Rev. F. Denison.

from the church, and began to hold meetings on the Sabbath for their mutual edification. In August of the next year, they were brought before the church to make known their reasons for this step. These reasons were, for substance, nearly the same which Mr. Backus elsewhere gives; namely, that persons were received into the church who gave no satisfactory evidence of conversion; that many were suffered to remain as regular members, without being dealt with, whose walk was evidently contrary to the Gospel; that the pastor declared his strong attachment to the Saybrook Platform, which had been renounced by the church before settling him; that, while many true doctrines were preached, the nature of conversion and of the soul's walk with God, the teaching of the Divine Spirit and the substance of experimental religion were not clearly held forth; and that many things were publicly and from the pulpit assailed, "which," says Mr. Backus, "my soul well knew to be the work of God." Complaint was also made by one or more of them, that Mr. Lord was no friend to "lowly preaching"[1] and had used his authority to prevent it. At an adjourned meeting of the church it was voted that these reasons were insufficient; at a subsequent meeting those who had thus separated "were publicly warned of their errors and admonished to return to the church;" and at a still later meeting, (Oct. 17, 1745), they were by vote "*suspended* from the communion and from special ordinances till they shall receive better Light and manifest a Desire to return," etc. The separation, however, was permanent. Mr. Backus and his associates became identified with a religious movement of the time. For the same reasons, in the main, which led them to establish a separate meeting, led within a few years to

1 i. e. that of uneducated men.

the formation of a large body of Separate or New-Light churches. It is therefore necessary for us to weigh these reasons deliberately and to describe the religious movement and organization which they brought into existence; for in no other way can we understand the times and the labors of him whose history we are writing.

In the first place, then, we find the "Half-way Covenant" generally approved at this time by churches of the standing order. Indeed men who entertained no hope themselves, and who gave no evidence to others, that they had been renewed by the Spirit of God, were often, if not generally, admitted to all the privileges and ordinances of the christian church. Mr. Stoddard taught that a man sometimes "may and ought to come to the Lord's Supper, who knows himself to be in a natural state," that this ordinance "is *instituted* to be a means of regeneration," and "that the direct end of it is conversion, when the subject that it is administered unto stands in need of conversion." And Mr. Williams, a defender of the Half-way Covenant, in opposition to Jonathan Edwards, mentions two ends contemplated by Christ in appointing the communion: viz. "That such as have grace already should be under proper advantages to gain more, and that those who have none, should be under proper advantages to attain grace." And Edwards himself, who utterly repudiated this view, was forced to lament, that "*owning the covenant*, as it is called, has in New England, it is to be feared, too much degenerated into a matter of mere form and ceremony; it being visibly a prevailing custom for persons to neglect this until they come to be married, and then to do it for their credit's sake, and that their children may be baptized."[1] In a word, it was held that the christian church

[1] Edwards, Vol. I., p. 115.

is but a continuation of the Jewish, the terms of admission remaining unchanged. The position laid down by Mr. Stoddard was practically maintained, viz. "That if unsanctified persons might lawfully come to the passover, then such may lawfully come to the Lord's Supper, — and they who convey to their children a right to baptism, have a right themselves to the Lord's Supper, provided they carry inoffensively."

But on the other hand, Mr. Backus and those who took the name of Separates, believed, — to use their own words, — "That at all times the doors of the church should be carefully kept against such as cannot give a satisfactory evidence of the work of God upon their souls, whereby they are united to Christ." The views which they cherished on this point were manifestly according to the New Testament and were triumphantly asserted by Jonathan Edwards in his work entitled; "Qualifications for full communion." To the argument drawn by ministers of the standing order from the "tares of the field" in favor of their practice, it was pertinently answered that, even if "the field" was intended by Christ to represent the visible church, — which however was called in question by many of the Separates, — still according to the parable the tares were introduced secretly, by an enemy, to grow and ripen as tares, and not openly, purposely and, by direction of the owner, to be changed ultimately under proper advantages of culture into wheat.[1]

The Separates were also charged with fanaticism, and especially with the error of supposing, that "the saints

[1] Perhaps some," says Jonathan Edwards, "would be ready to make the reflection, that those churches whose practice is agreeable to the loose principles Mr. W. espouses, do that at noon-day, in the presence of God, angels and men, which the devil did in the night, *while men slept!*"

certainly know one another by their own inward feelings." Doubtless in the heat of controversy the more zealous of the Separates were many times betrayed into the use of very extravagant language, and a few individuals, it is evident, embraced unscriptural opinions on the subject; but as to the great body of them, their views in regard to the proper evidences of conversion appear to have been sober and scriptural, differing in no important respect from those approved by evangelical Christians at the present day. Mr. Backus says: "When we first appeared against having the worthy and the unworthy partake together at the Lord's Supper, — which was a principal reason of our fathers' separation from the Church of England, — ministers told us as I have before proved, that *tares* and *wheat* must grow together in the church till the harvest; for they knew there were many, both in public and private stations, who, notwithstanding their form of godliness, appeared as plainly against the power of it, as the tares appeared by their fruit in the field. But because we would not confound church and world together as they did, they shifted about and accused us of assuming God's prerogative of searching the heart; asserting at the same time that we could not know who were saints and who not. And when it was replied that Christ said: *Ye shall know them,*[1] the return would be: What, are you infallible? Whereupon disputes have ensued which have been carried to extremes on both sides. I confess with shame that I have sometimes been thus ensnared, and so have given occasion to those who desired occasion against us."[2]

[1] "*Fruits,*" says Mr. Backus, in his discourse "On Faith and its Influence," "comprehend all that men *bring forth out of their hearts,* in their principles, experience, conversation and conduct; and hereby we are to *know them,* and to act towards them according to the clearest light we can gain."

[2] Examination of Fish's sermons, p. 49, 50.

In the second place, a reason for separation was found in the prevalent neglect of discipline by the regular churches. Not merely were those welcomed to full membership in the church who made no pretensions to genuine piety or a change of heart, but many "whose walk was evidently contrary to the Gospel," were allowed to retain their standing with the people of God. It was natural that all who looked upon the church of Christ as a spiritual temple which ought to consist of such only as are, in the judgment of charity, "lively stones," should be grieved at the indulgence shown to open transgressors, and should despair of any reformation in this respect while the Half-way Covenant was retained. In his reply to Mr. Fish, Backus testifies, "that it is a *professed* rule with many ministers, not to deal with any person in the church for moral evil, till he is[1] convicted in the state."

In the third place, Mr. Backus and his friends strenuously asserted the independency of every christian church, and opposed the Saybrook Platform. For this Platform not only referred all ecclesiastical questions of importance to the decision of a synod composed of regular ministers in each county and of (optional) messengers from their several churches, but also made every decision of this council final and authoritative, and the council's own action dependent on the concurrence of a major part of the ministers present.

In a previous chapter we have spoken of Mr. Woodward's share in the production of this scheme, of the trouble and separation which ensued between him and his people, and of the terms of settlement to which Mr. Lord subscribed when he became pastor of the church in Norwich. When now after many years Mr. Lord be-

[1] Substituted by the writer for "they are."

gan to express himself in favor of the Platform and even proposed to attend the association of ministers, though without compromising the independency of his own church, it is not strange that the grandson of Joseph Backus took the alarm and protested against his course. And just at this time opposition to the Platform was greatly strengthened by events which took place in Canterbury. For, in compliance with a major vote of the society, but against a strong major vote of the church in that place, the ministers of Windham County proceeded to ordain and settle (Dec. 28, 1744) Mr. James Cogswell over the church and society. In consequence of this action about fifty families withdrew and established worship by themselves. Moreover the expulsion of two young men, John and Ebenezer Cleaveland, from Yale College, because they chose to worship with the members who separated, served to extend the knowledge of these proceedings, to heighten the indignation of many at every species of religious coercion, and to awaken a strong, though not general, hostility to the existing union of Church and State.

In the fourth place, Mr. Backus and his associates did not think themselves edified by the ministry of their pastor. All of them assigned this as a reason for withdrawing and establishing worship by themselves. They were children of the great awakening, and longed for pungent, discriminating, zealous, Calvinistic preaching. While Mr. Backus acknowledged that the articles and covenant of the church were in general sound, and that many true doctrines were preached by the pastor, he nevertheless declared his conviction that such food was commonly given to the sheep of Christ as they could not live upon, and hence that personal piety or growth in grace demanded the separation. And when we bear in mind the intense religious thought and agitation which characterized this period, the radical and outspoken difference of opinion between the supporters and opponents of Whitefield as to what is the best kind of preaching, it is not strange that separation in almost every case was due in part to such a conviction as Mr. Backus and his companions expressed.

Mr. Lord is put down by the historian of Connecticut among those who favored the great revival, but not in the same class with Pomeroy, Wheelock and Bellamy, who were "the most zealous and laborious in the cause." We have already mentioned his visit to Jonathan Edwards in 1735, and the report which he brought back respecting the work of God under the labors of that eminent divine. We have also referred to the preaching of Dr. Wheelock and others in Norwich. And it may be added, that in 1743, Mr. Lord united with eleven neighboring ministers in a public declaration, which affirms their "persuasion that there has of late, for about three years past, been a great and wonderful revival of religion in the several places to which we minister, and in divers others which we are acquainted with;" and then, after alluding to imprudences and separations, continues thus: "and all of a bad nature and tendency, that we have seen, does not give us any reason to think that there has not been a great and glorious work of divine grace carried on among us, and a great reformation and revival of religion; for which we desire to praise and adore the sovereign mercy of God."

But in the year following, — a year of religious agitation, debate, and coercion in Connecticut, — he began, it seems, to lay more stress upon the disorders and innovations which attended the great awakening, to look with coldness if not suspicion upon the practice of relating "experiences," and to avow his approbation of the Saybrook Platform. The spirit of conservatism had gained the ascendency, and it was no doubt manifested in his preaching. He felt a degree of sympathy with those who would sustain the established order of churches by the civil power, and who were apprehensive of more evil than good from any considerable change. He often therefore "struck at those things from the pulpit" which were regarded by many as the work of God, and he also forbore to present some of those truths which they found to be most salutary and refreshing. Yet he should be classed, it is evident, with the more evangelical and earnest preachers of that period, and the Separates of Norwich had therefore less reason than many others to establish a distinct meeting for their mutual edification. The prospect of better spiritual food would not perhaps alone have justified them in resorting to such a measure; but this prospect was connected by them with the other reasons which have been mentioned.

Before taking leave of Mr. Lord, we add the following incident from the pen of Dr. Baldwin: "Previously to my baptism, I visited my friends at Norwich, Connecticut. I then took an opportunity of conversing with my former venerable pastor. He received me very kindly, and when at his request I related my religious exercises, was quite melted into tears. But when towards the close of the evening, he suspected, from some of my inquiries, that my mind was not established in the doctrines of Pedobaptism, he remarked to me, in rather a stern tone of voice: "Well, Thomas, if you renounce your infant baptism and are re-baptized, I shall reprobate you, notwithstanding all that you have told me.' I was shocked at the remark, and after a moment's silence replied: 'I hope, Sir, I shall be directed to do what is right.'" It appears, however, that the good man did not execute his threat. For we are informed that "after Dr. Baldwin had become a Baptist minister, his aged relative treated him with great kindness, invited him to preach in his pulpit, and indeed to the close of his life manifested towards him the most parental attention."

A brief narrative will cast still further light upon the Separate movement. By request of Rev. Ivory Hovey of Rochester, Mr. Backus and others met with the former in Beech Woods,[1] November 22, 1749, for a conference on their different sentiments and feelings. We give the rest of the account in the words of Mr. Backus. "After commiting the case to God, we began the conference. And first Mr. Hovey asked what we thought of the churches generally in this land. We answered that we believed they were churches of Christ, though greatly degenerated and corrupted. He said he was of the same mind. Next he asked what we thought of the ministers. We answered that we believed many of them were ministers of Christ. He agreed with us therein. Then he asked what were the reasons of our separation, and also how far we did separate from them. We answered, that the reasons were the corruptions which had crept into the churches, and that we desired to separate from nothing but their corruptions; that although we could not join in the communion of those churches, yet if any who remained in them and gave evidence of their being saints desired it, we could freely receive them to our com-

[1] A part of Middleboro'.

munion; and that we desired to join with them in anything that was right. Upon this we had much talk, but could not be of a mind. When he asked our views respecting the power of ordination, we told him that we held the power to be in the churches. He held the power of choosing [a minister] to be in the churches, but the power of ordaining to be in the ministers. Next he asked our minds concerning the knowledge of the brethren. I told him that the way I knew them, was by what came from them in word and action, and also that the rule which God has given us to know them by is a perfect rule; but as we are imperfect creatures, we may be imperfect in [applying] that as well as in other things. Here he agreed with me. Then he asked concerning visions, prophecies, etc. Herein we agreed that the Scripture is our perfect rule, and that we are not to give heed to anything contrary thereto. We then discoursed about persons' bodies being overcome; and herein we agreed that it was no certain evidence either for or against them. In the whole of our discourse we were kept very free from bitterness on both sides, and we agreed in all but two points. One is, he thought we ought not to separate, but to stay in the churches, groaning under the burdens and laboring for a reformation. The other relates to the power of ordination."

Such then were some of the reasons which led to frequent separations from the standing order in the period before us. The history of Mr. Backus for the next few years will give us ample opportunity to observe still more closely the character of this movement, and to discover the elements of weakness which it involved. It has been stated that Mr. Backus and his friends began to hold meetings by themselves in the beginning of 1745. For upwards of a year they continued to maintain religious worship without any ecclesiastical organization; but on the sixth of July, 1746, they united together in covenant as a church, and engaged to walk in the ordinances of the Gospel. Of their subsequent course — their labors and their sufferings — the limits assigned to our present work forbid us to speak. Yet the reader will be interested in a single letter written to Dr. Lord by one of those who were imprisoned in 1752. For this letter we are indebted to the "Historical Notes" of Rev. F. Denison. It probably illustrates the spirit with which many of the New-Lights suffered and acted.

"NORWICH GAOL, NOVEMBER THE 1st DAY, 1752.

"MR. LORD: Sir, I take this opportunity to present you with these few lines, which I should have thought you would have prevented by visiting us. Pray, Sir, consider whether or no you do not neglect to minister to Christ; for inasmuch as ye did it not to them, etc. And further if you come not to see us, there are other prisoners here, and as you sustain the character of a minister, see to it you neglect them not; and I should be glad of opportunity to see you. Ye lay heavy burdens and refuse to touch them with one of your fingers. You say it is the authority; Simeon and Levi are brethren; instruments of cruelty are in their habitations.[1]

"Pray, Sir, read the third chapter of Micah's prophecy, and may the Lord make the application. Consider also that our Lord Jesus hath told us that his kingdom is not of this world, also that he that taketh the sword shall perish by the sword. I could wish you a deliverance from mystical Babylon and from her merchandize. My soul looks

[1] Gen. 49: 5-7.

to and longs to see her receive the cup of the Lord's vengeance, and that all His plagues may come upon her in one day, and that God's children may come out of her, and that the kingdom may be given to the saints of the Most High. These lines, with our cause, I leave with God, who will I trust defend it, and so subscribe myself a prisoner of hope.

CHARLES HILL."

CHAPTER IV.

CALL TO THE MINISTRY.

UNCONVERTED MINISTERS OF THE STANDING ORDER. — PERSONAL PIETY AND AN INWARD CALL NOT ESTEEMED INDISPENSABLE. — VIEWS OF DR. CHAUNCEY. — OF THE MINISTERS OF CONNECTICUT. — A LIBERAL EDUCATION DEEMED INDISPENSABLE. — REMARKS OF JONATHAN EDWARDS. — REASONS FOR TENACITY ON THIS POINT. — OPPOSITE VIEWS MAINTAINED BY THE NEW-LIGHTS. — MR. BACKUS' ACCOUNT OF HIS CALL TO THE MINISTRY. — HIS SERMON ON THE NATURE AND NECESSITY OF AN INTERNAL CALL.

IT is well known that both Whitefield and Tennant insisted upon personal piety as an essential qualification for the work of preaching the Gospel, and that they had no confidence in the religious character of large numbers who then held the pastoral office. At the close of his first visit to New England, Whitefield wrote in his journal: "Many, perhaps most, that preach, I fear, do not experimentally know Christ." This remark has been condemned as uncharitable and imprudent, yet there was too much reason for him to doubt the piety of not a few. Certainly it is no more sweeping than the language of Gilbert Tennant: "It is true some of the modern Pharisees have learned to prate a little more *orthodoxly* about the new birth than their predecessor *Nicodemus*, who are in the meantime as great strangers to the feeling experience of it as he. They are blind who see not this to be the case of the *body* of the clergy of this generation."[1] Nor is it severer than the

[1] Backus, Reply to Fish, p. 33.

words of Mr. Porter of Bridgewater, who says of many graduates from college: "Alas, for the *encouragement* they meet with! No sooner do these *light*, *airy*, *fashionable* young men, who evidently *deny*, *oppose*, and banter, both publicly and privately, the great soul-humbling and Christ-exacting doctrines of the Gospel, and ridicule experimental religion as *enthusiasm*, and resolve christian experiences into an *over-heated imagination* and *disordered brain*, if not *fanatical delusion;* I say, no sooner do these young men come forth from the feet of *Gamaliel* into the world, and begin to exercise their gifts, but they are *at once* invited to preach and settle in the ministry; and there are *ministers* and churches enough that will ordain them, notwithstanding the *testimony* which the serious, and such as are concerned for the doctrines and interest of Christ, bear against it. This is too much the case at this day. We have *frequent* and *flagrant* instances of it; he that *runs* may read it, and he is *wilfully blind* that does not see it. And, alas, how dark the aspect on *these churches!* 'These things are a lamentation, and shall be for a lamentation.'"[1]

"Mr. Ruggles," says Trumbull, "was a scholar and a wise man; his morals were not impeachable; but he was a dull, unanimating preacher; had a great talent of hiding his real sentiments, never coming fully out, either as to doctrinal or experimental religion;" and there appear to have been at that time not a few in the pastoral office to whom this description of the Guilford minister was applicable.

When Whitefield proposed the question: "Are not unconverted ministers the bane of the Christian church?" Dr. Chauncey replied: "If, by unconverted ministers, you mean those who appear to be so by a faith or life visibly contradictory to the Gospel, I entirely agree with you.

[1] See Examination of Fish's Sermons, p. 68–9.

But if you intend, by unconverted ministers, those whom God knows to be so, though from what outwardly appears they ought to be well thought of, I doubt not but you are under a great mistake." And in his "Seasonable Thoughts on the State of Religion in New England," he offers this remark: "Conversion does not appear to be alike necessary for ministers in their public capacity as officers of the church, as it is in their private capacity." This view of the matter seems to have been quite prevalent before the great awakening. It is not, therefore, surprising that educated men, "if orthodox in doctrine and regular in their lives" were admitted without hesitation to the sacred office.

In 1712, the ministers of Connecticut at their general association, recommended that a candidate for the ministry should be required to give satisfaction to the association examining him, of his skill in the Hebrew, Greek, and Latin tongues, in Logic and Philosophy; of his acquaintance with the main grounds or principles of the christian religion and his assent to the confession of faith publicly owned by the united churches of the colony; and of his sober and religious conversation.

It will be observed, that "sober and religious conversation" is a very indefinite expression, by no means equivalent to "experimental religion," and that no allusion whatever is made to an internal or spiritual call to enter the ministry. Indeed, we do not find that such a call had ever been esteemed necessary by churches of the standing order in New England; and there is reason to believe, that from 1712, until the great revival, candidates for the ministry were not generally expected to give an account of their religious experience.

But when the "set time to favor Zion had come," and genuine converts to the faith were multiplied, better views of the new birth began to prevail, and the labors of spiritual men were anxiously desired. Yet many churches of the established order remained under the care of those who were strangers to vital piety. In many instances their people were for the most part content with such instruction as they gave; yet, had it been less satisfactory, a supply of educated and devout men could not have been found to take their places. For it must be remembered that no one was thought to be qualified for the ministerial office without a liberal education.

Even Jonathan Edwards wrote in opposition to the opinion, that the office of the gospel ministry need not be limited to persons of a liberal education. He remarks that "some of late have been for having others that they have supposed to be persons of eminent experience, publicly licensed to preach, yea, and ordained to the work of the ministry; and some ministers have seemed to favor such a thing; but how little do they seem to look forward, and consider the unavoidable consequences of opening such a door!" "Not but that there may probably be some persons in the land that have had no education at college, that are in themselves better qualified for the work of the ministry than some others that have taken their degrees and are now ordained. But yet I believe that the breaking over those bounds that have hitherto been set, in ordaining such persons, would in its consequences be a greater calamity than the missing such persons in the work of the ministry."

If one who knew the importance of religious experience to the minister of Christ could use this language, it is easy to imagine the bitterness and contempt with which less charitable and less spiritual men would speak of uneducated preachers. Yet we are by no means surprised that clergymen of the standing order in New England were resolved to welcome none but men of classical learning into their ranks. For they were convinced on the one hand that such learning is exceedingly desirable for religious teachers, and they were doubtless reluctant on the other hand to surrender a weapon — namely, the reproach of ignorance — which had done them good service against the Baptists. Several of the first Baptist preachers in New England, were, it is true, men of liberal culture; but this was not the case with all. The churches did not esteem an acquaintance with the dead languages *necessary* to qualify one for the ministerial office. Nor did they believe it right to close the approaches to this office against all who were unable to produce a diploma. It had therefore been found in many cases easier to abridge the influence of Baptist ministers by sneering at their ignorance than by replying fairly to their arguments from the Word of God; and hence, even christian men were disinclined to relinquish the advantage of using such a weapon. Nor is it strange, all things considered, that the Legislature of Connecticut made the following law in 1742: "And be it further enacted, that no person that has not been educated or graduated in Yale College, or Harvard College in Cambridge, or some other allowed foreign protestant College or University, shall take the benefit of the laws of this government respecting the settlement and support of ministers."

Those, however, who separated from churches of the established order were stanch advocates of "lowly preaching." They rated spiritual discernment far higher than classical learning. They held "that every brother that is qualified by God for the same, has a right to preach according to the measure of faith, and that the essential qualification for preaching is wrought by the Spirit of God; and that * * * the tongues and liberal sciences are not absolutely necessary; yet they are convenient, and will doubtless be profitable if rightly used; but if brought in to supply the want of the Spirit of God, they prove a snare to those that use them and all that follow them." They also believed "that all the gifts and graces that are bestowed upon any of the members, are to be improved by them for the good of the whole; in order to which there ought to be such a gospel freedom, whereby the church may know where every particular gift is, that it may be improved in its proper place and to its right end, for the glory of God and the good of the church."[1]

Mr. Backus heartily embraced these views; and soon after the Separate Church was organized in Norwich, he was led to devote himself to the ministry of reconciliation. We submit an account of his call to this holy work in his own language. "Hitherto a private life had been my choice and delight; but a new scene was before me, which I had no idea of, till I was led into it in the following manner. Being at a certain house where a number of the saints were met, the command, 'pray ye the Lord of the harvest that He will send forth laborers into his harvest,' was read and spoken upon. A conviction seized my mind that God had given me abilities which his church had a right to the use of, and which I could not withhold with a clear conscience. Soon after, a spirit of prayer for divine teaching was given me in a remarkable manner, and eternal things were brought into a near view, with a clear sight of the truth and harmony of the Holy Scriptures; also these words were impressed on my mind: "Son of

[1] See Confession of Faith of the Separate Church in Mansfield, Ct., in the Result of a Council of the Windham County Consociation, held at Scotland, January 13th, 1747. *Athenæum Library, Boston.*

man, eat this roll." Never did I more sensibly eat natural food than did my soul feast upon the solid truths of God's Word. Yet I did not then conclude that I should ever preach the Gospel in public.

"A few days after, our minister[1] invited me to go with him to Colchester and Lyme, where there was a revival of religion. I went accordingly, and on the journey two souls were hopefully converted. I returned home with rejoicing, and much life in my soul. The next day, September 27, 1746, new views were given me beyond those which I had before received. My business led me out to work alone in the woods, where, with none to interrupt me, I had such converse with my God as I never had before. His former teachings now came to this point, *that He called me to preach his Gospel.* And I was then led to count the cost of obedience to the will of God in this work, as distinctly as ever to cast up any particular sum. Many and great enemies appeared in my way, reproaches, losses, imprisonment, and death; but God showed me that He could make them all fly from my path as chaff flies before the wind. I thought of my own ignorance and weakness; but He gave me to see that He had knowledge and strength for me. I urged the plea that I was slow of speech and very bashful; but the answer came: cannot He who formed man's mouth, cause him to speak? I said if I should go and preach the Gospel with success, I might be lifted up with pride and fall as many others have done. This difficulty seemed to me like a great mountain, rising far above all the rest; but God said: *My grace is sufficient for thee;* the mountain was taken away and every excuse gone, so that it appeared like trifling with Divine majesty to make another objection. And though I looked upon

[1] Mr. Hyde, minister of the Separatist Church in Norwich.

6

the work as too great for an angel to go through with in his own strength, yet I saw it was easy for God to carry such a poor worm through it, make him faithful unto death, and give him at last a crown of life. So I was enabled then to give up my soul and body afresh to God, with all my interest, to serve Him in preaching his Gospel. He then gave me a particular message from the fifty-third psalm, to lay open the universal corruption of mankind. And as our church allowed each brother free liberty to improve his gift in teaching, I delivered that message the next day (Lord's day, September 28, 1746) with special clearness, and with acceptance to the church. And as I was then free from all worldly engagements, I devoted my whole time to that great work."

It may be well to notice in this place, a "Discourse on the Nature and Necessity of an Internal Call to preach the everlasting Gospel," published by Mr. Backus in 1753. In this Discourse he undertakes to show that "all true ministers of the Gospel are called into that work by the special influences of the Holy Spirit," and in the Preface he makes the following remark: "Much of what I have here written I knew experimentally before I did doctrinally." He puts it down as the belief of many, that ministers are authorized to license preachers of the Gospel, and that whoever engages in this work without their license runs before he is sent; that ministers and churches are to examine and ordain all the clergy, and that this action, and this alone, gives to the latter their commission and authority. He testifies that it was often asserted, both from the pulpit and in conversation, *That the call of man is the call of God;* that if a man has college learning and is regularly introduced according to their order, he is a minister of Christ and sent of God, though unconverted; and that one must have an understanding of the original tongues, or else he does not know whether he preaches right or wrong.

He speaks of his own view as novel, and therefore likely to encounter many objections; and he proceeds to answer briefly the most material of these objections, "though," he says, "I know that a man may as easily stop the winds from blowing with his words, as to still all the cavils of such as do not love to receive the truth." He protests against being regarded an enemy to learning, and grants that a knowledge of the original tongues may, by the help of the Divine Spirit, be improved for the good of others. He pronounces an acquaintance with the languages useful in itself, but considers it evident "that in our colleges many learn corrupt principles, not only about what makes a minister, but also about what makes a Christian." And he takes the ground that a true minister's qualifications consist more in divine enlightenings than in human learning, that his authority to preach depends more upon his being internally called by the Spirit of God, than upon his being externally sent by the voice of man.

According to this discourse, the Holy Spirit inwardly calls men to preach the Word, by giving them a specially clear view of the present state of the church and the world, by opening and committing to them the treasure of the Gospel, and by constraining them sweetly and powerfully to enter upon this great work at God's command. Mr. Backus concedes, however, that "the Lord deals variously with different persons as to the means and manner of their call," yet insists that all who are moved by the Holy Ghost to take upon themselves this ministry, have such views of the actual condition of immortal souls and of the glories of divine truth, that they are constrained by divine power, and animated by love to the children of men, and zeal for their good, to go and speak unto them all the words of this life.

He moreover denies that holding to an internal call invalidates external ordination in the least; for as a converted person, he argues, has an internal right to all the privileges of the Christian church, yet has no external right to them, till he is openly received as a member; so a person who is called to preach has no right to act in duties peculiar to an officer of the church, till he is publicly set apart therein. Praying, exhorting, and preaching, though duties to be performed in the church, are not so confined to it, that they may not rightly be performed where there is no church at all. But only those who have a visible standing in the church can administer special ordinances or act in cases of discipline, for these are things peculiar to a visible church.

CHAPTER V.

ITINERANT PREACHING AND SETTLEMENT.

MR. BACKUS BEGINS TO PREACH. — HIS DOUBTS RESPECTING HIS CALL. — VISITS TITICUT WITH MR. SNOW. — IS MOVED TO LABOR THERE. — DESCRIPTION OF TITICUT. — ECCLESIASTICAL PARTIES IN THE PLACE. — MR. BACKUS IS INVITED TO PREACH THERE FOR A TIME BY THE PRECINCT COMMITTEE. — FORMATION OF A NEW-LIGHT CHURCH. — MR. BACKUS ORDAINED ITS PASTOR. — HIS TREATMENT BY THE PRECINCT COMMITTEE.

No sooner was Mr. Backus assured of his call to engage in the work of the ministry, than he began to go and preach. About fourteen months of untiring labor were spent in various towns of Connecticut, Rhode Island and Massachusetts. And although a law had been passed by the Legislature of Connecticut in 1742, making it a penal offence for any person who was not a settled or ordained minister, to publicly teach and exhort the people in any parish without the express desire and invitation of the settled minister of such parish,— a law which Trumbull pronounces "an outrage to every principle of justice," and which led to the imprisonment of more than one true evangelist — yet Mr. Backus was suffered to prosecute unmolested his work. Many believers were quickened, several persons were hopefully converted, and not a few of the careless were moved to earnest reflection.

For the most part, he "labored with freedom and delight." Yet he did not escape severe trials. About three months after he commenced preaching, he was sorely tempted to relinquish the work. He found the path before him one of difficulty and danger. It was suggested to his mind that he had gone forth suddenly, without trying to resist the call; that if God had chosen him for this work, He would overpower all opposition to his will; and that the greatest sinner — the one who resisted longest — would be the greatest preacher, as the case of Paul illustrated. But on the other hand, he recollected that Zechariah was struck dumb because he would not believe the angel Gabriel without a sign; and notwithstanding the temptation which continued for a long time, he pursued his work until at length deliverance and liberty came. In answer to many earnest prayers for a wise and understanding heart, the truth was laid open to him with fresh clearness, and he was made willing to fulfil his ministry with any people to whom God should send him.

In December, 1747, Mr. Backus first saw the place where he was to labor more than half a century in the vineyard of his Master. On the 8th of this month, he paid a visit to Rev. Joseph Snow, pastor of a Separate church in Providence, and was urged by the latter to accompany him to Bridgewater on a preaching excursion, which he was soon to make. "After weighing the matter and committing the case to God," Mr. Backus concluded to accept the invitation. He accordingly went over to Attleboro' to spend the few days before their journey in preaching the Word. On the 18th, he proceeded from this place with Mr. Snow, to the house of Seth Hayward, a christian brother in Bridgewater, where they were kindly entertained. On the next day, says the subject of our narrative, we "visited several other Christians in the town, and had freedom in conversing with them. They appeared to be in reality hungering after gospel food. Towards night we came down to Titicut to brother Samuel Alden's, where brother Snow, who had labored in the place before, was welcomed with much rejoicing.

"After a little, I went out abroad and was enabled to bless God that He had helped us hitherto. When I had come in, and we were seating ourselves to partake of food, these words came into my mind with great light and power: 'Say not ye, There are yet four months, and then cometh harvest? Behold, I say unto you, Lift up your eyes, and look on the fields; for they are white already to harvest. And he that reapeth receiveth wages, and gathereth fruit unto life eternal; that both he that soweth, and he that reapeth may rejoice together. And herein is that saying true, One soweth, and another reapeth. I sent you to reap that whereon ye bestowed no labor: other men labored, and ye are entered into their labors.' By these words I was led to discover in this place a large field all white to the harvest. Other men had labored here in years past, and the Lord had wrought wonders by them, but now my soul was constrained by divine light, love and peace to enter into their labors. My heart was so drawn forth towards God and in love to this people, that I felt myself willing to impart unto them not only the Gospel but my own soul also. Thus the Lord bound me to this people ere I was aware of it and before I knew any of them personally."

Titicut parish, in which Mr. Backus was now to begin a long course of service, comprises a part of Bridgewater on the north, and a part of Middleborough on the south of Taunton River, which separates these towns. On account of their distance from any place of public worship, the inhabitants of this district had at one time petitioned the General Court to be incorporated into a town; but their request was not granted. They then desired to be made a separate parish or precinct, and an Act for that purpose was passed February 24, 1743. Eliab Byram had preached in this place about fourteen months with great success, in 1741–2, and the people were expecting to settle him as their pastor; but before the act of incorporation was obtained, he had gone to New Jersey, and was there settled. Subsequently, Silas Brett, Solomon Reed, John Wadsworth and some others had preached in the place. In the meantime there was brought to light a serious difference of opinion between the leading men of the parish and the professors of religion; the former were inclined to favor the standing order and to support religion by the power of civil law, while the latter were friendly to the New-Lights, and desired a total separation of church and state.

When, therefore, these brethren applied to the several churches with which they were connected for letters of dismission, that they might be organized into a church by themselves, their requests were, after some delay, uniformly denied; and disheartened by this refusal, they had forborne almost entirely to sustain religious worship in the place, during the year previous to the coming of Mr. Backus among them. While in this condition, Rev. Nathaniel Shepherd of Attleboro' visited them about the first of December, and delivered a sermon which led them to engage in holding meetings on the Sabbath for their mutual edification, and especially to pray that God would send them a pastor after his own heart. Their first meeting was on Lord's day, December 13; and on the Saturday following, Mr. Backus arrived in Titicut parish.

In the forenoon of the next day, Mr. Snow preached to a large assembly. At the conclusion of his discourse, Mr. Backus stood up to exhort the people. "Divine truth," he says, "seemed to flow through my soul like a river, and it was easier to speak than to refrain. Thus I went on for several hours, and the saints were greatly refreshed, while many sinners were struck under conviction. Towards night I preached from the second Psalm, and had perhaps greater assistance and freedom than ever before in my life. Glory to God alone." In the evening, Mr. Snow preached again; and during the ten days which he spent in this place with Mr. Backus, they preached alternately twenty-four sermons.

"Monday, Dec. 28. This morning the Precinct Committee came and requested me, in case I would be examined and approbated by the neighboring pastors, to preach to them as minister of the parish. I replied that I was clearly convinced of its being my duty to preach to this people for the present, and that I cared not how many came to hear; that I was willing to be examined by their ministers, and to give them the reasons of my hope and my practice; but that I should not consent to their proposal with any such understanding as this, that the precinct instead of the church had a right to lead in the choice of a minister, nor should I leave it to man whether I ought to preach the gospel or no. This answer did not please them; yet they requested me to preach to them for a while. I afterwards found great reason to bless God for enabling me to be steadfast, and to escape the snares which men were laying for my feet. If I had yielded to their scheme they would soon have sent me off."

Up to this time all the meetings had been in Bridgewater; but arrangements were now made to hold them every alternate Sabbath on the Middleboro' side. In the early part of January, Mr. Backus came before the people with a discourse on the Building and Government of the

Church of Christ as distinct from all worldly governments, and during the month he preached no less than thirty sermons. Meanwhile, Christians began to confer about the formation of a church, and they desired him to draw up Articles of Faith and a Covenant. He complied with their request, and in February (16, 1748,) sixteen persons signed the Articles and Covenant which he had prepared, and which, like those of the Separate churches generally, were peculiar for their high-toned spirituality, Calvinism, and republicanism. On the 31st of March, the church, which had now increased to thirty-four members, gave Mr. Backus a unanimous call to become their pastor. This call was accepted, and he was accordingly ordained April 13, 1748.

While the church and council were occupied with matters preliminary to the ordination, Benjamin White, Esq., rode up among the throng of people, and in the name of the Precinct Committee, of which he was a member, forbade all the proceedings. Yet this prohibition was disregarded, and Mr. Backus was solemnly ordained and set apart to the ministry of Christ and to the pastoral care of the church in Titicut.

It may not be amiss to add, that the Precinct Committee had previously, about the first of March, revoked their invitation to Mr. Backus to act as preacher for the parish. And the spirit which animated them may be inferred from the following circumstances. No compensation was made him for the services which he had rendered. His own language is this: "They never offered me a farthing for my preaching two months at their request." "Directly afterwards," he adds, "they called a precinct meeting and taxed me five pounds." This tax was for the support of religion in the place, and Mr. Backus, who was conscientiously opposed to the maintenance of religious worship by the civil power, refused payment. The result is given in the following memorandum. "Monday, February 6, 1749. This morning I was seized by the officer, who threatened to carry me to prison for the precinct-rate; but, glory to God, he gave me a sweet calmness and serenity of soul, so that I was able not to fear the officer, or treat him with any bitterness. I told him that they were going on in an unscriptural way to support the gospel, and therefore I could do nothing to countenance them in such a way. He told me that if I would not pay him he would immediately carry me to jail; but just as he was about to drag me away, there came in a man,[1] who called him out and paid him the money, so that he was forced to let me go." "After they had imprisoned one of our brethren, and made distress on one of my hearers, it appeared upon trial in our county court, that said tax was voted at an illegal meeting. Yet they sent an agent to Boston and obtained an Act of their Legislature to make it legal, and their supreme executive court turned the case against my hearer upon said Act. Thus was judgment turned into wormwood; and this is the natural effect of the use of the sword to support religious teachers."

[1] Capt. Abiezer Edson.

CHAPTER VI.

EARLY PASTORSHIP AND MARRIAGE.

QUALIFICATIONS FOR HIS WORK. — USEFULNESS IN TITICUT. — EXTRACTS FROM HIS JOURNAL.— LABORS AS AN EVANGELIST. — EXTRACTS FROM MEMORANDA OF PREACHING TOURS. — LETTER FROM MR. LEFFINGWELL.— EXTRACTS FROM MEMORANDA CONTINUED. — PARISH LINES DISREGARDED. — MARRIAGE. — ACCOUNT OF THE WEDDING.

Mr. Backus was now twenty-six years of age; his education was poor and his experience limited; but his health was firm, his mind vigorous, his hopes bright, and his zeal ardent. He looked upon himself as sent into this field by the Lord of the harvest in answer to prayer. His labors had been attended by the Master's blessing, and a genuine revival seemed to be in progress. Thus qualified and thus encouraged, he ventured to accept the office of a christian pastor; "an office," says Augustine, "than which there is nothing in this life, and especially in this age, more difficult, more laborious, more dangerous, or, on the other hand, more blessed before God, if a man conduct himself therein as a true soldier under the banner of Christ." The subject of our narrative endeavored thus to conduct himself, and before many years had passed he knew by experience the profound truthfulness of this language.

For a considerable time after his ordination, the religious

interest continued without abatement. Before the eighth of May, the church had increased to fifty members, and on the seventeenth Mr. Backus writes: "When I came into this place I did not expect to stay a fortnight, yet I have been here every Sabbath for five months, have preached an hundred and twenty sermons, a church has been formed and I have been ordained the pastor, and about twenty souls have been hopefully converted." At the close of this year, there were upwards of sixty members in the church, and during the next winter a good degree of spirituality was manifested by them. To illustrate the religious habits and feelings of Mr. Backus at this time, we have selected a few passages from the memoranda which he kept of his life.

Sunday, Nov. 27, he says: "For some days past, I have wrestled earnestly for the divine presence and blessing; and great strength and clearness were given me to-day in preaching."

A few weeks later, Sunday, Dec. 18, he writes: "Last week some of the saints were greatly blessed in private meetings, and this day I have enjoyed unusual freedom in preaching. It has been to many Christians a time of sweet refreshing. O Lord, return and purge away our sins, and take up thine abode with us forever!"

On Sunday, Jan. 1, 1749, he makes this record: "I have had little liberty through the whole day. O, my dear Lord, though I have begun the year so poorly, yet grant, I beseech thee, that I may spend it to thy glory."

But the next Lord's day brought a blessing to his soul, and he writes: "This day was a refreshing time with us. Glory to God alone."

Four weeks later, Feb. 5, he says: "In the forenoon I had some freedom, but at noon I could get no text to preach from, till just before I began to speak. Then the Lord gave me one, and gave me glorious liberty in preaching from it."

This notice is characteristic. Mr. Backus was at this period of his ministry in the habit of preaching many times during the week, and he does not seem to have given so much attention to the arrangement of his thoughts beforehand as is necessary in order to the clearest and most forcible exhibition of truth. His sermons contained, it is evident, much of the marrow of the Gospel, and when the Spirit of God touched his feelings in a special manner his exhortations became earnest and powerful. Then his natural diffidence gave way and he urged home the calls of mercy with glowing zeal upon the hearts of dying men.

"Thursday, Feb. 9. Two couples were married at Raynham; I was there and preached, but was remarkably straitened in spirit; yet in the evening I had delightful liberty. Blessed be God, that though he gives sore correction for sin, yet he will not take away his loving kindness from me."

"Lord's day, March 5. Both preacher and hearers were dull through most of the day; but, glory to God, he gave us some refreshing from his presence."

"Lord's day, March 26. This has been a very awful day. My soul has been fearfully straitened, and so were the saints in general. Sinners appeared to have their minds barred against the truth. O Lord, what shall I say unto thee, or what shall I do, if thou dost not return? Return, O Lord! and for thy name's sake, revive thy work."

"Lord's day, July 2. To-day the Lord made me to see that there was a great want of discipline in this church; and to warn the saints to arise and be faithful in this work."

"Friday, July 28. Being sensible that the Spirit of God is in a great measure withholden from us, and yet proposing, if the Lord will, to enjoy the ordinance of the Supper next Sabbath, we did therefore keep this day in fasting and prayer. After the people came together, I offered prayer; then one of the brethren followed, and during his prayer the wind of the Spirit began to breathe upon us. Then I went on to show the duty of renewing covenant with the Lord, and with one another; and the Lord did gloriously assist me for several hours."

We have seen that Mr. Backus began his ministry as an evangelist; and it may be added, that after his settlement as a pastor, he made frequent and sometimes extended journeys for the purpose of preaching the Gospel. This practice of going from place to place to declare the word of life, was not, however, peculiar to him, but was characteristic of the Separate ministers generally. They were stimulated and encouraged by the success of Whitefield and Tennant, and were ready, for the good of souls, to labor in the humblest manner. The work which they performed was, on the whole, similar to that which occupies an army of colporteurs at the present day. It consisted mainly in preaching the gospel, but for the most part, to small companies in private houses. Yet the New-Light ministers were also in the habit of visiting and assisting one another, and of preaching without hesitation wherever people were inclined to hear. They paid but slight regard to parish limits, and continually trespassed on fields that were claimed as their own by clergymen of the standing order. We subjoin a few passages from the diary of Mr. Backus, in illustration of these remarks.

Jan. 22, 1749, he visited Mr. Snow and his people, and speaks thus of their condition: "Their trials have been coming on for some time; chiefly for this reason. Last year they had a wonderful revival, but they now found that they had sometimes followed imagination instead of faith, and had made too much of sweet feelings and transports. At this discovery, Satan comes in with an attempt to drive them over to the opposite extreme, trying to have them settle down upon a doctrinal knowledge of the truth, and a mere belief of the fulness there is in Christ, without the Spirit of God to lay open and apply divine things with power to the soul. Some were caught in the meshes of this subtle error, and then others set up bars against them for it."

Feb. 20. "This morning we set out for Harwich, and found the Lord was with us on the way directing our steps, refreshing our souls, and giving us liberty in witnessing for him in sundry places where we stopped."

Feb. 23. (Harwich.) "The Lord favored us wonderfully through the whole day, (in the ordination of Mr. Nickerson). In the evening, as we were about parting, some of us were at a loss in respect to our duty, and we joined in prayer to ask counsel of God. He did gloriously answer us, showing the ways in which we should severally go, and pouring down into our souls such divine blessings that we had not room enough to receive them."

Feb. 28. "This morning we left Barnstable. I believe God has a remnant there whom he will yet bring in to taste of his grace. O Lord, wilt thou not send help to that dear people, for thy name's sake? Oh that thou wouldst water that dry and barren place with the showers of grace, and show them thy mercy according to the days wherein they have seen evil."

April. 25, 1750. "Reached Rehoboth in the afternoon, and found the saints met together. I preached from 2 Sam. 15:22, and though I felt like a guilty wretch before God, yet now I found real assistance from above in laying open the awful nature of sin, and the nature of true submission."

May 11. "We returned in the evening from Colchester to Norwich. I conversed on the way with dear brother Leffingwell, and I trust we felt something of that which the two disciples felt when going to Emmaus."

We insert the following letter as an interesting specimen of New-Light correspondence. Among the letters which Mr. Backus preserved are several from the same hand.

"NORWICH, JANUARY 12, 1747-8.

"DEAR BROTHER: — Wishing you to abound in the gifts and graces of the Spirit of God, I have taken this opportunity of writing to you, to let you know something of the affairs of Christ's kingdom with us. Since your departure, the Lord has added two to his mystical body; namely, your honored grandmother, that mother in Israel, and the wife of Ebenezer Grover. The Lord has also made some sweet and blessed addition to us in grace, as well as in number. Last Sabbath there was the shout of a king in the camp of Israel. Our dear sister Martha[1] proved to be a Mary indeed, and a laborer also. Many others were sweetly refreshed and solemnized by the grace of God, and aged sinners were awed. And now, dear brother, to speak particularly of myself, through the goodness, grace, and mercy of our God, I am in bodily health at present, but in soul lean from day to day, to my shame and blushing. Remember me in these bonds. * * Dear brother, remember the Captain of your salvation goeth before you, leading on the way through the ranks and armies of your enemies; therefore fear not, though an host should encamp against you, and be in nothing terrified by your adversaries. It

[1] Col. Lathrop's wife.

may be to them an evident token of perdition, but to you of salvation, and that of God. Dear brother, you are not called to the honors of this world, but to be cast out of men, and to be brought before kings and rulers for Christ's sake. * * It is not for the servant to be above his master, nor the disciple above his Lord; 'if they have persecuted me, they will also persecute you,' says our dear Lord and Master.

I remain your loving brother,
in the dear Lord Jesus. Amen.
JOHN LEFFINGWELL, JR."

"This brother Leffingwell," says Mr. Backus in a note on the back of the letter given above, "is dear to me; and he hath been a blessed helper in the church of God at Norwich."

May 13. "My heart has been rejoiced sundry times since I have been here (at Norwich), in conversing with some of these dear lambs (that have lately been converted), and in seeing the sweet temper, and love, and solemnity they discover. Oh that God would keep and lead them forward."

Attleboro', June 11. "Went to brother Daggett's and conversed with him until late in the evening; found it truly edifying. He told me that he perceived the error of making the Spirit the rule instead of the Word to be creeping into the church."

Beech Woods, Sept. 26. (Second conference with Mr. I. Hovey, of Rochester.)[1] "Upon the whole I find that much disputing is hurtful in many respects; and in such public debates, I find it very difficult to manage so as to secure any real benefit."

Oct. 1. "In the forenoon I felt too much of careless-

[1] See p. 51.

ness, yet some degree of watchfulness, and cries after God; in the afternoon I preached from 1 Thess. 5:15, to a larger number than we could expect by reason of the rain. I was enabled very plainly to lay open the nature of the operations of God's Spirit, and it was a time of glorious refreshing — such a meeting as I have not seen for many weeks."

Dec. 2. (Lord's day.) "Found divine sweetness in treating the words: 'Thy time was a time of love;' and in the afternoon had uncommon clearness in showing the difference between the two covenants. In the evening I preached at mother's, to a house crowded full of people. It was a solemn and refreshing season. My dear grandmother was so overcome that she could not refrain from speaking. Glory to God for his boundless mercies."

Dec. 4. (Barnstable.) "Just at night we called at a house, where I had the greatest enlargement of soul that I 've had for several years. Heaven seemed to come down to earth. We joined in singing and prayer, and were really of one heart and of one soul. Then I went on to call upon all not to look upon creatures, but to behold our God; and I did solemnly demand entertainment for the King of Glory; and I went on to set forth his glories, till I was entirely swallowed up in admiration, and could only cry: 'Oh, the height! the depth! etc.'"

Truro, April 8, 1751. "We found more than two hundred people met together, and (Rev.) Mr. Avery, of Truro, and (Rev.) Mr. Lewis, of Billingsgate, with them. Then I went on to preach from 2 Cor. 13:5, and God was with me, of a truth, aiding me to declare how Christ is in every saint, and that this may be certainly known. The word was refreshing to many. Then these ministers desired to have some discourse with us. So we began, and Mr.

Avery asked what right we had to preach in his parish, without his leave; concluding, from a passage in Romans, that Paul would not build on another man's foundation, and from one in 2 Corinthians, that he would not go into another man's line, that my course was wrong. Then Mr. Lewis took the matter up, and went on with a long discourse upon many things. When I could have liberty to speak, I told them that if we would talk to edification, we must not run upon many things at once. As to the first passage brought forward, I told them Paul was showing that his lot was more especially to preach to the heathen, but that he had a right to preach among any saints when he had opportunity; and as to the other passages, I held that he was showing the Corinthians that his line reached as far in discipline as it did in preaching; for he says: we are come as far as you in preaching the gospel. We then proceeded to other things, and I suppose we disputed two hours and a half or three hours. During the whole I felt peace of mind, and I believe that many were convicted of their wrong. Once Mr. Lewis called for witnesses against me in a particular thing, but none would answer, till two or three witnessed against him that he had treated me unfairly. I bless God for giving me so much clearness in standing for truth."

But while Mr. Backus addressed himself thus earnestly to the work of a pastor and evangelist, he found time also to make provision for a life of domestic happiness. And no reader of these pages will be surprised to learn, that before acting in this affair he besought the direction of God with fasting. On his first visit to Massachusetts, he had preached in Rehoboth (Jan. 18, 1747), and had then conversed on the subject of religion with *Miss Susanna Mason*, of that place. Their brief acquaintance was renewed from time to time, and seems to have ripened into mutual esteem, and then at length into true affection. "We solemnly covenanted together in July," says Mr. Backus, "were published in September, and were married November 29, 1749. Thus Susanna Mason, of Rehoboth, became the companion of my life for nearly fifty-one years,[1] and the greatest temporal blessing which God ever gave me; for which I trust I shall praise him to eternity."

A further notice of this wedding may not be without interest to some of our readers. It took place at Miss Mason's home, where a goodly company of friends and neighbors assembled. A psalm was read by Rev. Mr. Shepard, of Attleboro', a hymn was sung, and prayer offered. "Then," says Mr. Backus, "I took my dear Susan by the hand, and spoke something of the sense I had of our standing and acting in the presence of God, and also how he had clearly pointed out to me this person to be my companion and a helper meet for me. Then I declared the marriage covenant; and she did the same. Thereupon Esquire Foster solemnly declared that we were lawfully *husband and wife*." The bridal salutations are described in the following manner: "Brother Shepard wished us a blessing, and gave us a good exhortation, and so did some others." Another prayer was offered; after which all united in singing the one hundred and first Psalm; this was followed by a short sermon from Mr. Backus himself. The account closes thus: "I think I can truly say that Jesus and his disciples were at the wedding. My soul is astonished at the goodness of God. Oh, that I may never forget His benefits!"

[1] These words were written when he was more than eighty years old.

CHAPTER VII.

CHANGE OF BELIEF RESPECTING BAPTISM.

DECLENSION IN TITICUT. — BAPTIST TENDENCIES OF THE SEPARATES. — DIVISION RESPECTING BAPTISM IN THE TITICUT CHURCH. — MR. BACKUS PERPLEXED. — HASTILY PREACHES IN FAVOR OF BELIEVERS' BAPTISM. — RELAPSES INTO HIS FORMER BELIEF. — JOURNEY TO NORWICH. — RETRACTS THE VIEWS OF HIS SERMON ON BAPTISM.— SECESSION OF CERTAIN BAPTIZED MEMBERS FROM HIS CHURCH. — TRIES IN VAIN TO EXCLUDE THE PAINFUL TOPIC FROM HIS MIND. — EXTRACTS FROM HIS JOURNAL. — HIS REFLECTIONS ON INFANT BAPTISM. — DAY OF FASTING, PRAYER, AND INVESTIGATION.— FINDS NO AUTHORITY IN THE WORD OF GOD FOR INFANT BAPTISM. — IS BAPTIZED.

But we must turn from this glimpse of domestic joy to follow the subject of our narrative through a long period of trial. According to his own testimony, sad tokens of a decline in vital piety began to appear in his parish soon after the beginning of 1749. Whispering and backbiting prevailed to a fearful extent, especially among the young people; and warnings from the servant of Christ did not avail to arrest the evil. Gospel discipline was also greatly neglected, and a melancholy change in the state of religion was but too evident. This was a severe affliction to the young and zealous pastor.

But this was not all. The Separates had embraced substantially Baptist views of the Christian church. They affirmed with great unanimity that only those who give satisfactory evidence of piety are entitled to the privilege of membership in the church, and that only those who are regenerated by the Spirit of God are "Abraham's seed, and heirs according to the promise." Some of them, it cannot be doubted, saw more or less clearly the inconsistency of these declarations with the practice of infant baptism. In the Articles of the Mansfield church there is one which reads: "Though *most* of us agree in the Article of infant baptism, yet a difference in that particular doth not break the spiritual communion of saints; therefore it is no just bar to our covenanting and partaking of the ordinances together wherein we are agreed." Others perceived more distinctly than the New-Lights themselves whither their doctrine of a "spiritual church" was likely to conduct them. As early as May 17, 1743, Rev. A. Croswell, of Groton, Conn., thus writes to Rev. Mr. Prince, of Boston: "I may hereafter print something about the times, showing wherein I have seen reason to alter my judgment, particularly with reference to *exhorters*. For though I was the first in New England that set them up, I now see, too late, that the tendency of their ways is to drive learning out of the world, and to sow it thick with the dreadful errors of Anabaptism, Quakerism, and Antinomianism!" And in 1741, the Consociation of Windham County, Conn., objected to the article cited above, because it tends "to let in Anabaptists, and seems more agreeable to the inclination of parties than the Word of God." We will now proceed to give, from the papers of Mr. Backus, and nearly in his own words, written from time to time as the events took place, an account of his change of views in respect to the ordinance and subjects of baptism.

At a church meeting, August 7, 1749, Ebenezer Hinds and Dea. Jonathan Woods declared that they had embraced the Baptist principle. This led to much discourse on the subject, and sundry of the brethren were ready to follow their example. They advocated the opinion that plunging is the right way of baptizing, and that infants are not qualified for this ordinance. The question thus introduced became a very prominent topic of thought and of debate. Those who had adopted Baptist sentiments were persuaded that they could convince the rest of the church, and therefore improved every opportunity to discuss the matter. Bitter clashing and contention followed, by which the remaining life of religion was destroyed. All the evil was traced by one party to the Baptist principle, and by the other, to fear and resistance of the truth. In reality, however, it sprang chiefly from the unchristian temper which these brethren displayed toward one another.

For a time Mr. Backus strove not to meddle with the new doctrine. From the ill behavior charged upon Baptists of former and later times, he was led to fear that some mischief lurked in their principles, and that these were now sent as a delusion in judgment upon them. But he could not exclude the topic utterly from his thoughts. About the 20th of August, he began to give it close attention; but he was dreadfully perplexed, and his mind was tossed this way and that. When he carefully searched the Scriptures, light seemed to be clearest for the Baptist doctrines; but when he looked at his own guilt and that of his people, the fear returned that these things were sent in judgment upon them. On Saturday night, August 26th, while crying to God for help and direction, he found there were many things very dear to him which yet he could freely give up into the hands of God, but that in this case he felt a sensible pulling back. At length this conclusion suddenly came into his mind: namely, *the Baptist principles are certainly right, because nature fights so against them.* The next day he felt a secret hurrying on to preach upon this subject; which he did in the afternoon, taking for his text, Romans 6 : 4, and maintaining that none have any right to baptism except believers, and that immersion seems to be the only correct mode.

In the evening, after this premature discourse, occasioned by a hasty decision, darkness began to fill his mind, and on the forenoon of Monday this darkness became well nigh total. A little light, however, seemed to dawn upon him in the afternoon, and the next morning he was enabled to cast his burdens on the Lord. He now saw in the dreadful gloom we have noticed, an indication that the doctrine maintained in his sermon must be wrong; he remembered also how the Bible everywhere represents the Lord as granting many favors and blessings to the children of saints for their fathers' sakes; he thought of God's covenant with Abraham and the tenor of his promise: "I will be a God to thee and to thy seed after thee," and found this to be the covenant with Christians still; and he concluded in the light of these considerations that the children of believers have a right to baptism. These reflections appeared to satisfy his mind, and he set out cheerfully on his way to Norwich.

Making a flying call upon his friends in Rehoboth, he went into Providence on Thursday, August 31st, and there met with three of his flock at the house of Rev. Joseph Snow. They had started from home with the purpose of being plunged; but Mr. Snow spoke so clearly upon Infant Baptism that one of them without further delay turned his steps homeward. Mr. Backus proceeded to Norwich, and after spending some weeks in preaching, visiting, and attending to secular affairs, returned to his parish on the 23d of September.

Meanwhile, he had become, as he thought, fully settled

in his former opinion, that only[1] believers and their infant seed are entitled to baptism, and that as to the mode, every one must be fully persuaded in his own mind and act accordingly. His intercourse with ministers of the Separate order during this journey may have aided in bringing him to such a conclusion. Yet he was sometimes sorely puzzled to fix the line beyond which one had no right to baptism; for he knew that Abraham circumcised not only children under age, but also his three hundred servants. From this difficulty, however, he took refuge in the plea of ignorance, confessing, as Paul does, that "now we see through a glass darkly."

Arriving in Titicut, he soon learned that in his absence Elder E. Moulton, of South Brimfield, now Wales, had come to Bridgewater by invitation, and had plunged, Sept. 17th and 18th, nine members of his church, with one other person.[2] Here then, was a new trial; but it does not seem to have modified his own course. At a meeting of the church, Tuesday, September 26th, he made a full confession, and retracted the sentiments expressed in his sermon upon baptism. Those who had been immersed were disappointed and offended at this recantation; and on the next Lord's day they met by themselves for reli-

[1] "Only believers," etc., for the New-Lights were all opposed to the Half-way Covenant, which admitted to baptism the children of those who made no claim to personal piety.

[2] Their names were, Jonathan Woods, (Dea.) Joseph Harvey and his wife Mary Harvey, Joseph Leach, William Richards, William Hooper, Ebenezer Hinds, Nathaniel Shaw, and Timothy Bryant. Joseph Leach was not a member of the church. It will be noticed that Mr. Backus uses the word "plunged"; doubtless with the same feeling of contempt for the rite which leads to the choice of this term or the word "dipped" to describe the ordinance at the present day. We trust the time will at length come when good men will employ something better and nobler than ridicule in treating of Christian ordinances.

gious worshsip.[1] But Mr. Backus was ready to make his relapse into the common belief still more public and practical. In the afternoon of the following Sabbath, Oct. 8th, he discoursed upon the submission of David: "Here am I, let Him do with me as seemeth good unto Him," and then spoke of his sorrow for preaching against infant baptism, going so far even as to declare that he was willing to venture into eternity on that practice; and proceeding thereafter "to baptize a child of sister Richmond."

But in the present case also he was guilty of rashness; and he afterwards, (in 1752) made this record: "Though I really thought that way to be right, yet those expressions which I delivered publicly, concerning venturing into eternity on that practice, did carry in them a much greater certainty than I really had at the time in my own soul, which has often since caused me to mourn before the Lord."

Soon after the events which we have recited took place, Mr. Backus resolved to dismiss all anxiety and inquiry on the subject, and to treat infant baptism as an ordinance of the gospel. But it had been determined otherwise; and before many weeks were passed he was brought to a stand in his course by the question: *Where, and in what relation to the church of God do those stand who have been baptized and yet are not believers?* The question was proposed to him by no one, — unless by the Spirit of God, — and he

[1] In the evening of February 3, 1750, seven of these persons united together as a church, and soon after Mr. Hinds began to preach among them. But this church dissolved within a few months; Mr. Hinds and Mr. Shaw united with the Second Baptist Church in Boston; and several others became members of the First Baptist Church in Swanzey. Mr. Hinds was afterwards pastor of the Second Baptist Church in Middleboro'; and Mr. Shaw was for more than fifty years a faithful deacon of the First Baptist Church in that town.

could not exclude it from his mind. But he now moved slowly, and only after two years of painful suspense and study did he reach a satisfactory conclusion. It will be profitable to know some of his feelings during this period.

Lord's day, Dec. 31, 1749. "My unsettled state about baptism wounds and weakens my soul; but this day I was favored with considerable tenderness and clearness in preaching."

Feb. 4, 1750. "For some time in the evening I felt such guilt and distress that I was ready to cry: 'A wounded spirit who can bear?' The promised joys of sin were turned into pain, and my soul was in agony. Lord, when thou hidest thy face, who can behold thee?"

Feb. 17th. "This day I feel much as I have done for a long time. There is a constant load upon my mind. Yet at times I am intensely engaged in study; though I have scarce any strength or heart to act for God."

April 8th. "I find considerable strugglings in my heart against declaring the whole truth, because I practise no more of it myself. O Lord, deliver me from the power of this temptation!"

July 15th. "I have worried along now for some months, sometimes feeling so guilty and ashamed in viewing my past conduct and present case that I hardly wanted to see anybody. * * * But in the midst of all this various turning of things within and without, I find my soul is held, as a ship by the anchor is held in the boisterous waves, either from dashing on the rocks or driving off into the wild ocean."

July 23d. "Felt as if I were laid aside by God and man; could find scarce anything to do; yet the Lord gave me instruction out of all this. At night a few of us had a meeting at brother Alden's, and near the close of it I had such glimpses of the heavenly glory and such drawings of divine love as I have n't felt before these many weeks. Oh, one taste of love is infinitely sweeter than all that earth can afford."

Sept. 5th. "Labored with my hands most of the day; dull and stupid; but in the evening the Lord gave me sweet enlargement in secret prayer. I was enabled to come as a child to a father, tell him all my wants, and lay open my very heart to him."

Sept. 9th. "Enjoyed considerable freedom in preaching, and some of the hearers were refreshed. We then partook of the Lord's supper. Two offered themselves for communion with us, and told their experiences. One was the wife of Isaac Pierce, of Beech Woods, who was received; the other was my dear wife, who had blessed clearness in describing the dealings of God with her soul, and the whole church seemed to be affected thereby. We then attended to the ordinance itself, which by reason of the difficulties among us had not been observed for more than a twelvemonth. Sundry of the saints were divinely refreshed while partaking of the supper."

Nov. 11th. "This forenoon I had no remarkable assistance, but in the afternoon I was led to treat of the hope and comfort of the saints, and to lay open the horrid falseness of the notion entertained by carnal hearts, that a life of holiness is an uncomfortable life. There is no true happiness here or hereafter but in being conformed to God in heart and conduct."

Dec. 19th. "Was much depressed in the morning by a sense of my vileness and by a view of the miserable case of this people. The waters came into my soul."

Dec. 31st. "Spent much of the day in reading. In the evening I preached to a little number at brother Alden's. Alas, I had but a poor ending of the year. Almost the whole of this year, 1750, has been a season of heavy trial to my soul. If any one had told me a twelvemonth ago that I should meet with all which I have gone through since, I should have thought it insupportable. Hence the reasonableness of Christ's word: "Take no thought for the morrow, for sufficient unto the day is the evil thereof."

Feb. 13, 1751. "Was called in the afternoon to visit a sick woman, and found some assistance in praying and conversing with her. But in the evening I felt horrid temptations even to Atheism and Infidelity, which taught me the danger we are still in, if left of God."

April 5th, (Harwich.) "My soul was brought to such a view of the discipline of God's house and the want of it among our people, that I could not but solemnly engage before God to be faithful in that work, and I called all the saints to witness against me if I was not; and I felt such a salvation as I had not for a year or two before."

Aug. 13th. "Had a short conference with some of our brethren concerning our church affairs; our case appears exceedingly difficult still."

And, long after, Mr. Backus thus refers to his reluctant and protracted inquiries at this time in respect to baptism: "No man, who has not experienced the like, can form a proper idea of the distress I endured for two years." We are now in some measure prepared to trace the mental and moral process by which his views on this subject were changed, to draw near and sympathize with this servant of God, while, by "agonizing prayer" and "intense study," he slowly emerges from darkness into light, from painful suspense into assured belief.

When the question, "where, and in what relation to the

church of God, do those persons stand, who have been baptized and yet are not believers?" presented itself to the mind of Mr. Backus, he was unable to find a satisfactory answer. He perceived that during the former dispensation, all who had been circumcised were in the church, which was national. He also saw, and had clearly seen for many years, that under the new dispensation, none are in the church, but saints who are built *up as lively stones*, etc. He found no gospel standing-place for half-way members. In spite of all he could do, he felt constrained to omit the practice of infant baptism, and for upwards of a year his mind continued in nearly the same posture of indecision, "suffering trials which no tongue can express." On the fifth of April, 1751, he made a solemn promise to the Lord to attempt the restoration of faithful discipline in the church. He succeeded at first in leading his brethren to engage in this work; but after a time some of them said they could go no further in disciplinary labor, till they knew how the case would turn with him as to baptism. Discouraged by this obstacle, he felt himself compelled to let the work drop.

Having thus borne for almost two years the tortures of doubt respecting the subjects and mode of baptism, he set apart Saturday, July 20, 1751, as a day of secret fasting and prayer, to seek once more the direction of God. After confessing his sins, and earnestly imploring divine help, he took Wilson's Scripture Manual, and seriously examined every particular passage of God's Word which relates to baptism, and was forced to "give in" that the sentiments of Mr. Wilson appeared to be according to the mind of Christ. Then, still looking to the Most High for direction, he went on to examine several portions of the Sacred Record, which speak of God's blessing his people and their seed with them. He carefully reviewed the account of Noah's preservation with his family, the promises made to Abraham and his seed, to David and his posterity, and the descriptions given in the Old Testament of the Messiah's reign; and he concluded in view of all these, that God had promised to manifest himself to his people in the latter days, and to pour out his Spirit upon them in a very extraordinary and glorious manner; also, that he had given to believers great encouragement to bring their offspring to him, praying and hoping for large blessings upon them; *for they shall all know him, from the least to the greatest.* But he was led at the same time by this comprehensive and prayerful survey to conclude that none ought to be baptized, and thus have the outward mark of Christ's disciples put upon them, except those who give evidence of having believed in him. This settlement of the question gave him some degree of peace. "But yet, alas!" he says, "I feel like a weak creature still, having but little strength and boldness to come forth in the truth in this evil day. Lord, I commit my all to thee."

At a meeting of the church, July 25th, he made known to his brethren the character and result of his inquiries, declaring his full conviction that there is no scripture warrant for infant baptism. Much discourse followed. On the 29th he writes: "I have had some distressing views of my case, and of the danger of being left as a stumbling block to others, or as a barren useless creature. I went to pour out my soul to God, and I was enabled to confess my sins, and with earnestness to plead, that he would either bring my soul forth to act for him, or take me out of the world. For I had rather be hid in the grave, than to live a burden to his creation." He also spent the 30th of this month in fasting, humiliation and prayer, and closes his record of it with these words: "O Lord, bow down thine ear and hear; for I am poor and needy. We are made a strife to our neighbors, and our enemies laugh among themselves. Turn us again, O Lord of hosts, and cause thy face to shine upon us, and we shall be saved."

Mr. Backus was now fully satisfied in respect to his duty. He therefore sent for Elder Benjamin Pierce of Warwick, Rode Island, to administer the ordinance of baptism; and on the 22d of August, 1751, he was baptized with six members of his church, on profession of faith in Christ.

CHAPTER VIII.

COUNCIL UPON COUNCIL.

POSTURE OF MR. BACKUS.—IS CENSURED WITH OTHERS BY THE FIRST COUNCIL.—VISITS NORWICH.—RETURNS HOME AND IS RESTORED TO OFFICE.—TWO OPPOSING BRETHREN ARE ADMONISHED BY THE CHURCH.—A SECOND COUNCIL ADMONISHES THESE TWO BRETHREN, AND THEN THE CHURCH.—EFFORTS TO RESTORE PEACE.—A THIRD (EX PARTE) COUNCIL CENSURES MR. BACKUS AND JUSTIFIES THE TWO BRETHREN—REMARKS ON THIS ACTION. MR. BACKUS EXCLUDED FROM THE CHURCH.—HIS LETTER TO THE SAME ON INFANT BAPTISM.—VISITS STURBRIDGE; CONDITION OF THAT CHURCH; COUNCIL THERE.—OPPRESSION IN NORWICH.—FOURTH COUNCIL IN TITICUT.—GENERAL MEETING OF NEW-LIGHTS IN EXETER, R. I.—FIFTH COUNCIL IN TITICUT.—GENERAL CONVENTION AT STONINGTON, CT.—PROCEEDINGS.—RESULT.

No one can be surprised that Mr. Backus came with great reluctance to the conclusion above described. His early education, his attachment to a large circle of relatives and to ministers of the Separate order; his prejudice against the Baptists, whose name was literally cast out as evil, and his unwillingness to recant a deliberate, public, solemn recantation, thus exposing himself afresh to the charge of fickleness, fully explain this reluctance. But at length, to use his own language, believing that "truth is to be received and held for its own sake, and not upon any exterior motives; and that it is never to be violated or forsaken for any consideration whatsoever," he had been able "to leave good men and bad men out of the question, and inquire: *What saith the Scripture?* Hereby a settlement was granted, and he was baptized."

But this act did not bring him to the point of rest. Slowly, with careful inquiry, and impelled by the pressure of truth, was he to pass on step by step to his final position. At this time he did not look upon himself as a Baptist, nor desire to become connected with that denomination. His purpose was to abide with the flock over which he had been placed by the Holy Ghost; and as several of the members believed the practice of infant baptism to be scriptural, he proposed to have the rite administered, when desired, by neighboring clergymen. In this way, it seemed to him possible for the whole church to remain together in peace and without violence to the convictions of any.

But the church was in a very sad condition; brotherly love was almost gone and discipline had fallen to the ground. Every day it became more evident that the pastor had given serious offence to some of his flock.

In this posture of affairs it was deemed expedient to seek the advice of other churches. A council was therefore called, which met on the 2d of October, 1751, and continued in session three days. From the records of this council we present a summary of its action. The first day was devoted chiefly to an examination of the "travail of Isaac Backus" in respect to the ordinance of baptism. But this examination was at length interrupted and the further prosecution of it deferred until inquiry had been made as to the standing of the church. Most of the second day was spent in making this inquiry; and it was found not only that diverse opinions and great confusions prevailed in the church, but also that some of its members had a controversial disposition.

On the third day, the church covenant was read and sixteen members gave themselves up afresh to the service of God, promising to walk together in the ordinances and discipline of Christ's house. Notwithstanding their previous neglect of gospel discipline, these and some others were voted by the council to be regular members. It was also voted that Isaac Backus, by neglecting to discipline some that were scandalous walkers, by not putting, in many respects, the laws of Christ's house in execution, by falling out of the testimony and not standing in the authority of his office, has violated his pastoral covenant and is a transgressor of the laws of Christ's house. As such an one he was admonished. Those who refused to enter into covenant with the sixteen mentioned above, were then censured by the council and declared to be persons of irregular standing. According to the testimony of Mr. Backus, those who renewed covenant at this time were charged to follow the irregular members till they were either restored to fellowship or cut off by discipline. In the course of two or three weeks four of them were restored. As to Mr. Backus, he had, at the time, no courage to unite with the sixteen, and was therefore left under censure by the council.

On the 15th of October he set out for Norwich with his wife and his mother. The former he left with her friends in Rehoboth. Proceeding to his native place with his excellent mother, he began after a few days to feel a "real thirsting" of spirit for an opportunity to bear testimony for God and to preach his gospel, before leaving the town. But he says, Oct. 22d: "I had some discourse with brother Hide, and he seemed to throw a block in the way; for though I felt some freedom in my soul towards God, and the load of guilt was to a considerable extent removed, yet because there remained some darkness in my mind as to how I should go on in the ordinance of baptism, he thought the censure was not taken off, and so he could not encourage my preaching as I now stood. These things brought fresh distress upon my poor soul. Some part of the evening I felt dreadful wranglings of mind, and then a view of these did increase my burden; so that I was ready to choose strangling and death rather than life. On the morning of the next day I still felt this distress for a while, until it seemed that I could live no longer. Then I withdrew to pour out my complaint to my God, and he assisted me to draw near and order my cause before him. And as I was condoling my case and pleading that he would appear for the honor of his own name, that promise which was given me when I was first called to preach, was brought afresh to my mind,—*my grace is sufficient for thee.* This did renewedly take hold of my soul, and I was enabled by it to lay hold of the girdle of God's faithfulness and to wrestle with him as really as ever Jacob did. Oh, how dreadful was that place! God's majesty and glory appeared, and I was strengthened to bring forth sundry enemies to have them slain before him; also to renew covenant with him, in a most solemn manner, to go on in his work; and my soul had a measure of sweet deliverance. In the evening the saints met, and I told them something of my travail, and was enabled to dedicate myself and all I have to God, to be the servant of his church for Jesus' sake. They received me, and I preached from 1 John, 3: 8, with considerable clearness. Glory to God for his amazing goodness to such a wandering creature!"

Much affected by the loving-kindness of God, Mr. Backus, on the 2d of November, returned to his peaceful home and to his distracted flock. Meanwhile, during his absence, the Lord had been in the place, some of the saints had enjoyed refreshing seasons, and the spirit of love and fellowship seemed to be resuming its control. In the evening after his return, we find him saying: "An Indian man, one of my neighbors, came in, and I found him under deep conviction. The Lord gave me remarkable enlargement in laboring with him for an hour or two. I have not seen a person under more powerful conviction for a year. Glory to God!"

November 8th. The church restored him to fellowship and to his office as pastor. But Samuel Alden and Robert Washburn would not give their consent to his reässuming the pastorship, unless he would baptize infants. A private brother, although rejecting this practice, might, indeed, remain in the church; but a minister, they insisted, who thought it to be without scriptural warrant, could not be tolerated. And, therefore, "after much labor, they were admonished as offenders, and suspended from church communion, because they held to that which tended to divide the body of Christ." Those persons also who had been baptized by Elder Moulton, and who believed in restricted communion, were admonished and laid under censure.

But the end was not yet. Although a large part of the church sustained Mr. Backus, the two recusant brethren adhered to their position, and refused to accept him as pastor. At their request a council was called, which met on the 27th of May, 1752. After examination, the council expressed a belief, that Samuel Alden and Robert Washburn were guilty of setting up a bar which they ought not against the reception of the pastor by the church, while he could not engage to baptize infants; but at the same time the council declared itself not clearly satisfied that the church as a body was right in admonishing them.

All on both sides were then invited to come forward, give up themselves to God, and renew covenant one with another to go on in his ways. The response to this invitation was not satisfactory; and the council accordingly "gave its testimony, that the pastor and church as a body lay under the defilement of sin in neglecting to go on in gospel discipline, and did admonish and call upon them to arise and be faithful now to strengthen the things which remain, which are ready to die, as they would escape the dreadful judgment of God's departing."

Here then was no progress, no relief. It is not enough, the two brethren still insisted, for Mr. Backus to agree that all who wish to have their children sprinkled, may call in ministers to do it who believe in the rite; he must, as pastor, do this himself. On the other hand, it was impossible for him to perform this ceremony without doing violence to his religious belief. In this condition of affairs he made another effort, along with some of the brethren, to bring about a union and to prosecute the discipline of the church. They not only strove to avoid all controversy about the ordinance of baptism, but sought not to mention it even; and after a time, having excluded the two contentious brethren, they began to hope for prosperity.

But their hopes were doomed to be disappointed. For these two brethren sent to three churches for advice, and a council met at the house of Joshua Fobes in Bridgewater, on the 1st of November, 1752. Although this was an *ex parte* council, Mr. Backus and the church did not object to having the course which they had taken with Alden and Washburn thoroughly examined by it.

After organizing, the council proceeded to inquire:

1. Whether the covenant of the church was agreeable to the Word of God, particularly concerning infant bap-

tism? And the reply was, that "we find the above mentioned covenant, particularly in respect to infant baptism, to be no way contrary to the Word of God, but agreeable thereto.[1]

2. Whether Isaac Backus has broken said covenant, or the two aggrieved brethren, Samuel Alden and Robert Washburn? And this answer was given: "We find that the above named Isaac Backus hath broken covenant, particularly in respect to infant baptism;" alleging his declaration, that he could venture into eternity upon it, and in contrast with this, his subsequent re-baptism and refusal to baptize the children of members belonging to the church under his pastoral care.

3. Whether there should be any difference, as to their being received into a church, between a pastor and a private member, who are alike wanting or destitute of divine teaching and establishment in infant baptism, or who have fallen from it? And it was said in reply: We find there is a great difference. First, because a pastor must be so taught and established in the truth that he may be able to teach others also, and by sound doctrine convince the gainsayers, etc. And, secondly, because the pastor has also to administer the sacraments of the New Testament, according to Christ's appointment, and if he is not established in the practice of infant baptism, the church is deprived in part of the outward means whereby Christ communicates the benefits of redemption.

4. As to the conduct of the above-named brethren, and their behavior towards the said Isaac Backus, pastor? — it was responded, that we can find no just charge to bring against them. Having been laid under church censure for holding their principles agreeable to their covenant, they

[1] Gen. 17:10. Acts 2:39. Gal. 3:29. 1 Cor. 1:16.

were thereby rendered incapable of dealing with the said Isaac Backus as a covenant breaker, otherwise than by a council. It was further declared to be the judgment of the council, that pastor and church and all who joined with them in suspending and excommunicating Samuel Alden and Robert Washburn, had acted contrary to the rule of the gospel and given just cause of offence to said brethren and to all who were in fellowship with the church at its organization. They were therefore solemnly charged, in the name of the Lord Jesus, with having caused a division and an offence contrary to the doctrine we have learned; and were solemnly exhorted to consider from whence they had fallen, and repent, and do their first work, lest Christ come quickly and remove the candlestick, etc.[1]

It may be remarked, that this council did not inquire of Mr. Backus respecting the reasons which had led him to renounce infant baptism; yet, in the result, he is said to have offered no scriptural warrant for his belief and action.[2] Neither was he asked to explain the strong expressions of confidence in that rite which he had once made; yet those expressions were emphatically and repeatedly brought forward in the result. It may also be observed that this council censured the church for doing the very things which the council of October 2d, 1751, had charged it to do. Solomon Paine was the moderator of both councils,

1 Rev. 2: 5.

2 Under the fourth count of the doings of this council, these words are addressed to the pastor; "You offer no scriptural warrant for your baptizing persons who have been baptized in the name of the Father, Son, and Holy Ghost, and for refusing to baptize minors upon the term of their being the household of believers, and have debarred your brethren not only of this, but of all the privileges which your covenant, made with them, holds forth, only because they would not have fellowship with such unfruitful works of uncertainty," etc.

and seems to have controlled in a great measure their action. The change which had taken place in his views will find an explanation in the sequel.

The proceedings of this council led to the exclusion of Mr. Backus from the church; though some few of the members seem to have adhered to him in the darkest hour. The majority, however, with Alden and Washburn at their head, established a meeting by themselves, which was sustained for a short time and then died away.[1] On the 18th of November, Mr. Backus sent the following letter:

"To the members of the Church in Bridgewater and Middleboro', who now profess to stand and act as the church:

"DEAR BRETHREN: Since you expressed, last week, when I was with you, that you were willing to receive light, if any could communicate it, concerning this point which is so much controverted among us; viz., of believers being the only proper subjects of baptism; and as my soul has a desire that you may be brought to see things as they are, therefore I have thought it expedient to write to you a few lines upon the matter. 1. One great argument brought to prove that it is right to baptize infants, is this—that the covenant which believers stand in now is just the same as that which was given to Abraham, to which circumcision was a seal. But it seems strange to me that any can hold it so. For the covenant, in the seventeenth of Genesis, plainly includes a promise to Abraham of a numerous posterity, and that kings should come out of him, and that they should have the land of Canaan for an everlasting

[1] Robert Washburn subsequently left Bridgewater and settled in Plainfield, Ct., where for some years he continued to be a strong advocate for infant baptism, and then relinquished it as an unscriptural practice.

possession, as well as that the Lord would be a God to that people. And circumcision was the seal of the covenant, which included all the ceremonial law, and the Jewish forms of worship. And there is one prescription expressed plainly, in first mentioning the time when children should be circumcised; viz., at eight days old. The reason for this was, that by the ceremonial law, they were not clean before, as is plainly expressed, Leviticus 12 : 3. Now, to say that baptism seals just the same covenant, is most strange and absurd.

"2. It is commonly said that the subjects are the same, only the seal is altered. But I never yet saw the person who practised so. The subjects then were all who would profess that religion, and their whole households, let them be old or young. A foreigner, or hired servant, was not to be taken in, but all the males who were property were to be circumcised.[1] Observe here, God says expressly—'Every man's servant who is bought with money (let him be as old as he may), when thou hast circumcised him, then shall he eat the passover.' Now I never saw one yet who practised according to this in baptism, and I hope I never may. There, the servant, let him be ever so old, was circumcised on his master's account; and it is plainly expressed that when they had circumcised him, he should eat the passover. So that, did I believe the subjects of baptism remained the same, I should not dare to shut off one of the children or servants of believers from this ordinance or from the Lord's Supper either.

"3. Another argument, which seems to be of great weight with many serious people, is, that our privileges are not less now than theirs were then. But in this, there seems to be much of the spirit of those ancient fathers who came

[1] Gen. 17: Ex. 12: 44, 45, 48.

out of Babylon, who despised the day of small things,[1] and wept when the foundation of the second temple was laid,[2] because the outward glory of it, when compared with the first temple, appeared as nothing. But God said, 'The glory of the latter house should exceed the former.'[3] The glory of the Jewish church stood much in outward things; (as of circumcision, God says — 'My covenant shall be in your flesh.') Now, as to the outward glory, they exceeded all churches which have existed in gospel times in many things. The prosperity and blessing in temporal things, which they enjoyed at times, I suppose, went greatly beyond what any church of Christ has had since he suffered; and the temple of Solomon was undoubtedly more magnificent than any house of worship on earth. But shall we say, therefore, that our privileges are less? No, surely. Again, they had three yearly public feasts, at which all their males were to appear before the Lord; but there is only one stated ordinance in the New Testament church; viz.: the Lord's Supper. But is it right to say that our privileges are cut short on that account? Once more, the gospel ministry as really comes in the place of the priesthood, as baptism does in that of circumcision; and the priesthood was confined to Aaron and his descendants. Now, is it good reasoning to say that gospel ministers have not so great privileges as the priests had, because they have no right to bring their children into the ministry? I believe no serious person will say so. Not a whit more of reason is there for saying, that the privileges of believers are now less, because they are not now allowed to partake of the ordinances of Christ's house until the Lord converts them and prepares them for it. The truth is, those things were types and shadows of heavenly things;[4] and

[1] Zech. 4:10. [2] Ezra 3:12. [3] Hag. 2:3, 9. [4] Heb. 8:5.

we have a more clear and glorious revelation of divine things; and our children have vastly greater advantages of being taught in the things of salvation by Jesus Christ. And it highly concerns every saint to use all gospel means and methods to bring his family as well as others to believe in Christ; so that they may have a right to all the privileges of the sons of God. And I wish I could see all those who are pleading so earnestly for infant baptism more engaged to train up their children in the ways of God.

"Thus, my brethren, I have hinted to you some things which were upon my mind concerning these matters. And I desire that you may be as noble as the Bereans were, and search the Scriptures daily, to see if these things are not so. And now, as to the line you are going on in, in admonishing all, as covenant breakers, who hold that none are the proper subjects of baptism but saints; I verily believe that in this you are striking against divine truth; though I hope it is ignorantly; and therefore, though I am not much concerned what you will do to me, yet I must say, *Do yourselves no harm.*

So I remain your souls' well-wisher,

ISAAC BACKUS."

We have found no record of the manner in which this letter was received or of the effect, if any, which it produced. The excluded pastor, however, continued his ministry with such as still approved his course; and after a few weeks it was deemed expedient to call another council.

Mr. Backus therefore set out (Jan. 1st, 1753,) on a journey for the purpose of requesting certain churches to send messengers to this council. And he soon perceived that many of his brethren among the Separates were deeply affected by the censure which had been passed upon him. This was particularly the case with those who had from the first held the immersion of believers to be the only baptism authorized by the New Testament, but who were at the same time decided advocates of open communion. Several of the New-Light ministers were to this extent Baptists when they were ordained; e. g., Samuel Drown, Stephen Babcock, Nathaniel Draper, and Peter Werden; and these were of course prepared to appreciate the convictions of Mr. Backus, and to sympathize with him in this hour of trial.

During this journey, he visited Sturbridge, January 7, being led thither by the peculiar condition of the church in that place. It appears that John Blunt, when settled as pastor over this church, was a believer in the practice of infant baptism.. After a while, however, he renounced that practice, and was himself immersed. He subsequently "buried with Christ in baptism," almost a hundred others. Yet he had lately come out once more in favor of infant baptism. Hearing of all this, Mr. Backus was drawn to Sturbridge, although he had no thought of going there when he left home. At noon, he told the saints (for it was Lord's day,) wherefore he had come, and that on hearing of their case these words were impressed upon his mind: "When thou art converted, strengthen thy brethren." In the afternoon he preached upon the "nature of a gospel establishment." "At night," he says, "I went home with brother Blunt, and he gave me a narrative of his travail, and how he was now brought to embrace infant baptism. After weighing his discourse deliberately, it was evident to me that his views had been changed principally by observing effects; viz.: some running into errors, making division among the saints, and the like; rather than by seeing scripture light for infant baptism. I therefore told him that I believed he must search deeper before he would have clear establishment."

On the following Tuesday, a council met to consider the difficulties between Mr. Blunt and the church. After organizing, "brother Blunt," it is said, "brought in a written copy of the church's admonishing him for his instability about baptism. Then he brought forward his complaint, saying he was grieved at the church for going off from the covenant which they first adopted, and also that he thought the church had broken covenant, by hindering him from baptizing infants. But after deliberately hearing and weighing the case, it was found by the council, that the pastor and church did all unitedly change their principles, and afterwards their articles, about baptism, and that brother Blunt went on to baptize upwards of ninety persons by immersion. So the council judged that he had broken covenant by his late course, and that the church did right in admonishing him. These things showed me that the question in respect to baptism is becoming more close and urgent. Oh, that the Lord may keep us from a party spirit, and enable us always to contend for the truth in love."[1]

Returning by way of his native place, in order to see his friends, he makes this record January 17: "I would here review a little what I have seen at Norwich. This last year the enemies have done more at haling the saints to prison for rates, than they have done ever before since our separation; but it is remarkably evident that, as it was with Israel, so it has been here: 'The more they oppressed them, the more they grew.' This congregation, I think, is nearly as large again as it was the last time I was here before. The Lord has indeed wrought wonders among them."

[1] See Appendix A.

On the 20th of January, he reached home; and on the 31st, the proposed council was held, and the following result was reported. "We find a peculiar difficulty subsisting among them[1] which affects the whole number of the Separate churches; therefore we refuse to give our opinions or judgments until the number of the faithful, by their messengers, meet together in a general assembly, to settle points of communion, * * * at Exeter, R. I., * * * on the 23d of May next." A copy of this was to be sent to all the Separate churches in fellowship in the land.

Twenty-five chuches were represented at the General Meeting in Exeter. After much deliberation and conference it was concluded: (1) That we do not find it to be a censurable evil for one who has professed and practised the baptism of minors, to turn from that to the baptism of adults by immersion; and (2) That we do not find it to be a censurable evil for one who has professed and practised re-baptizing by immersion, to turn from it and give up his children or minors in baptism. The word "censurable" refers of course to ecclesiastical censure. This, now, was thorough and consistent testimony in favor of mixed communion. And it may be worthy of remark, that the New-Light ministers who held to believers' baptism, were nearly or quite all present, while several of the more prominent defenders of the opposite view did not appear; e. g., Solomon Paine and Thomas Stephens.

On the second day of its session, this meeting took into consideration the case of Mr. Backus, and advised him to choose four elders to visit Middleboro' and sit in council on the troubles there. Accordingly, he made choice of elders Sprague, Werden, Lee and Peck. These, with the exception of Lee, met at Middleboro', July 11, 1753, and were

[1] That is, Mr. Backus and his people.

joined by some others. The conclusion to which they came was this: that Mr. Backus and his brethren were to blame for excluding Samuel Alden and Robert Washburn; and also for dealing with Jonathan Woods, Ebenezer Hinds, and others. When this result had been read, twelve persons[1] renewed covenant, and after having been cordially received into fellowship by the council, proceeded to revoke their former acts of exclusion, and to confess their faults one to another.

Yet peace was not even now restored. Discordant opinions still existed in the bosom of the church; its members did not all see eye to eye; they could not in the fullest sense declare their acceptance of one Lord, one faith, one baptism; and therefore they were unable to illustrate the New Testament idea of a spiritual brotherhood, the oneness of faith and purpose and action, the mutual confidence, fidelity, watchcare and sympathy, which are implied in such a brotherhood.

And what was true in this particular church, was to a great extent true of the Separate ministers as a body, and of the Christians whom they served in the gospel. Agitation was therefore to be expected, and agitation was sure to make their present position untenable. A few days after the meeting at Exeter, Oliver Prentice was ordained at Stonington, Connecticut, May 29, and Stephen Babcock declined acting with Solomon Paine in the services. When subsequently called upon by the church in Stonington for an explanation, he mentioned his belief that Mr. Paine had abused the Baptists in general, and Isaac Backus in particular. For making this statement to others before

[1] Namely; Isaac Backus, William Hooper, Joseph Phinney, Jabez Eddy, Onesimus Campbell, Timothy Bryant, David Alden; and Patience Eddy, Lydia Richmond, Esther Hayward, Martha Paddleford, Susanna Backus.

coming with it to himself, Mr. Paine commenced a labor with Elder Babcock. The latter, however, sustained by his church, decided not to hear the charges of the former. But these two ministers finally agreed to call a general meeting of the New-Lights at Stonington on the 29th of May, 1754.

We may here cite a passage from the papers of Mr. Backus. "Nov. 8, 1753. Stayed at Robert Washburn's, who moved from Bridgewater to Plainfield last spring. With him I had considerable discourse last night and this morning upon our former differences about baptism; and from all I could learn he and his church have now a zealous disposition to cut off from their communion all who are fully of the mind that there is no gospel warrant for infant baptism, let their behavior apart from this be such as it may. Brother Solomon Paine and others seemed to be running in the same path, and this, I fear, unless the Lord prevent, will make a sad rent and sore divisions among the godly."

Forty churches[1] of the "Separate Constitution" responded to this call by their ministers and messengers. Messrs. Paine and Babcock occupied the first day and a half in laying their difficulty before the Conference; and in the afternoon of the second day this body decided by a

1 "Elders and brethren from forty churches then met, viz., from twenty-four in Connecticut, eight in Massachusetts, seven in Rhode Island, and one on Long Island." — *Backus' History.* In his examination of Mr. Fish's Sermons (p. 118), it is said that "the messengers of about thirty-five churches came together." The former of these statements is undoubtedly correct. It will be seen that Mr. Backus speaks of delegates from *twenty four* Separate churches of Connecticut. Yet Mr. Trumbull remarks: "There were ten or twelve churches and congregations of this denomination in the Colony." The historian of Connecticut seems never to have examined the writings or the statistics of the New-Lights with sufficient care.

major vote, that Mr. Babcock, by his conduct, had violated the gospel rule. On the next day the meeting proceeded to consider his complaint against Mr. Paine. The result of the Council of May 1st, 1752, was read and criticized. After much discourse, it appeared by vote that thirty-seven regarded the result in question as no just cause of offence to the Baptists; while thirty-five thought otherwise, and five were undecided. "Then dismissing the consideration of particular facts, Paine and Babcock were desired to bring out plainly their principles. Paine then confessed, that when he joined the Baptists in communion and in Babcock's ordination, he did not so critically examine the foundation of things as he ought to have done. He thought *then* that they might go on together, but *he now found that they could not.* He read a paper concerning his principles, the sum of which was: That if any godly people, who do not hold infant baptism, confessed that it might be their *darkness* that they did not hold it, he would commune with them; but *he could not commune* with those who said it was their *light* and not their darkness which made them reject infant baptism. Then Babcock manifested that he was of the same mind as when he was ordained, making a difference of opinion on baptism no bar to communion; and so the Baptist brethren in general appeared to stand. But many on the other hand showed a disposition to *draw off from them.* So the meeting broke up in a sorrowful manner. On the whole, it appeared evident that Paine and Stephens, with some others, meant to break with the Baptists, and yet to cast the blame of it upon them; which was the main point in these labors of three days."

In another place Mr. Backus says: "At the close of the meeting, several of the most noted leaders on the side of the Pedobaptists openly declared that though they could yet commune with saints who did *not see* light for infant baptism; yet they did withdraw the hand of fellowship from all such as professed *to see* that there was no warrant for bringing infants to that ordinance."[1] To show the feelings of Mr. Backus at this time, we insert the following letter to his mother:

"STONINGTON, Jan. 1, 1754.

"MY DEAR MOTHER: I understand that you expected me to come to Norwich now, but I think my circumstances wont admit of it. I left my family well on Monday morning, and it is a time of health among our people; yet souls are very stupid. Now, as to the affairs of Zion, my heart is greatly grieved and burdened — for the divisions of Reuben there are great searchings of heart. Alas, what will be the end of these things! The transactions of this sorrowful meeting have often made me think of an observation of Mr. Flavel concerning divisions and contentions that happened in his day about the same points. He says they rose to such a height that it seemed as if one party would devour the other; yet God would not suffer it to be so, but let in the enemy, who laid hands on them; and now, says he, we have an opportunity of making acquaintance again in prison. God knows whether it may not be so now, if repentance and reformation don't prevent; which may God in infinite mercy grant. I can't enlarge further now; but close with my duty to you and love to all my friends. Amen.

ISAAC BACKUS."

This Convention, the largest ever held by the New-Lights, served unquestionably to divide rather than to

[1] "A Fish caught in his own net," p. 118.

unite them. Its doings foreshadowed a separation of ecclesiastical elements, which had been brought together by the force of common sympathy, at a single, vital point. But as yet there was no formal rupture. And with the hope, it seems, of averting this issue, fifteen churches thought proper to call another meeting to be holden at Exeter on the second Tuesday of September, 1754, for the purpose of settling terms of fellowship and communion at the Lord's table. Representatives from twelve churches only appeared. David Sprague was chosen moderator, and Isaac Backus clerk; both of them belonging to the Baptist wing. The result of the General Council at Exeter, May 2d, 1753, was then publicly read and fully canvassed; some approving and others disapproving its *form*. At last the following question was proposed: Whether, if a Congregational brother should come to a Baptist church in the fellowship of the gospel, and desire to commune with them at the Lord's table; but two or three refused to sit down with him; — whether said church will receive that brother to communion, or not? And it was answered fully in the affirmative: "Because we dare not shut out such as Christ evidently receives."

This appears to have been the last meeting of the Separate churches as a body; and it may be well to bear in mind, that the Baptist section of this body was amply represented and was found to be in favor of open communion, while the Pedobaptist leaders were absent and their sentiments were understood to be inclining towards restricted communion. No man wielded such an influence among them as Solomon Paine; and it is manifest that he had, in effect, refused to commune with every Baptist who had either intelligence or self-respect.

CHAPTER IX.

BACKUS BECOMES A REGULAR BAPTIST.

EFFORTS TO LIVE IN PEACE. — FAILURE. — MR. BACKUS REVIEWS THE QUESTION OF COMMUNION — FINDS THE ARGUMENTS OF BUNYAN INCONCLUSIVE. — RELINQUISHES OPEN COMMUNION. — FORMATION OF THE FIRST BAPTIST CHURCH, MIDDLEBORO'. — EXTRACTS FROM HIS MEMORANDA OF PREACHING TOURS; (1.) TO CAPE COD. — ORDINATION OF MR. CHASE. — (2.) TO SOUTHERN NEW HAMPSHIRE. — LETTER TO MR. CHASE. — (3.) TO MARTHA'S VINEYARD. — (4.) TO THE CAPE. — (5.) TO DURHAM, N. H.

BUT it is time for us to withdraw our attention from the Separates as a body and fix it upon Mr. Backus and his church. In Titicut precinct both pastor and flock were heartily committed to the practice of open communion. Serious and persistent efforts were made to "keep the unity of the Spirit in the bond of peace," and to move on harmoniously in the service of Christ. If any member of the church desired to have his children baptized, he had full permission to call in a minister from abroad to perform the act; and if any member who had been sprinkled in infancy wished to be baptized, full permission was granted Mr. Backus to administer this rite. Moreover, it was agreed, that no one should introduce any conversation which would lead to remarks on the subjects or the mode of baptism. But this mutual agreement could not stand the test of practice; and these persistent endeavors to avert dissension and live in peace were unavailing. For when infants were sprinkled the Baptists showed their dissatisfaction, yet without leaving the house. And when

Mr. Backus baptized certain members of his own church, the Congregationalists would not go to witness the immersion, but called it re-baptizing and taking the name of the Trinity in vain. And when the members of the church met for conference, they were afraid to speak their minds freely, lest offense might be given; and this fear led to an unbrotherly shyness. Hence, for fifteen months before they dissolved, they could not agree to meet at the Lord's table, and some of the members went back to the churches with which they were previously connected.

These things finally induced Mr. Backus to enter upon a fresh inquiry, and search after their cause. He reviewed the arguments of John Bunyan in favor of communing with sincere souls, though unbaptized, of which the two following are the most important, viz., *That in ancient times plain laws were dispensed with for such persons*, and *That God hath communion with them.* As illustrations of the first, Bunyan had appealed to David's eating the shew-bread, which it was not lawful for him to eat, and to the people's eating the Passover, in the time of Hezekiah, otherwise than had been prescribed. Heretofore, Mr. Backus had looked upon this argument as conclusive; but he now discovered in it a great mistake, forasmuch as *extraordinary cases are brought forward to establish a general rule.* To the second argument, also, he found grave objections. For he observed that many of God's ways cannot be imitated by men. And while he believed that Christians ought, so far as they are able, to walk together in divine truth, he now perceived that *one rule ought not to be broken over in order to unite in another.* "Baptism," he says, "and the Lord's Supper, appear to be ordinances of Christ of equal weight, and the one to be placed before the other; and therefore, after many cries for divine direction and much searching of the Scriptures, I was constrained to give in that we ought not to receive any to the Lord's table who have not been baptized according to the gospel rule. I was brought to see that we had made Christians our rule, instead of the Word of God; for his Word requires a credible confession of saving faith, in order to baptism; and if we come to the Holy Supper with any who were only sprinkled in infancy, we commune with unbaptized persons, which Pedobaptists themselves do not profess to do.

"Evidence of union and communion with our glorious Head lays the foundation of communion with each other, as his members; but the question arises, whether this be all which is needful for admission into the visible church? Some have answered in the affirmative, and yet, upon trial, have found that there are things not essential to salvation, which are necessary in the visible building. For instance, those who hold the church to be national cannot build with those who hold it to be congregational. Something more than an evidence merely of heart religion is therefore necessary, in order to build together. And what is it? A consideration of some general rules, such as: 'Love the truth and peace,'[1] 'Follow peace with all men, and holiness,'[2] 'Follow after the things which make for peace, and the things whereby one may edify another,'[3] may help to answer this question. To promote truth, peace and holiness, then, should be our great concern in all our religious exercises, and whatever interferes therewith should be avoided. Mutual edification is also one great design of a visible church, and whatsoever mars it we ought likewise to shun. Well, then, to apply these rules to the case in hand, I conceive that it is vain for

1 Zech. 8:19. Heb. 12:14. Rom. 14:19.

those who hold that a profession of saving faith is necessary, in order to baptism, and those who hold that believers ought to bring their children to this ordinance, to try to build together. For this latter belief lays the foundation of a national church, as has been found in our land. Nay, it tends to make void believers' baptism; for if infant baptism universally prevailed, there would never be another believer baptized, and so Christ's command would be made void through this tradition."

These and similar considerations led Mr. Backus to relinquish the position which he had so long and so heartily maintained. In a letter to his mother, dated Jan. 26, 1756, he says:

"We have been so broken and divided as to be incapable of acting as a body for some time, though greater numbers have latterly met for public worship than used to do. By long experience and a more thorough search of God's Word, I am convinced that it is neither agreeable nor expedient for those who differ so widely about the first ordinance of the gospel (viz., baptism) as we do, to build together, or, in ordinary cases, to try to go on together in the special ordinances of the church; yet, at the same time, I would earnestly labor to maintain all christian love and freedom in things wherein we are agreed. After several free conferences and having our way made clear, six of us being of this mind, did, in a meeting for that purpose, on January 16, solemnly and renewedly sign covenant together; I trust, with some real freedom and sense of divine things. And I can't but hope that this people will yet be blessedly delivered. But, for aught I know, this news may be grievous to your mind; which [grief] the tenderness of love between us would be loath to cause; yet I am persuaded you are sensible that every one must practise according to the clearest light he has, let who will be of a different mind. And we may doubtless in these things rest upon the text, Philippians 3:15, 'If in anything ye be otherwise minded, God shall reveal even this unto you.' Now, committing our case into his hands, with desires to be remembered by you at the throne of grace, I remain yours, in nearer regards than I can express.

I. BACKUS."

In a discourse subsequently published, he argues that the Lord's Supper is properly an ecclesiastical ordinance; that Christ has required baptism prior to church membership or privileges; and that a close union of those who observe and those who disregard this order must be productive of alienation and strife. At a much later period, he thus refers to the years of transition and trial through which we have traced his path: "After renewing grace was granted, I was such a dull scholar in Christ's school, that I was thirty-two years in learning a lesson of only six words, namely, 'one Lord, one faith, one baptism.' It took ten years to get clear of the custom of putting baptism before faith, and near five more to learn not to contradict the same in practice; after which, above seventeen trying years rolled over us, before we could refrain from an implicit acknowledgment of more than 'one Lord' in religious affairs." The last clause of this retrospect will be illustrated in the progress of our narrative.

On the 16th of January, 1756, several baptized believers met at the house of Mr. Backus, and, after earnest prayer to God for wisdom and help, and the preaching of a sermon, six persons entered into covenant as a Baptist church.[1] Three more were joined to this little body on the 22d of March, and on the 6th of April, Nathaniel Shaw was received from the Second Church in Boston, and chosen deacon. At the same time, Mr. Backus was unanimously invited to become their pastor. The invitation was accepted, and on the 23d of June he was publicly installed. Thus was organized the first Baptist church between Boston and Rehoboth, a distance of almost fifty miles, and between Bellingham and the end of Cape Cod, a distance of more than one hundred miles. And thus, too, did the subject of our narrative find himself in a position, as to his religious views, from which he never saw reason to depart.

It will be interesting, before closing this chapter, to peruse a few notices, from his own pen, of his labors and feelings as an itinerant preacher. In December, 1751, he attended a council at Harwich, for the purpose of assisting the saints in that place to settle certain difficulties, and to ordain Mr. Chase as their pastor. The difficulties were soon happily removed, and Mr. Backus thus speaks of the ordination:

"Dec. 11. Brother Chase gave an account of his conversion, of his call to preach, and of his call to take the care of this church. Now, also, in a clear and solemn manner, did he give himself to God and to this people, and they did receive him according to the gospel. Then I preached and prayed, brother Carpenter gave the charge, brother Ewer the right hand of fellowship, and brother

1 Viz., Isaac Backus, Timothy Bryant, John Hayward, Susanna Backus, Mary Caswell, and Esther Fobes. The Confession of Faith and Covenant adopted by them were drawn up by Mr. Backus, and may be found in Appendix B. "Before this time there were only about eighteen Baptist churches in the Massachusetts, New Hampshire, and Vermont."

Nickerson made the last prayer. The Lord gave us the witness of his presence, and afterwards, on our taking leave of this dear people, a great many of them were swallowed up wonderfully in the divine love."

"Dec. 12th. Came over to Barnstable and found the saints met together. I preached just at night, and it was a blessed season. The saints had great wrestlings and fervent cries for brother Silas Ewer, who has been for some time possessed with a spirit of pride and bitterness, and carried away with notions of great things, so that his intellectual powers are much disordered."

"Dec. 13th. The case of sister Lovell, who has been under doubts about the work of God in this day, and has been assailed by great temptations, took such hold of my mind that I could not with clearness leave the place without going to see her. I went, therefore, with two of the brethren, and we found her sorrowful and tempted. Her father came in and tried all he could to hinder our conversing with or preaching to her. But at last her husband said that he did not choose to be prevented from hearing a sermon by these things. So I went on to preach from the words: 'Simon, Simon, Satan hath desired to have you, that he may sift you as wheat,' etc.; and the Lord did give me remarkable clearness in laying open Satan's temptations, and in mentioning some things to comfort God's people under them. After we came away, I felt such flowings of divine love, and such peace in my soul, that I wanted heaven and earth to help me praise my God."

"Dec. 14th. In reviewing what God has wrought in this journey I had great satisfaction. He gave me uncommon clearness about coming, has directed me from day to day, has wrought a wonderful deliverance for his people at Harwich, and has given my soul at sundry times blessed refreshings of divine love; so that, all things considered, I think the grace of God to me in this journey exceeds all that I have experienced in any journey of my life. Oh, that I could be more active in praising my divine Master!"

Towards the close of January, 1752, Mr. Backus made an excursion, with Rev. William Carpenter, into the southern parts of New Hampshire, in order to proclaim the gospel. He thus writes:

"Jan. 28th. Travelled to Exeter, and were kindly received at the house of Elias Ladd. In the afternoon we had considerable discourse with brother Sweet and some others. In the evening I preached to more than a room full of people on the dreadfulness of putting God afar off; and he drew near and enabled me to lay open the truth in demonstration of the Spirit, and to press it home. Brother Carpenter, also, had sweet liberty in exhorting; many were seized with conviction, and the saints were refreshed. A solemn season it was, the most blessed of any that I've seen since I came from home. My soul desires to thank God and take courage."

"Jan. 29th. In the morning we had much discourse with the man where we stayed. He appears to have been greatly enlightened, and now stands in a very critical and dangerous place. May the Lord deliver his precious soul! We afterwards set forward, came to Durham, and held a meeting at Esquire William Odiorne's. I preached, but was very much straitened, so that I could scarce find any sweetness in truth, and hardly deliver the plain doctrines of the gospel without blundering, and I felt ashamed to look anybody in the face. Oh, how foolishly do I wander away from my God! Let me be fastened to Thy cross rather than lose Thy sight."

"Feb. 1st. Felt something low both in body and mind. We held a meeting, and brother Carpenter preached. The Lord came down by his power, sundry saints were set at liberty, and did shout forth his praise, sinners were seized with conviction, and some cried out in distress. Glory to God in the highest!"

"Boston, Feb. 7th. Had opportunity last night and this morning to peruse Mr. Davies's account of the state of religion in Virginia, and my soul was refreshed in hearing of the wonders which God hath there wrought, and was filled with insatiable longings for the spread of Christ's kingdom through the whole world."

The following letter will not be without interest to some as showing the sobriety of mind and christian fidelity of Mr. Backus at this period of his life.

"To Richard Chase, in Yarmouth.

"Dear Brother: Old Father Eldridge informs me that you have declared it to be your duty, as you are pastor of the church, to take a basin of water and wash the disciples' feet after the Supper. Now, knowing the friendship and intimacy which has been between us, I shall, without any apology, freely in simplicity, give you my thoughts upon that point.

"1. As to the literal sense of washing feet, we find that it was commonly practised when persons who had been journeying came from their journey.[1]

"2. It seems that the work was commonly done by servants, and was looked upon as a menial employ.[2] And, therefore, it did greatly express the humility as well as the brokenness of heart which Mary felt, when she washed the feet of our Lord.[3] Therefore:

[1] Gen. 18: 4; 19: 2; 24: 32: and 43: 24. Ju. 19: 21., etc.

[2] 1 Sam. 25: 41.

[3] Luke 7: 38.

"3. I apprehend that Christ's washing the disciples' feet did set before them a pattern of humility, and that herein he showed them that they should never become so great as not to be ready to do the meanest office of kindness to each other; as indeed he seems to explain it himself, 18: 14, 16. 'If I your Lord and Master have washed your feet, ye ought also to wash one another's feet. The servant is not greater than his Lord,' etc.

"But then I do not think that washing the disciples' feet literally, is a work to be performed by ministers in the church now, for the following reasons:

"1. Because the need and occasion of it have ceased. I observed before, that in old times they washed the feet of travellers; the occasion of which I take to have been, that they went with their legs naked, and only sandals on their feet, and these I suppose to have been pieces of leather, merely tied on with strings, and protecting the soles of their feet, so that their ankles and feet were covered with dirt and defiled in travelling, and needed washing before they retired to rest. But in general, you know, there is not the same need and occasion for it now. And this, by the way may help to answer the Quakers' objections against the external use of all ordinances, if we neglect this; for there is as much need of being stirred up in remembrance of a dying Saviour now, as ever; but there is not the same need of washing the disciples' feet. But again:

"2. If we did practise it now, yet it is not office-work in the church. Paul mentions it as a work done by virtuous women. 1 Tim. 5: 10. 'If she have lodged strangers, if she have washed the saints' feet,' etc. And our Lord in the 13th of John, mentions it as a work of humility and kindness which the saints should do to each other. v. 19. 'Ye ought to wash one another's feet.'

"Thus I have briefly hinted to you my mind; but if the practice seem to you to be clearly required by the truth, and you apprehend that you have clear light, yet I hope you will take these lines as tokens of unfeigned love from your friend and brother,

ISAAC BACKUS.

MAY 10th, 1752."

In August of this year he again visited the same region with Rev. Mr. Hide of Brookline.

"Aug. 15th. Dined at brother Sweet's in Exeter, and while our bodies were feeding on temporal food our souls were gloriously refreshed with divine grace."

"Aug. 18th. We proposed to have gone to Portsmouth to-day, but Providence seemed to shut the door. So we spent the day in visiting and conversing. Once I had great strength and freedom in secret prayer for Capt. Odiorne and his wife, also for my dear family and the church. At night we went and heard Mr. Prince, the blind man, and he delivered many truths, but in a legal dress. After he had done, I had freedom to deliver a few words for my God, and then had some comfortable discourse with him."

"Aug. 21st. Mr. Hide preached a sermon with sweet assistance; sundry saints were really brought near to God, but one man came in and openly expressed his rage at his wife for her religion. After the meeting was dismissed, I went into the other room, and there found one soul under deep conviction. As I began to converse, my heart was enlarged towards God for the deliverance of this person and two others; and for an hour or two I was enabled to agonize for them in prayer as I scarce have done for any sinners these four years past. It was, indeed, a solemn and glorious season; many saints were brought into the bosom of divine love, and sundry of the unconverted were crying out in view of their sins. A night much to be remembered!"

"Aug. 23d. A great number of people came together, so that we could not meet in the house, but went out under a shady tree. After preaching, we went on to partake of the Sacrament. Several offered themselves to the church, and one was received. The lot fell upon me to administer the ordinance, and I had remarkable clearness therein."

In March, 1753, he paid a visit to Martha's Vineyard. We subjoin a few notices:

"Falmouth, March 14th. Read some in the "Travels of Ungodliness," and was affected at seeing so many of the schemes of wickedness laid open. My heart was stirred within me to press forward in laboring to destroy the works of the devil."

"March 15th. By the way, (to Martha's Vineyard,) I had earnest outgoings of heart to God and desires that he would guide and help me in this place, where I am entirely a stranger."

"March 17th. In the afternoon I went with brother Butler down to the water side, and had some comfortable conversation with his uncle. I then went to see Mr. Newman, the minister here, and we soon fell into a discourse about qualifications for, and introduction into, the ministry. He held it to be necessary for a man to have the original tongues, or else, said he, 'A man does not know whether he divides and delivers the Word right or wrong.'"

"March 18th. I heard him both parts of the day, and he delivered truth; but he read nearly all, and he did not come so close upon men's consciences as I should have been glad to have heard. In the evening I preached at brother Butler's. People were very differently affected.

Some said, 'he is a good man,' others said, 'nay, but he deceiveth the people.' Some said, 'he is a Quaker;' others said, 'we have n't heard such a sermon these seven years.' And thus I found I must pass through evil report and good report."

From the record of a journey which he made to the Cape in the early autumn of 1753, we select the following item.

"August 23d. We met in council at Harwich to consider the case of brother Chase and this church, who were dealt with by a council last December as disorderly walkers for forsaking infant baptism. Brother Carpenter, who was moderator of that council, openly confessed his fault and asked their forgiveness for dealing so with them; and they freely forgave him. We then proceeded to revoke their censure and publicly to declare fellowship again with this dear church. After this I preached a sermon from 2 Timothy, 2: 19. My heart was drawn forth in an astonishing manner to treat with immortal souls, and I trust the Spirit of God was sweetly moving among them. We then, at brother Clark's, had further conference with the church about certain difficulties. I did not intend to have another sermon to-day, we were so spent; but in the evening a crowd of people filled the room, and it touched my heart to see their earnestness. So I preached to them concerning the great trumpet of the gospel,[1] with very little fatigue. To see souls eager to hear, animates my heart, and oh, how great has been God's goodness this day! All glory to his name!"

"24th. I hear that sundry vain young persons were seized with strong convictions last night, and were crying, "what shall we do to be saved?" Went this morn-

[1] Isaiah 27: 13.

ing to brother Nickerson's and preached; then went to Nathaniel Gage's, and brother Carpenter preached. After meeting, brother Chase came out and told how he was convinced that he ought to follow Christ's example in going into the water to be baptized, and he spake with great tenderness towards others, and exhibited such a gospel temper that no objections were made against it, and I could do no less than go down to the water and baptize him."

"25th. Preached my farewell at the house of Isaac Chase, and God's glory appeared in such a manner, while I was treating with souls about the great salvation,[1] that I was ready to cry: 'How dreadful is this place; it is none other than the house of God and gate of heaven.'"

"June 27, 1754. Came down to Harwich and preached twice at brother Clark's. The people seemed very earnest to hear, and urged my staying longer, but I could not. I fear many of them are ready to idolize a poor worm; and alas, my heart is too apt to be taken with the applause of frail men — which I find a dreadful snare."

"Norwich, September 15, 1754. Preached both parts of the day in brother Hide's meeting-house to the largest auditory which I ever saw there; and in the afternoon my soul had glorious clearness in treating of the inside of religion."

"September 17th. This morning my aged grandmother came to see me; her soul seems to live in sight of the glorious prize."

"January 15, 1755. Came forward, [on his way to Durham, New Hampshire,] and my soul had some meditation on the road respecting Baptist principles, which are so much controverted at the present time. From this I was

[1] Hebrews 2: 3.

led to think of my education and the way I was trained up in; and I could say that, instead of despising my ancestors because I had left the principle in which I was nurtured as to baptism, my heart did bless God for their faithful instruction and government as well as for their prayers and godly example; from them my thoughts were led higher to the great Author of my being, in thankfulness for a religious ancestry and for his grace to my poor soul."

CHAPTER X.

JOY IN SERVICE.

SETTLED BELIEF. — ABUNDANT LABORS. — MEMORANDA OF PREACHING TOURS; 1. TO NORTHERN MASSACHUSETTS AND SOUTHERN NEW HAMPSHIRE; 2. TO CENTRAL MASSACHUSETTS AND CONNECTICUT; 3. TO NORWICH THRICE; 4. TO THE CAPE. — LETTERS OF MR. BACKUS TO HIS MOTHER; 1. SPECIAL VIEWS OF TRUTH; 2. COMFORT IN AFFLICTION; 3. CONCEALED PIETY; 4. SECOND BAPTIST CHURCH IN MIDDLEBORO' GATHERED; 5. SIGNS OF A REVIVAL. — LETTER TO REV. BENJAMIN WALLIN; 1. MISTAKES OF THE PLANTERS OF NEW ENGLAND; 2. MINISTERIAL EDUCATION; 3. NOTICE OF THE GREAT AWAKENING; 4. REVIVALS.

WE have accompanied the subject of our narrative through a long period of inward conflict, and have seen the issue of his prayerful search for the path of duty. From this time to the close of his life, we shall find no traces of a mind wavering as to the proper constitution and ordinances of a christian church. Whether right or wrong in his belief, he was henceforth a Baptist, firm, consistent, earnest, charitable.

Without turning back to rail at those whom he had left, his energies were faithfully applied to the great work of preaching Christ at home and by the way. From year to year the little church under his care grew in numbers and in strength; neglected districts were made glad as heretofore by his occasional but zealous proclamation of the Gospel; and feeble interests were kept alive by his wise counsels and stout-hearted faith. But for a considerable period we have no record of particular events in his life.

The only memorials of this period, preserved to us from his own pen, consist of certain letters to his excellent mother, several sketches of preaching tours, and lists of the conversions which took place in his society, the persons whom he baptized, the texts from which he preached, and other items of a similar nature. From these sources it appears that, during a space of eleven years, from 1756 to 1767, he baptized sixty-two individuals, preached two thousand four hundred and twelve sermons, and travelled beyond the limits of his own parish fourteen thousand six hundred and ninety one miles.

That this quiet, yet laborious and useful period of his life may not be altogether unknown to the reader, we have selected a few passages from his memoranda of journeys to preach the Word, and from the series of letters to his mother, mentioned above.

Near the close of March, 1756, he started on a visit to Haverhill, Methuen, and Newton, New Hampshire. He was at Newton, Lord's day, March 28, and writes: "Preached twice to this people, and the Lord did draw near of a truth and give my soul sweet enlargement. Such bowels of compassion for sinners I have n't felt for a long while. Oh, that the Lord would appear for the deliverance of these precious souls!"

"March 30th (Methuen.) After meeting in the evening I spoke with a young woman who gave me a clear account of her conversion. I hear that some others have been recently converted in this place. How blessed a thing it is to see a new-born soul!"

He reached home on Saturday, April 3d, and finding his family in good health, concludes thus: "The divine favors have been distinguishing here; and while I have been gone, the assistance which I have enjoyed in preaching and the conversions which I have seen among sinners, together with the language of new-born souls, have made it the most comfortable journey to me that I have taken this winter. Oh how reviving was it to hear in this dark day 'the voice of the turtle' in our land!"

In October he made a journey, visiting several towns in Massachusetts and Connecticut. We take the following notices of it from his journal:

"Oct. 18th. Came over (from Sutton) to Dr. Green's in Leicester; and they were earnest for a meeting. So I tarried and preached, the Lord giving me special assistance."

"Oct. 19th. I can but admire how the doctor is able to get along as he does; having a great deal of farming business to manage; multitudes of sick to take care of; several apprentices to instruct in the art of physic; and a church to care for and watch over; — yet in the midst of all he seems to keep religion uppermost, to have his mind bent upon divine things, and to be very bold in Christian conversation with all sorts of company."

"Oct. 30th. (Norwich). Found all my friends tolerably well, except aunt Lord and grandmother Backus. I found the latter still bent and engaged in divine things, though her bodily strength and her intellectual powers have apparently decayed since I last saw her."

"Nov. 4th. Took my leave of my dear mother and friends. Called to see grandmother; found her low in body and the tempter trying to worry her mind; yet when she came to speak of her past experiences, both as to her conversion above sixty years ago, and as to several revivals since, she had a fresh taste of the same thing and could not but own that God had done great things for her. She now looked to me like a shock of corn fully ripe and just ready to be gathered into the divine garner. I prayed with her and took my leave, never expecting to see her again till we meet in glory."

In September, 1757, he visited the Cape; and his account of an ordination at that time will be in place.

"Sept. 28th. We proceeded to Yarmouth; and for our satisfaction concerning elder Chase's gifts we prevailed with him to preach in the evening. And though in the fore part of his discourse he was straitened, yet afterwards he was more enlarged."

"Sept. 29th. We met at the widow Clarke's in Harwich. Elder Round was chosen moderator and myself scribe. Their confession of faith and covenant, also their choice of Elder Chase and his acceptance thereof, were looked into and gave satisfaction. So we proceeded: — I preached a sermon from Malachi 3: 6, with clearness of mind; Elder Round offered the ordaining prayer, while both of us laid our hands on the candidate; after this he (Elder R.) gave the charge; then I gave the right hand of fellowship and made the last prayer. Through the whole exercise good attention was given by the people, and there appeared evident movings of the divine Spirit in the assembly."

The next day Mr. Backus attended a wedding at Truro, which is thus described:

"We arrived near night, and found some hundreds of people assembled. So matters being prepared, Esquire Paine of that town married them; while, at his motion, I prayed before, and gave a word of counsel after the transaction. Then (also at his desire) brother Hinds offered prayer; we sang part of the 45th Psalm, and brother Hinds preached an excellent sermon from Solomon's Song 5: 9."

In November, 1757, Mr. Backus paid a visit to Norwich, and thus writes:

"Nov. 28th. Preached in the evening at mother's; and grandmother Backus came a mile on foot to meeting. As her natural strength holds out wonderfully (she being eighty-eight years old and upwards), so, though her memory fails, her soul is most intensely engaged in pursuing the heavenly journey. Her discourse this night was very affecting; may I never forget it!"

About a year later he was once more in his native place, and has left the following note:

"Nov. 14, 1758. I visited my aged grandmother, who has lived to enter her ninetieth year; and though her strength of memory is exceedingly broken, her strength of body remains, so that she can walk two miles a day. Her wisdom in divine things continues likewise, so that she can yet discourse wonderfully on the inside of religion. A hoary head is a crown of glory, when found in the way of righteousness."

In August of the next year he made still another visit to Norwich, finding both his mother and grandmother alive and rejoicing in the service of Christ. We close these extracts with a passage from his account of a journey to the Cape.

"May 25th (Truro). Preached three times at the house of brother Rich; and though but few met together, yet God was evidently present both by a spirit of conviction and also of consolation. I was favored with uncommon strength and solemnity in treating with immortal souls, as one who must give account of himself before God.

"May 26th. Came back to brother Harding's, and preached in the forenoon with real clearness; but after meeting some found fault because I would not direct sinners to do something before they come to Christ by faith. This is indeed a cutting point to carnal hearts, and it appears to be the *hard saying* which offended so many of Christ's nominal disciples of old. He asserted their perishing condition without Himself, and at the same time, that 'No man can come unto me except the Father draw him.' This was so offensive that many of them went back and walked no more with him. Yet if rightly considered, the declaration that all the help for undone sinners is in Jesus Christ, is the most blessed news ever heard in these dark regions."

The letters written by Mr. Backus to his mother breathe a most dutiful, affectionate and christian spirit. If we may judge of his daily experience by these simple effusions of the heart, religion was constantly uppermost in his desires and aims; he was strict in self-examination, importunate in prayer, and assiduous in the study of God's Word. We do not recollect having ever seen so many letters, not treating professedly of religion, in which this divine theme occupied so large a place. The following specimens are submitted to the reader:

"MIDDLEBORO', Nov. 29, 1756.

"DEAR MOTHER: I readily embrace this opportunity of informing you that I have been favored with comfortable health since I saw you. My wife and most of the children have been ill with colds, but we are now all about. The sickness round us is also abated; though a terrible breach was made in our community while I was away. * * * In religion, things remain much as they have been of late. But yesterday morning, before day, my soul was favored with some special views of divine truth. I awoke with these words of our Lord in my mind: 'I speak not of myself; but the Father that dwelleth in me, he doeth the works;' from which I was led to see that if Christ spoke and acted only by the Father who dwelt in him, then surely it is the greatest vanity for any of his people to think they can do anything without him. My soul had a view of the blessedness of yielding our powers of mind and members of body to his influence, to be improved entirely by him, and I was led to dedicate my all afresh to God, entreating him to cleanse my soul and body from every pollution and ever use my powers and members for his glory. And I trust he did in some measure use them that day to treat with immortal souls. To him be all the glory! * * * *

"My consort joins me in duty to you and in affectionate regards to our brothers and sisters. * * * *

From your obedient son,

ISAAC BACKUS."

"MIDDLEBORO', MARCH 22, 1757.

"MY DEAR MOTHER: As the Holy Ghost witnessed to the apostle Paul, that in every city bonds and afflictions awaited him, so the Scriptures and our constant experience show that sorrows and troubles attend us in all our journey through this thorny maze. Some rumor of death among my friends I heard in January, but I had no particular intelligence until the 14th of February. I was then informed that grandmother Backus, sister Abell, and Rufus, were dead. About that time I met with several trials of another nature, by all of which my thoughts were turned upon 1 Pet. 1: 16., and I preached from this text the next Sabbath. I was led to observe: (1) That manifold trials attend God's people in this world. (2) That these are sent because we have need of them; * * * to kill pride, to cure us of worldly mindedness and love to the creature, to rouse us from our sloth, and to quicken our regard to eternal things, etc. (3) That these temptations and sorrows continue but for a short season. And, (4) That in the midst of them God gives his saints springs of great joy. And blessed be the name of the Lord, I did not preach an unfelt religion. I have seldom seen affliction bear a more pleasant face than it did then. * * * *

"Last week I preached in Dartmouth and Rochester, where many thoughtless souls have been awakened to some concern about their eternal welfare; * * * and it is observable that in the former stir these towns were almost entirely passed by. * * * My companion joins me in dutiful respects to you, feeling some sympathy with your various afflictions. * * * *

"No more at present, from your obedient son,

ISAAC BACKUS."

"MIDDLEBORO', AUG. 29, 1757.

"BELOVED MOTHER: These lines come with my dutiful regards to you, and love to my brothers and sisters; and to inform you that we are still continued in health through God's forbearing mercy. * * * * We have much cause to lament our coldness and the stupidity which prevails. Of late, the mere liberty we still have of meeting freely for divine worship, has appeared to me a great thing; how long it may be allowed us, God only knows. Yet we have not only this privilege, but some tokens also of God's presence in these dark times. A week ago yesterday, a man from Raynham joined this church. For many years he has appeared to be a sober man, but much reserved; and with many others I was not aware of any special change in his feelings. So foolish was I, that when he talked of offering himself publicly, I felt in my heart unwilling to have him do this. Yet he gave such a relation of experience as carried conviction, I believe, to every conscience present, that he had been really born of God. And what is more wonderful still, this work was experienced twenty-three years ago, in the seventeenth year of his age, in dark times where he heard none speak of vital piety. But the Lord found a way to his heart by means of afflictive providences, etc. * * * *

"I remain your dutiful son,

I. Backus."

"Middleboro', Feb. 12, 1758.

"Loving Mother: * * * * A church was gathered in the south part of our town on the sixteenth of November, and brother Hinds was ordained pastor, January 26th past. I was over there again at the ordination of their deacons last Thursday; and I can but hope that God has many blessings in store for that people. Week before last I preached on Tuesday, Wednesday, and Thursday, among the old Baptist Societies in Rehoboth and Swanzey; and souls seemed to drink in the Word, as the thirsty earth does the rain. There is an encouraging prospect of a glorious work of grace in that region, where Arminianism has so long prevailed. * * * * I must conclude with those dutiful regards which are ever due from your obedient son,

I. Backus."

"Middleboro', Aug. 4, 1762.

"Honored and beloved Mother: With joy I embrace this opportunity to write you. I have often had reason to mention with thankfulness, that we and our neighbors are favored with health, even as now; but I have still better news to send you to-day, namely, that King Jesus is evidently returning to visit us with the blessings of his grace. Some tokens of his approaches I have seen for many months past, but lately we have had more visible signs of his presence. Lord's day, July 11th, I exchanged with brother Carpenter of Norton; he preached three times here, and among other happy effects, two souls, we believe were savingly converted; and on July 24th, a man above forty years old met with a great change at home; I hope a saving one. People generally not only flock to hear preaching, but they have also set up neighborhood meetings for prayer, exhortation, etc. * * * *"

"MIDDLEBORO', SEPT. 27, 1762.

"BELOVED MOTHER: I wrote to you some time ago of the work at Fresh Meadows, and that two or three were hopefully converted among us in July. I have now the comfort of saying that the work prevails and increases among us still. A young woman was brought out of darkness into marvellous light at a meeting on the 3d inst. This had a great influence upon others, and many are now under concern. Yea, in truth, the fields appear to me to be white unto the harvest. I daily look upon myself as a vile creature, yet the worth of souls and the great concerns of the kingdom of Christ, have, I think, engaged my mind as fully as ever in my life, to labor in his vineyard. Oh, these are golden moments, and woe to those who trifle them away.

So I remain,

Ever yours,

ISAAC BACKUS."

It would be easy to fill many pages with extracts similar to those now given from the letters of Mr. Backus to his mother. And, as we have before remarked, her letters to him were equally spiritual. Their thoughts were busy a large part of the time about the affairs of the Saviour's kingdom, and they gave free expression to these thoughts in a delightful correspondence; from which, however, we must now turn reluctantly away.

Part of a letter to Rev. Benjamin Wallin of London, will furnish a fitting conclusion to this chapter.

"Nov. 16, 1764.

"* * * * New England, I suppose you know, consists of four governments, (formerly of seven); three of which, viz., the provinces of Massachusetts Bay, New Hampshire, and the colony of Connecticut, were planted for the most part by Christians of the Congregational persuasion. Many of them were eminent for religion in its life and power. Yet they had their mistakes; and among these this may be reckoned a great one, viz., that they were not content with establishing their religion by the civil law, and taxing the inhabitants generally to support it, but they also undertook to keep out errors by the civil power. Many, therefore, who appeared to be of different sentiments from themselves, were disciplined by their courts, and at last banished. This gave birth to Rhode Island Colony, where many Baptists, Quakers, and others, repaired and obtained a charter from home.

"Such treatment, you may easily imagine, laid the foundation for stronger bars between them than the colony lines; and they have been handed down to posterity, even to this day. And as two schools or colleges were erected, one at Cambridge, and the other at New Haven, to educate persons for the ministry, so by degrees it got to be a received point with the Pedobaptists in general, that none might be admitted into the ministry but such as were educated there; while all such, in general, might, if they would. Moreover, as many people were compelled to support such ministers, contrary to their minds, strong prejudices were aroused in the minds of great numbers, against learning and supporting ministers, so that a great part of the Baptist ministers in the country have had but little either of learning or of support from the people. The consequences, on the one hand, of setting up human learning as a principal thing in a minister, and on the other hand, of this prejudice against it, you may well think, have been very melancholy. Indeed, we were reduced to such a state that our Lord's charge against the church of Sardis,[1] was eminently true of New England generally. In such an awful state we lay, when He whose thoughts and ways are not like ours, instead of destroying us with his vengeance, appeared in the latter part of the year 1740, in a marvellous manner, to pour out of his Spirit for the conviction and conversion of great numbers; and the work prevailed gloriously through the following year in various parts of the land.

"But the instruments used therein, being nearly all Pedobaptists, against whom the Baptists had a strong prejudice, most of the latter were very much barred against the work. It may be further observed, that a number of ministers of the common denomination were much used in that work, while many others of them bitterly opposed it and called it delusion. The work was also greatly promoted by private meetings for prayer, exhortation, etc.; and in process of time, some gifted brethren were moved to teach and expound the Scriptures, frequently to the satisfaction of many. But this was soon called an intrusion into the ministerial office. And as the former sentiments

[1] Rev. Chap. 3d.

were still held that none should be received into the ministry but such as were educated for that purpose, the ministers in general, both those who had favored and those who had opposed that blessed revival of religion, united their power and endeavored to stop all such proceedings. This caused many struggles and contentions among us, which issued in a separation of many from the established ministers and churches. The civil authorities exerted themselves not a little to reclaim these, but this only made the breach wider, and it would weary your patience to hear of the effects produced by all these movements. Many said that the state of religion was worse among us than before the revival.

"Well, in the year 1749, the pure doctrines of grace in their power gained considerable ground in several places of Rhode Island Colony, where ignorance and irreligion had terribly prevailed. And about the same time, the doctrine of believers' baptism obtained a footing in several of our Separate congregations in the other governments. Among these, ours was one, though the hot disputes which ensued seemed as if they would have eaten out all the life of religion. And to add to our other calamities, there appeared in some places, as zealous advocates for that doctrine, a number of persons who assumed the power to baptize without any ordination, and some of them went so far as to declare in express terms, that they were perfect and immortal, — whose folly has since been manifest to all men.

"From these hints you may form some conception of the mountains of difficulty with which God's people seemed to be encompassed on every side; and we might well say: 'By whom shall Jacob arise, for he is small?' Yet he who makes the mountains flow down at his presence, has of late appeared, to work like himself. Things have been on the gaining hand among us for these seven years, and two or three years ago, there were several remarkable seasons of conviction and conversion in sundry places, and so at times since; and it seems like Ezekiel's waters, to rise higher and higher.

"I have had many direct accounts of a revival, which commenced at Ipswich about the beginning of last winter, and has so prevailed that near or quite a hundred souls, it is thought, have been converted there since. The work has spread into Newbury and other places lying thirty or forty miles north-east of Boston, and also into several parts of the province of New Hampshire, from which I have had very late intelligence of a good time. We have not been without some sprinklings of this spiritual shower in our society, and we hope for a greater rain. Oh, that it may be hastened! I have not only heard but seen great things elsewhere. In the town of Providence, which is very populous, and which has been a place of much profaneness and irreligion, a revival began about the middle of last winter, and increased through the spring, and has affected all sorts of people. Some deists, leaders in gaming, and many profane persons, as well as others more civil, have been hopefully converted. I have been among them sundry times, and the joy of seeing such a marvellous change in the town, is better felt than expressed. To hear the profane praising Jesus, to see the irreligious thronging to a place of divine worship, and to discover such a heavenly temper in many, was surely enough to fill a cold heart with love and praise. * * * * Yet I must not omit the place of my nativity. I was there about a year ago, and the face of things in that part of the town where I was born appeared to me more melancholy than I had known it to be for twenty years. But a revival began soon after and increased to a blessed degree. I was there to see a dying brother, in February, and the satisfaction which I had from what then appeared of the work, quite overwhelmed the sorrow of parting with a near friend. Yet much greater things have been seen there since. These glorious visitations have not been confined to New England. I have seen three written accounts from Mr. S. Buel, a Presbyterian minister at East Hampton, on Long Island, in the province of New York, of a work begun there last winter, which has exceeded what has been described in any of the above mentioned places. Among the rest, he says, there has been a Jew remarkably converted; and I hear that the work spreads over a great part of that island. And Mr. James Manning, a young man of our persuasion, who was educated at the college of New Jersey, and came from there to settle in Warren, R. I., informed me last week that he had very late intelligence of a great work going on and increasing in various parts of New Jersey, also in the city of New York, and a great deal of it among the people of our denomination. * * * * Oh, for a heart ever to glorify our God for these astonishing wonders to the children of men!

"Dear Sir, I hope you, and the people of God with you, will help us to praise and pray also; for, indeed, a great and effectual door is opened unto us, and there are many adversaries. An old saint, who formerly came from England, but died in my native place, once said that she never went to God for another without getting something for herself. May King Jesus go on still, from conquering to conquer in these ends of the world, and also return with increasing displays of his glory to our Mother Island! which is the unfeigned prayer of your younger brother,

ISAAC BACKUS."

CHAPTER XI.

WIDER INFLUENCE.

DISCOURSE, THE BOND WOMAN AND THE FREE.—LETTER TO DR. LORD OF NORWICH. — WAR ADVERSE TO PIETY. — DISCOURSE ON THE DUTY OF FAMILY PRAYER. — DISCOURSE, TRUE FAITH WILL PRODUCE GOOD WORKS, AGAINST SANDEMANIANISM. — FOUNDING OF RHODE ISLAND COLLEGE. — LETTER TO GILL. — IS A TRUSTEE OF THE COLLEGE THIRTY-FOUR YEARS. — FORMATION OF THE WARREN ASSOCIATION. — ITS USEFULNESS.

IMMEDIATELY after the organization of the Baptist church in Titicut, Mr. Backus published a discourse on "The Difference between the Bond-woman and the Free," showing in particular "that none are proper subjects of the special ordinances of the gospel church but real saints." In 1763 he published another discourse, maintaining that "spiritual ignorance causeth men to counteract their doctrinal knowledge." From this sermon we make the following extract, which indicates the reason for its publication: "After great declensions and stupidity, and the awful prevailing of iniquity in our land, the Lord has been pleased, in infinite mercy, to revive his work in various places, particularly in Middleboro' and the borders of some towns adjoining; and yet great numbers, both of ministers and people, treat it either with disregard or opposition, notwithstanding the evidences of its being a divine work are such as these: namely, many that formerly scarce showed any regard to religion, and rarely attended public worship, now rarely neglect any stated or occasional opportunity to hear the Gospel preached; great numbers of young people who were before bent upon vanity, now show more engagement and delight in religious exercises, public and private, than they ever did in their merry meetings; some intemperate persons are become sober and regular in their conduct; many that were inordinately bent after the world, are brought to lament their folly in pursuing earthly things to the neglect of heavenly; numbers which had old grudges are reconciled, etc. Those who are looked upon to be converted, though many circumstances of their change are various, yet all agree in acknowledging the purity and strictness of the divine law, and that their hearts as well as lives have been filled with sin; and from thence give in to the justice of God in their condemnation, and hold their justification to be entirely by Christ's righteousness, received by faith. Yet a view of that is so far from making them careless in their behavior, that they discover an earnest desire to know and conform to all Christ's commands and ordinances. They show much love to God's people, earnest concern for the salvation of souls, and the like. Indeed, I am far from thinking that there has been no intermixture of things that are not good; though, from the most careful observations that I have been able to make, I really believe that this work has been more clear from such things than the work was twenty-one years ago; particularly the impressions that have been made, either of a sorrowful or joyful nature, have been more upon the understanding, and less on the imagination, now than then. Hence I have heard of no *trances* among us; also, Christians have been more solemn in their joys and less bitter in their zeal, than in the former work."

In 1764 he published a letter to his former pastor, Mr. Benjamin Lord, of Norwich, who had put in print "some harsh things * * against those who have dissented from his sentiments about the ministry, the church, and baptism." Mr. Lord had declared, for example, that no just cause of withdrawment from the standing order could be produced by the New-Lights. He had charged "those that imagine the fulness of the Spirit (or singular gifts which they think they possess) doth warrant their assuming the character and entering on the work of ministers of Christ," with coveting to be "above their Master." And he had joined with six neighboring ministers in saying: "Do not the late separations, and one separation from another, already discover their nature by their fruits? in that some have by this time apostatized even from all religion; while some others are renouncing infant baptism, and going fast to the like dreadful apostasy. It is hid from them that 'evil men and seducers wax worse and worse'; it is hid from them, or rather they will not see, that they have fell *into the way of Cain*, and are in danger of *perishing in the gainsaying of Core*."

In reply to these charges, Mr. Backus explained and vindicated his belief, and that of the New-Lights generally, respecting an internal call to preach the gospel. He then proceeded to show that the right to ordain ministers is vested in the church and not in the clergy alone. Finally, he defends the doctrine of believers' baptism as scriptural, and repudiates that of infant baptism as unscriptural. We cite the following recapitulation of his argument:

"Now, sir, since Christ's forerunner warned the Jews against thinking to come to baptism in Abraham's right, and told them they must bring forth fruits meet for repentance; since Christ himself called little children to come to him, but says not a word of their being brought to baptism before they do come to him; yea, instead of that, he, in the commission, orders that *all nations* be *taught* and *believe* before they are baptized; and since his ministers, in obedience thereto, baptized those that gladly received the Word at Jerusalem, those that believed Philip's preaching in Samaria, and such as heard and believed at Corinth, etc., but there is no account of their baptizing any but such;—and, on the other hand, since God declares that the new covenant is not according to that which he made with *Israel* when he brought them out of Egypt, and that one special difference is, that all who are in this covenant know him and have his law written in their hearts; and since no custom like circumcising children on their parents' account was to be observed among the believing Gentiles;—I dare not follow the multitude in bringing children to the initiating ordinance of the gospel church on their parents' faith, let there be as great or good men as there will that do it, knowing that I have but one Master in all these things, to whom I must give account. And I believe his orders are, that none should be admitted into the ministry but "faithful men," or "men full of faith and the Holy Ghost;" and that none ought to be received into the church but real believers, that is, those that give credible evidence of saving faith."

But his attention was not directed solely to denominational questions. It is evident from his private memoranda that he earnestly longed for an increase of vital godliness in the saints, and carefully observed the religious tendencies of society from year to year. He often referred, in language of great solicitude, to the signs of the times in this respect. When he perceived indications of a genuine revival, his mouth was filled with praise; but when the hearts of men seemed to be drawn away from the service of God, he made record of the fact with mourning. While the French and English war was in progress, he had frequent occasion to lament its effects upon the state of religion. In a letter to his mother, June 9, 1745, he says: "The world seems in great commotion and extensive warlike preparations are making among us. Many appear very light and vain in their going forth, and a general stupidity prevails over the land. But I am ready to look upon these things as the beginnings of sorrow. What the end will be God only knows. Oh, may he prepare us for his holy will!"

After mentioning, in a subsequent letter, May 27, 1756, that scarce one of the soldiers who had lately returned from Nova Scotia had escaped a fit of sickness, he adds: "As to religion, it is a time of hardness among sinners, and most of the saints seem very dull." In another letter, dated March 22, 1757, he remarks: "Affairs in general look very dark for our land. Sixteen men are now called for, out of our town, to go into the war, and scarce a man goes without being hired. Generally the price is fifty or sixty dollars, and some have seventy; which lays heavy burdens on the poor. And worst of all, the complaint in Amos 4th is justly made against us: 'Yet have ye not returned unto me, saith the Lord.'" A year later, May 10, 1758, he writes: "'Tis remarkable to see what a martial spirit prevails among us. Nearly twenty soldiers are going out of Titicut precinct; among whom are brethren Harvey, Campbell and Wood; likewise Joshua Fobes, John Wood, and many others who attend our meeting. * * There appears in our parts of the land an uncommon forwardness to enlist." Two months later, July 22, 1758, he employs the following language: "The rumors of slaughter and garments rolled in blood, which we have from our army, fill many with distressing agitations of mind. * * The absence of so many in the war seems to form an excuse for those who are left to spend all their *time* in the world, and God knows how much of the *heart* is there also. Thus the means which he is using to show us the vanity of earthly things are perverted to ensnare our souls therein. Miserable creatures that we are!" These extracts illustrate the interest which he felt in current events as related to the kingdom of Christ, and his perpetual solicitude for the increase of vital piety.

In 1766 he published a discourse on the duty of family prayer. His reasons for this step are thus given in a prefatory note to the reader: "New England has formerly been a place famous for religion in general, and for family worship in particular. But of late, the neglect of this, as well as of other religious duties, has evidently been growing upon us; which has caused much grief to pious souls. But I have not heard that any discourse has been published upon this subject here these many years. And as there have lately been numbers remarkably awakened in some parts of the land, who were trained up in the neglect of family prayer, and who are still at a loss about the scriptural authority for the daily practice thereof; therefore the following considerations, by the advice of friends, are humbly offered to the public." It is not too much to say of this sermon, that the argument is Biblical and convincing, the reply to objections thorough and fair, the application full, earnest and direct.

In the autumn of 1764, Robert Sandeman came over from Scotland to America, and, after travelling somewhat extensively, gathered a church in Portsmouth, New Hampshire. Within two years, however, this church was scattered, and Mr. Sandeman became pastor of a small society in Boston, Massachusetts. His peculiar views must be known to most of our readers, through the writings of Andrew Fuller, who, at a later period, exposed their unscriptural character with signal ability.[1] To counteract the influence of this man, as well as to clear the Calvinistic doctrines of grace from undeserved reproach, Mr. Backus, who had become a very well read and discriminating theologian, published a discourse, in 1767, from the words: "Purifying their hearts by faith,"[2] and bearing the title, "True Faith will produce good Works." From the introduction, we select the following paragraphs, as casting light upon the period before us:

"The neglect of right conduct in many who have made great professions of faith, has given occasion for the builders on works to exert themselves afresh; and the writings of a religious nature, which have had the most current spread in this land for some years past, are such as, under the pretence of promoting morality and good order, have been levelled against many of the peculiar doctrines of Christianity; yea, some of them even against the true deity of its great Author.

"In the mean time, we have one (Mr. Sandeman) who makes a show of appearing for those great doctrines, and to stir people up to look into them, that yet has artfully mixed such a potion as tends to settle men in a dead sleep. And since his writings have been a means of hardening many in iniquity, and of entangling or perplexing some serious minds, I shall attempt to point out some pernicious principles which he has interspersed among many choice truths."

Before closing this chapter, it is proper to notice two

[1] See Appendix, C. [2] Acts 15: 9.

important and progressive movements of our denomination, namely, the founding of a college in Rhode Island, and the formation of the Warren Association. Since the year 1707, the Philadelphia Baptist Association had been in existence, and at an early period had begun to project plans for the education of a suitable ministry. In 1762, this association was led, by the influence of Rev. Morgan Edwards and others, to form the design of establishing, in Rhode Island, "under the chief direction of the Baptists, a college in which education might be promoted, and superior learning obtained, free from any sectarian religious tests."[1] The leader selected for this important work was the Rev. James Manning, a native of New Jersey, and recently a graduate at Princeton. In July, 1763, he accordingly visited Newport, and proposed the subject of his mission to several gentlemen of the Baptist denomination; among whom were the Hon. Samuel Ward, Governor of the Colony, Hon. Josiah Lyndon, who was afterwards Governor, Col. John Gardiner, Deputy Governor, and twelve others of the same persuasion. They readily concurred with the proposal, and at once entered upon the measures necessary for the accomplishment of the object. After various struggles and difficulties, a charter, reflecting the liberal sentiments of the people in matters of religion, was obtained from the Legislature, in February, 1764, "for a college or university, in the English Colony of Rhode Island," etc. One provision of this charter is as follows: "And furthermore, it is hereby enacted and declared, That into this liberal and catholic institution shall never be admitted any religious tests; but, on the contrary, all the members hereof shall forever enjoy full, free, absolute, uninterrupted liberty of conscience; and that the places of

[1] Backus' History, Vol. II., Chap. 13.

Professors, Tutors, and all other officers, the President alone excepted, shall be free and open for all denominations of Protestants; and that youth, of all religious denominations, shall and may be freely admitted to the equal advantages, emoluments, and honors of the college or university, and shall receive a like fair, generous, and equal treatment during their residence therein, they conducting themselves peaceably, and conforming to the laws and statutes thereof; and that the public teaching shall, in general, respect the sciences; and that the sectarian differences of opinions shall not make any part of the public and classical instruction."

"The government of the college is vested in a Board of Fellows, consisting of twelve members, of whom eight, including the President, must be Baptists; and a Board of Trustees, consisting of thirty-six members, of whom twenty-two must be Baptists, five Friends or Quakers, four Congregationalists, and five Episcopalians. These represent the different denominations existing in the State when the charter was obtained. The instruction and immediate government of the college rests in the President and Board of Fellows."[1]

Mr. Backus felt a lively interest in this college from the beginning. In 1765 he was chosen a member of the Board of Trustees, and continued to serve the institution in this capacity thirty-four years. A letter from his pen to Dr. Gill, with whom he corresponded for many years, will indicate his feelings at the beginning of this enterprise.

"REV. AND DEAR SIR:—I did not think of writing to you again till I should hear from you, which I am hoping

[1] Taken from a sketch of Brown University, by its accomplished Librarian, R. N. Guild.

and expecting to do; but an occasion has presented itself, which I have thought it expedient to take notice of. To introduce this, it may be proper to give a little sketch of the state of the Baptist churches in our land. One grand objection made use of against believers' baptism, has been that none but ignorant and illiterate men have embraced Baptist sentiments. And there was so much color for it as this, namely, that ten years ago, there were but two Baptist ministers,[1] in all New England, who had what is called a liberal education; and they were not clear in the doctrines of grace. But three others have lately come from the Southern governments, namely: Mr. Samuel Stillman, who is settled in Boston; Mr. Hezekiah Smith, who has had remarkable success at Haverhill, where he has gathered a large society; and Mr. James Manning, who is settled at Warren, Rhode Island. And as the Baptists have met with a great deal of abuse from those who are called learned men in our land, they have been not a little prejudiced against learning itself; but latterly there has been considerable alteration in this respect. A charter was obtained from the General Court of Rhode Island Colony, in February, 1764, incorporating a number of Trustees and Fellows, for founding and endowing a college for the education of youth (of which you will be likely to hear more in due time); and this corporation, at their annual meeting, last September, chose the aforesaid Mr. Manning President. He has commenced a school, which appears in a likely way to increase fast. But as there are scarce any books, suitable for such business, to be sold in that colony, he has thought of sending to London for a quantity; and as he is unknown there, he requested that I would write a few lines in his favor. Therefore, my dear sir, if my poor

[1] Mr. Jeremiah Condy, of Boston, and Mr. Upham, of Newport, R. I.

testimony may be thought worthy of any notice, I desire that you would mention to Mr. Keith, to whom he has thoughts of sending, that from near two years' acquaintance with him, I am well satisfied that he is a man of piety, integrity and ability, who will make conscience of fulfilling his engagements.

I remain, Sir, your humble servant,

ISAAC BACKUS."

This letter appears to have been written in the early part of 1765. In 1799, he resigned his place on the Board, not, however, as will be seen by the following correspondence, from any diminution of interest in the college, but from inability to serve it longer:

"To the Corporation of Rhode Island College:

"REVEREND AND HONORED GENTLEMEN: Having been a member of this corporation above thirty years, in which it has advanced from small beginnings to great responsibility, * * * * as my age and infirmities are such as to render it very difficult to attend your meetings any longer, I request liberty to resign my place in your corporation; praying that the divine blessing may ever attend the seminary of learning, for the good of mankind, to the latest generations.

I remain your hearty friend and servant,

ISAAC BACKUS.

MIDDLEBORO', Sept. 2, 1799."

"COLLEGE CHAPEL, PROVIDENCE, Sept. 5, 1799.

"At a meeting of the corporation this day, voted, That the thanks of this corporation be presented to the Rev. Isaac Backus, for his long, eminent, and faithful services as a member of the incorporation.

GEORGE BENSON, Deputy Secretary."

The Warren Association was formed in 1767; and chiefly, it is said, by the efforts of James Manning, President of the infant college then located in Warren. Mr. Backus, who was chosen clerk of the first meeting, thus commences the minutes of this association: "Whereas there hath of late years been a great increase of Baptist churches in New England, which yet have not such an acquaintance with each other and orderly union together as ought to be, it has been thought by many that a general meeting or association might be a likely means to remove this evil and to promote the general good of the churches. Therefore a number of elders, being occasionally together last year, did appoint a meeting at Warren in Rhode Island colony, on September 8, 1767; and sent an invitation to others of their brethren to meet them there, to confer upon these affairs. Accordingly, a considerable number of elders and brethren met at the time and place appointed; and elder John Gano, from New York, opened the meeting with a suitable sermon from Acts 15: 9."[1]

Eleven churches were represented at this meeting; but although "they generally manifested a good will toward this attempt for promoting the union and welfare of the churches, most of them thought they were not prepared to join in an association." The pastors and messengers of but four churches were at this time ready to unite. The other brethren present seem to have hesitated through fear of some usurpation of authority by the associated body over the particular churches composing it; an evil which they were determined, if possible, to avoid. Besides, they were not altogether satisfied with the plan of organization and action now adopted. This plan was borrowed sub-

[1] See Appendix D.

stantially from the Philadelphia Association, and was thought to give undue authority to the united body. It was, however, soon after so explained and amended as to be less exceptionable to the churches. Yet ultimately, a new plan, drawn up by President Manning, was substituted for the original one; and gradually the association won the confidence of nearly all the Baptists of New England.[1] It linked together the scattered and feeble churches of our communion by a yearly meeting; it provided supplies for many a little flock which could not sustain a pastor; it transmitted pecuniary assistance to young men who were studying for the ministry; it encouraged those who were called to bear the spoiling of their goods; it sent forth appeals in behalf of religious liberty which hastened the separation of church and state; and it contributed in various ways to the spread of truth and the increase of piety. In the progress of our narrative we shall have occasion frequently to notice the enterprise and usefulness of the Warren Association; the earliest fraternal organization which united the Baptist churches of New England.

[1] The first Baptist church in Middleboro' united with the association in 1770. "They waited," says Mr. Backus, "until they could be satisfied that this association did not assume any jurisdiction over the churches, before they joined. And they now joined upon the express condition that no complaint should ever be received by the association against any particular church that was not of the association, nor from any censured member of any of our churches."

CHAPTER XII.

LEGISLATION FOR THE CHURCH.

REASONS FOR DESCRIBING MR. BACKUS'S EFFORTS FOR RELIGIOUS LIBERTY. — SKETCH OF EARLIER LEGISLATION FOR THE CHURCH DESIRABLE. — PARTICULAR LAWS. — ROGER WILLIAMS BANISHED. — LAWS AGAINST QUAKERS. OTHER LAWS. — CAMBRIDGE PLATFORM. — MALDEN CHURCH FINED. — OBADIAH HOLMES WHIPPED. — LAWS AGAINST QUAKERS. — FOUR EXECUTED. — APOLOGY FOR THIS ACT. — BAPTIST MEETING IN BOSTON. — DECLENSION IN PIETY. — THE NEW CHARTER. — BAPTISTS TAXED UNTIL 1728. — ACTS OF EXEMPTION PASSED, IN 1728. — IN 1729. — IN 1734. — IN 1740. — IN 1747. — IN 1753. — IN 1757.

To pass by in silence the exertions of Mr. Backus in behalf of religious liberty would be at once unjust and ungrateful; unjust, because those exertions are to be classed with the most resolute, conscientious and protracted labors of his life; and ungrateful, because we are enjoying this day a "freedom to worship God," which is to a considerable extent the fruit of his faith and perseverance. "With a great sum" did the fathers of our denomination in New England obtain that religious equality which is our acknowledged birthright. They were driven into the wilderness, were scourged by order of the civil power, were spoiled of their goods, were cast into prison, were pelted by the violence of mobs, were falsely accused, were reviled and defamed and treated as the filth and offscouring of mankind; their principles were caricatured, their purposes maligned, their integrity questioned their petitions slighted, and their hopes deferred; yet trusting in God they were in general true to their Master and their mission, while not a few of them, like the subject of this narrative, were distinguished for their moral courage and their assurance of ultimate deliverance. It would therefore be most ungrateful in us to exclude from this account a record of their exertions to establish religious equality.

But besides what is due to the memory of those who were ready to suffer loss, in order to secure the triumph of right principles, something also is due to those now living, and to those who will come after us, lest some of them by reason of ignorance should be left to undervalue their birthright of soul-liberty. We shall therefore give our readers some account of the labors which Mr. Backus performed in this department of christian service.

And for the purpose of assisting them to appreciate more fully the nature and the need of those labors, we shall, in the present chapter, briefly trace the course of action on religious affairs pursued by the civil authorities of Massachusetts, from the planting of this colony down to the period when his labors were commenced. In view of the object contemplated, the value and interest of this sketch will be increased by presenting it, for the most part, in the language of authoritative documents.

In 1631, the General Court of Massachusetts "ordered and agreed that, for time to come, no man shall be admitted to the freedom of this body politic, but such as are members of some of the churches within the limits of the same." Four years later, the elders and brethren of every church within the jurisdiction were entreated to "consult and advise of one uniform order of discipline in the churches, agreeable to the Scriptures, and then to consider how far the magistrates are bound to interfere for the preservation of that uniformity and peace of the churches." In 1636, all persons were ordered to take notice "that this court doth not, nor will hereafter, approve of any such companies of men as shall henceforth join in any pretended way of church fellowship, without they shall first acquaint the magistrates and the elders of the greater part of the churches in this jurisdiction with their intentions, and have their approbation herein." And this same year, Mr. Roger Williams, one of the elders of the church in Salem, was ordered "to depart out of this jurisdiction within six weeks now next ensuing, for divulging divers new and dangerous opinions against the authority of the magistrates, and for writing letters of defamation, both of the magistrates and churches here."

The next year, all Jesuits were banished from the colony, and it was provided that should any one be taken a second time in the same, he should be put to death. In 1638, it was ordered "that whosoever shall stand excommunicate for the space of six months, without laboring what in him or her lieth to be restored, such person shall be presented to the court of assistants, and then proceeded with by fine, imprisonment, banishment, or further,—as their contempt and obstinacy, upon full hearing, shall deserve." Also in the same year, "that every inhabitant in any town is liable to contribute to all charges, both in church and Commonwealth, whereof he doth or may receive benefit;" and that whoever shall not "voluntarily contribute, proportionably to his ability, with other freemen of the same town, to all common charges, as well for upholding the ordinances in the churches as otherwise, shall be compelled thereto by assessment and distress, to be levied by the constable or other officer of the town, as in other cases." This law was applicable to all, whether freemen or not.

Three years after this date, it was declared "that the civil authority here established hath power and liberty to see that peace, ordinances and rules of Christ be observed in every church, according to his word;" and likewise, that "all the people of God within this jurisdiction, who are not in a church way, and be Orthodox in judgment, and not scandalous in life, shall have full liberty to gather themselves into a church estate, provided they do it in a christian way," and provided "they shall acquaint three or more magistrates dwelling next, and the elders of the neighbor churches where they intended to join, and have their approbation therein."

In 1644, it was ordered "that if any person within this jurisdiction shall openly condemn or oppose the baptizing of infants, or shall purposely depart the congregation at the administration of this ordinance, after due means of conviction, [he] shall be sentenced to banishment." "About this time one Painter of Hingham was ordered to be whipped, not for his opinion, but for reproaching the Lord's ordinance of baptism, and for his bold and evil behavior both at home and at the court." In 1646, it was ordered that "wheresoever the ministry of the word is regularly established, every person shall duly resort and attend thereunto, on pain of forfeiting five shillings for every unnecessary absence. Moreover, that every person who shall go about to destroy or disturb the order of the churches established in this county, by open renouncing their church estate, or their ministry, or their ordinances dispensed in them," "shall forfeit to the public treasury forty shillings for every month, so long as he continues in his obstinacy." And that, "if any Christian, so called, shall behave himself contemptuously toward the Word preached, or the messenger thereof, he shall for the first scandal be convented and reproved openly by the magistrates at some lecture, and for a second offence shall either pay five pounds into the public treasury, or stand two hours openly upon a block four feet high, on a lecture day, with a paper fixed on his breast with this, A WANTON GOSPELLER, written in capital letters."

In 1648, the Cambridge Platform was approved, "for the substance thereof" by the General Court. This platform says: "It is the duty of the magistrate to take care of matters of religion, and to improve his civil authority for the observing of the duties commanded in the first as well as in the second table. The end of the magistrate's office is, not only the quiet and peaceable life of the subject in matters of righteousness and honesty, but also in matters of godliness. Idolatry, blasphemy, *heresy*, venting corrupt and pernicious opinions that destroy the foundation, open contempt of the Word preached, profanation of the Lord's day, disturbing the peaceable administration and exercise of the worship and holy things of God, and the like, are to be restrained and punished by the civil authority." Among the chief reasons for calling the synod which drew up this platform we copy the following: "Whereas, in most churches, the ministers do baptize only such children whose nearest parents, one or both of them, are settled members in full communion with one or other of these churches, there be some who do baptize the children if the grandfather or grandmother be such members, though the immediate parents be not, and others * * * do much incline thereto * * *; on the other side, there be some amongst us, who do think that whatever be the state of the parents, baptism ought not to be dispensed to any infants whatsoever," etc. And the following year the General Court wrote to the Plymouth colony, reproving them for conniving at Anabaptists, and entreating them "to take care as well of the suppressing of errors as of the maintenance of truth, God equally requiring the performance of both at the hands of christian magistrates."

In 1651, the church in Malden made choice of a minister without consulting the neighboring churches, and proceeded to ordain him against their advice conveyed by letter. At its next session, the General Court fined all the actors in this affair, except those who had given satisfaction for their fault. The same year, three men of the Baptist persuasion, John Clarke, Obadiah Holmes, and John Crandal, were arrested in Lynn for holding religious worship in a private house, re-baptizing, etc., were taken to Boston and cast into prison. They were soon tried before the court of assistants, "by whom Clark was fined twenty pounds, Holmes thirty, and John Crandal five, or each to be well whipped." Two of them were released; but Mr. Holmes was confined until September, and then publicly whipped with great severity. We cite a few words from his account of this infliction.

"I told them, moreover, that the Lord having manifested his love towards me, in giving me repentance towards God and faith in Christ, and so to be baptized in water by a messenger of Jesus, in the name of the Father, Son, and Holy Spirit, wherein I have fellowship with him in his death, burial and resurrection; I am now come to be baptized in afflictions by your hands, that so I may have further fellowship with my Lord, and am not ashamed of his sufferings, for by his stripes I am healed. And as the man began to lay the strokes upon my back, I said to the people, 'Though my flesh should fail and my spirit should fail, yet God would not fail.' So it pleased the Lord to come in, and to fill my heart and tongue as a vessel full, and with an audible voice I brake forth, praying the Lord not to lay this sin to their charge, and telling the people that now I found he did not fail me, and therefore now I should trust him forever who failed me not; for in truth, as the strokes fell upon me, I had such a spiritual manifestation of God's presence as I never had before, and the outward pain was so removed from me, that I could well bear it, yea, and in a manner felt it not, although it was grievous, as the spectators said, the man striking with all his strength, spitting in his hand three times, with a three-corded whip, giving me therewith thirty strokes. When he loosed me from the post, having joyfulness in my heart and cheerfulness in my countenance, as the spectators observed, I told the magistrates: "You have struck me as with roses;' and said, moreover: 'Although the Lord hath made it easy to me, yet I pray God it may not be laid to your charge.'"

In 1652, the "New Church" in Boston chose for their pastor one who had not received a liberal education; but the civil authority forbade his ordination, lest it should tend to the subversion of an able ministry. Three years after it was enacted that the "county court in each shire, shall, upon information given them of any defect of any congregation or town within the shire, appoint what maintenance shall be allowed to the minister of the place, and shall issue out warrants to the selectmen to assess the inhabitants, which the constable of said town shall collect and levy as other town rates."

In 1656, it was enacted, that any commander of a vessel, who shall bring a Quaker into the colony, shall pay a fine of one hundred pounds, and that all Quakers arriving in the colony from any place whatsoever "shall be forthwith committed to the house of correction and at their entrance be severely whipt, and by the master thereof be kept constantly to work, and none suffered to converse or speak with them during the time of their imprisonment." As soon as possible they were to be removed from the colony.

In the following year, the Court advised a general council to consider the question, whether all baptized persons, not scandalous in life, ought not to be treated as members of the church in all respects, except in partaking of the Lord's Supper. It was determined that all baptized persons ought thus to be considered members of the church and entitled to bring their children to baptism. More stringent laws were also passed this year and the next against Quakers. They provided that if a Quaker returned into the colony after banishment, he was to have one of his ears cut off; if he returned again the other ear was to be treated in the same way; if he came back a third time his tongue was to be bored through with a hot iron, and if found in the colony after the time limited for his departure, he was to be punished with death. During the following year, 1659, two men suffered death, according to the final provision of this law, for refusing to leave the jurisdiction, and the next year a man and woman for the same reason. Twenty more were in prison. But the General Court saw fit to pause in its course. For the satisfaction of weak consciences a defense of its action was duly published.

Moreover, an address was prepared for the king, in which it is said, respecting the Quakers: "Such was their dangerous, impetuous and desperate turbulency, both to religion and the State, civil and ecclesiastical, as that how unwillingly soever, could it have been avoided, the magistrate at last, in conscience both to God and man, judged himself called, for the defense of all, to keep the passage with the point of the sword held towards them. This could do no harm to him that would be warned thereby; their wittingly rushing themselves thereupon was their own act, and we, with all humility, conceive a crime bringing their blood on their own head. The Quakers died, not because of their other crimes, how capital soever, but upon their superadded contempt of authority; breaking in upon us notwithstanding their sentence of banishment made known to them." And yet farther on, in the same address, they use this noble and touching language: "We could not live without the public worship of God. We were not permitted the use of public worship without such a yoke of subscription and conformity as we could not consent unto without sin. That we might therefore enjoy divine worship without the human mixtures, without offence either to God, man or our own consciences, we, with leave, but not without tears, departed from our country, kindred and fathers' houses, unto this Patmos, in relation whereunto we do not say our garments are become old by reason of the very long journey, but that ourselves, who came away in our strength, are by reason of very long absence, many of us become gray headed, and some of us stooping, for age."

This address seems not to have made the intended impression on the king's mind; and the next year, 1661, in obedience to his command, it was ordered "that the execution of the laws in force against Quakers, as such, so far as they respect corporal punishment or death, be suspended until the Court take further action." They were never revived. In 1664, it was ordered, also in obedience to a letter from the king, "that henceforth all Englishmen, presenting a certificate, under the hands of the ministers or minister of the place where they dwell, that they are orthodox in religion and not vicious in their lives, and also a certificate under the hands of the selectmen of the place, that they are freeholders, and are for their own proper estate ratable to the place where they live, to the full value of ten shillings, or that they are in full communion with some church among us, it shall be the liberty of all and every such person or persons, — to present themselves and their desires to this Court for their admittance to the freedom of this Commonwealth."

In 1665, a few brethren established a Baptist meeting in Boston. They were fined and imprisoned for so doing by the General Court, but after several years of great suffering they began to be recognized as a christian church.

It 1679, it was enacted, "that no persons whatsoever, without the consent of the freemen of the town where they live, first orderly had and obtained at a public meeting, assembled for that end, and license of the county court, or, in defect of such consent and license, by the special order of the General Court, shall erect or make use of any (meeting) house," on penalty of forfeiting both the house and the land on which it is built to the county.

Thus did the civil government of Massachusetts, under the first charter, endeavor to suppress error and maintain the truth. Law was piled upon law and penalty annexed to penalty for the purpose of eradicating heresy; but in vain. The only weapons which can prevail against religious error are spiritual, but these were carnal. Meanwhile the union of Church and State was bearing its legitimate fruits. The deep toned piety of the fathers was not implanted in the hearts of their children. The half-way covenant was introduced, and the declension of vital godliness accelerated. The magistrate might indeed "improve his civil authority for the observing of the duties commanded in the first as well as in the second table," but he could not reach the heart; he could compel men to an outward worship of God only. Yet far more than this was necessary to preserve the substance of Christianity in the land of the Pilgrims. And happily, notwithstanding the pernicious effect of relying upon civil power in the last resort to maintain the church in her purity, there were many who still possessed the living faith of the fathers, and who did much to withstand the encroachments of indifference and formality. Yet these were but a small minority, and the process of deterioration went on. This process was not thoroughly arrested in any considerable portion of New England until the period of the Great Awakening. Then, as we have already seen, the vital forces of Christianity repudiated, to a considerable extent, all civil restrictions and established usages.

In 1691, a new charter of Massachusetts was issued by William and Mary. This charter granted "liberty of conscience in the worship of God to all Christians, except Papists, inhabiting or which shall inhabit or be resident within our said province or territory." "But this most important article," says Backus, "was construed by the ministers as meaning that the General Court might, by laws, encourage and *protect* that religion which is the general profession of the inhabitants." Laws were therefore directly enacted, providing that the minister elected by a majority of the inhabitants of any plantation should be the minister of the place, and that his salary should be levied by a rate upon all the inhabitants.

From the year 1692 to the year 1728, the Baptists were everywhere, except in Boston and some few other towns, taxed for the support of Congregational ministers. The fact of their maintaining worship by themselves was not allowed to be a sufficient reason for exempting them from rates to sustain a ministry, which in point of conscience they could not hear. For their refusal to pay such rates, we are told that they "oftentimes had their bodies seized upon, and thrown into the common jail, as malefactors, and their cattle, swine, horses, household furniture, and implements of husbandry, forcibly distrained from them, and shamefully sold, many times at not one-quarter part of the first value." And it is added "that the heavy pressures and afflictions occasioned by these distraints, imprisonments, and the losses consequent thereupon, made many of the Baptists bend, almost ruined some of our people, and disheartened others to such a degree, that they moved, with the remaining effects they had left, out of the Province."

At length, after repeated applications to the General Court for relief, the first act of exemption was passed, 1728, entitled, "An act to exempt persons commonly called Anabaptists, and those called Quakers, within this Province, from being taxed for and towards the support of ministers." This act was entirely unsatisfactory, both because it merely exempted the polls, and not the estates, of those concerned, and because it was limited to persons living within five miles of the place where the meetings of their church were held. Renewed applications were therefore made, and the next year an act was passed, exempting their estates also from ministerial taxes. It was, however, to remain in force but five years.

At the expiration of this period, application was again made, by persons of the Baptist persuasion, for relief; and a third act, more explicit than either of the preceding, was thereupon passed. It provided that "the assessors of each town where any of the said Anabaptists live, or their lands in their own actual improvement lie, shall take a list of all such persons, and forthwith transmit the same to the Clerk of the town, which list shall be entered on the record of such town by the Clerk, that so any of the people called Anabaptists, or any members of their society, thereto appointed, may view such list, have a copy thereof, if they desire the same, paying only sixpence therefor; and if any person of that denomination shall be omitted in such list by the assessors taken, and the assessors shall be certified thereof in writing, under the hands of two principal members of that persuasion, appointed thereto by the respective societies, that such persons not inserted in their list they believe to be conscientiously of their persuasion, and that they do frequently and usually attend their meeting, for the worship of God, on the Lord's day, the assessors shall also exempt the said persons, so omitted, and their estates in their actual management and improvement, as well as all others inserted in the said list, from all rates and taxes, by the said assessors to be made, for the support of the minister or ministers in their towns, or for erecting places of public worship; this act to continue five years," etc.

But this act, in like manner with the preceding, failed, in a great measure, to accomplish the purpose for which it was passed. No penalty was annexed to a refusal or neglect of the assessors to perform the service required of them. When, therefore, the Baptists "at some times reminded the assessors of their omissions herein, they were generally snubbed, and in a contemptuous manner answered, that the assessors knew nothing of any such act, nor would they concern themselves therein. Other assessors, more knowing and intelligent, insisted upon it, that as there was no penalty affixed on the non-performance of taking such lists of the Anabaptists, they would not trouble their heads about it." Hence the lists described in this act were taken in scarcely a single town of the province. This omission put the Baptists to no inconsiderable trouble and expense, in procuring the requisite certificates; besides the unpleasantness of being thus treated by their fellow Christians.

Upon the expiration of the third act, in 1740, a similar one was procured, not without much cost and trouble, to continue in force seven years. The same course was also pursued by the assessors generally, as under the preceding act, and the same vexations were experienced by the members of our denomination.

When this act expired, in 1747, the Baptists, it is said, were on the point of making application to the king for more permanent and complete relief; but they were prevented from so doing by an unsolicited renewal of the law exempting them from ministerial rates, to remain in full force ten years; for this spontaneous act of justice led them to look for peace and rest for the term of ten years at least. But in 1753, an act in addition to this was passed, which contained this provision: "That no person, for the future, should be esteemed to be an Anabaptist, but those whose names are contained in the lists taken by the assessors, or such as shall produce a certificate, under the hands of the minister and of two principal members of such church, setting forth that they conscientiously believe such person or persons to be of their persuasion," etc. And further, "that no *minister* nor the *members* of any Anabaptist church, as aforesaid, shall be esteemed qualified to give such certificates, as aforesaid, other than such as shall have obtained *from three other churches*, commonly called Anabaptists, in this or the neighboring Provinces, a certificate from *each respectively*, that they esteem such church to be one of their denomination, and that they *conscientiously believe them to be Anabaptists*," etc.

This law proved to be very oppressive. For there had come into existence since the great awakening, by means of the New-Lights, quite a number of Baptist churches which were not yet in fellowship with the older churches of our denomination, and which therefore could not obtain the certificates now required. Moreover, this act made it necessary for Baptists to certify their conscientious belief of a point which they were known not to believe, viz., that they and their brethren were Anabaptists or Re-baptizers. Strenuous efforts were made to procure the repeal of this additional act. Mr. John Proctor, a member of the Second Baptist Church in Boston, was chosen by his brethren as their agent to bear their complaints to England. He drew up a spirited remonstrance on the subject, which was presented to the assembly in May, 1754. Says Mr. Backus: "It stated matters so plainly, that a motion was made by some to take the signers of it into custody; but Governor Shirley, newly returned from Europe, convinced them of the impolicy of such a step; and then they appointed a committee to confer in a friendly way with the Baptists. Matters were shifted along until the war came on and their design for England was dropt."

In the year 1757, a new law was made for the relief of Baptists and Quakers. It provided that none were to be exempted from ministerial taxes as Baptists, but those "whose names shall be contained in a list or lists to be taken and exhibited on or before the twentieth of July annually to the assessors of such town, district, precinct or parish, and signed by three principal members of the Anabaptist church to which he or they belong, and the minister thereof, if any there be, who shall therein certify that the persons whose names are inserted in the said list or lists are really belonging thereto, that they verily believe them to be conscientiously of their persuasion, and that they frequently and usually attend public worship in said church on the Lord's days." This act was continued in force thirteen years until 1770; "and no tongue or pen," says Mr. Backus, "can fully describe all the evils that were practised under it."

It is now proper for us to close this survey. For the sake of brevity, we have in the second part of it traced the course of action pursued by the civil authority in matters of religion, only so far as it related expressly to members of our own denomination. A sketch of this action thus far at least seemed necessary in order to any just appreciation of the state of affairs when Mr. Backus began his labors in behalf of religious liberty; for those labors were called forth chiefly by the wrongs which, in his judgment, were suffered by his brethren of the Baptist faith.

CHAPTER XIII.

EFFORTS FOR RELIGIOUS LIBERTY.

DESIGN OF THIS PART OF OUR NARRATIVE. — COMMITTEE OF GRIEVANCES APPOINTED BY THE WARREN ASSOCIATION. — THEIR ADVERTISEMENT. — REV. JOHN DAVIS CHOSEN AGENT. — HIS LETTER TO MORGAN EDWARDS — PETITION TO THE GENERAL COURT. — NEW CERTIFICATE LAW UNSATISFACTORY. — TREATMENT OF MR. DAVIS.— OPPRESSION IN MONTAGUE, IN CHELMSFORD AND IN BRADFORD. — LETTER OF MR. BACKUS TO A MEMBER OF THE ASSEMBLY. — EXTRACTS FROM THE SAME. — CHARACTER AND DEATH OF MR. DAVIS.

To set forth in detail the efforts of Mr. Backus for the separation of church and state, according to the principles first applied by Roger Williams, would require more space than can be devoted to this topic. Besides this, the preparation of such a narrative is rendered well nigh impossible by the loss of his diary for the period when he was most engaged in this department of service. Yet it will not be difficult, from the records of this period still remaining, to ascertain some of the principal tasks which he performed, to exhibit specimens of the oppression which he felt himself called upon to resist, and to describe the general course of his activity. In doing this, it will be our aim, in harmony with the design of this volume, to describe also, so far as may be practicable, the labors of his brethren in behalf of the same cause.

The ministers of the Warren Association for the year 1769 certify that "many letters from the churches mentioned grievous oppressions and persecutions from the standing order; especially the one from Ashfield, where religious tyranny had been carried to great lengths." A committee, on which Mr. Backus was assigned a place, was therefore appointed by the Association, to draft petitions for redress to be presented to the general courts of Massachusetts and Connecticut. They were accordingly drawn up, read and approved; and another committee was chosen to present them. The following gentlemen were also appointed to receive accounts of "well-attested grievances," to be transmitted to Rev. Samuel Stillman of Boston; viz. Rev. Hezekiah Smith of Haverhill, Rev. Isaac Backus of Middleboro', Mr. Richard Montague of Sunderland, Rev. Joseph Meacham of Enfield, and Rev. Timothy Wightman of Groton[1] in Connecticut. These "grievances" were to be employed in the petitions and memorials by which the Association was determined to seek a remedy for oppression, "where," it is said, "a speedy and effectual one may be had."

The petitions, prepared by the Association as mentioned above, seem to have been wholly disregarded by those in authority. The committee of grievances were therefore still more anxious to know the exact truth as to any instances of unjust taxation. Accordingly, the following advertisement was published in the Boston Evening Post, August 30, 1770. "To the Baptists in the Province of Massachusetts Bay, who are, or have been oppressed in any way on a religious account. It would be needless to tell you that you have long felt the effects of the laws by which the religion of the government in which you live is established. Your purses have felt the burden of ministerial rates; and when these would not

[1] In the manuscript, "Thomas Whitman of Grattan."

satisfy your enemies, your property hath been taken from you and sold for less than half its value. These things you cannot forget. You will therefore readily hear and attend, when you are desired to collect your cases of suffering and have them well attested, — such as, the taxes you have paid to build meeting-houses, to settle ministers and support them, with all the time, money and labor you have lost in waiting on courts, feeing lawyers, etc., and bring or send such cases to the Baptist Association to be holden at Bellingham; when measures will be resolutely adopted for obtaining redress from another quarter than that to which repeated application hath been made unsuccessfully. Nay, complaints, however just and grievous, have been treated with indifference, and scarcely, if at all, credited. We deem this our conduct perfectly justifiable; and hope you will pay particular regard to this desire, and be exact in your accounts. Boston, July 31, 1770."

The Warren Association met on the eleventh of September, and such accounts were brought in to this body as led to a "unanimous resolution to send to the British court for help, if it could not be obtained in America." This resolution indicated very clearly their determination to make a systematic and vigorous resistance to the unjust exactions in support of the Standing Order; for, as a denomination, the Baptists were strongly opposed to the tyrannous course pursued of late by the English government towards the colonies, and were therefore exceedingly reluctant to lay their complaints at the foot of the throne. The Rev. John Davis, pastor of the Second Baptist Church in Boston, was appointed agent for his brethren, to use his best endeavors, with the advice of their committee, to obtain a full deliverance from ministerial taxes.

Isaac Backus was reäppointed on the committee, and though residing at a considerable distance from the centre of action, was one of its most efficient members. The following letter from Mr. Davis to Rev. Morgan Edwards, seems to show that the proceedings already described began to be looked upon as serious and important.

"BOSTON, SEPT. 26, 1770.

MY GOOD FRIEND: I have just time to tell you that when we published our advertisement, Dr. Channing pretended to me to be much interested in our affairs, and said he would join us in an address to the General Court, and a good deal to that purpose. In consequence of which I called the committee together; when it was agreed to suspend further publication till we had asked the Court to give us a law, and if they refused, to prosecute the matter with all the spirit we could. I sent for Mr. Smith, of Haverhill, who is now in town. We have drawn a petition which we propose presenting as soon as convenient after the Court goes upon business. I waited yesterday on the Lieut. Governor, who said many things to encourage us, and said he would do all he could for us, if we could make our way through the General Court. I asked him whether it would be proper to say *they had no right by charter to establish a religion*, etc. He told me such a thing might do beyond the water, but would not here. I mentioned the evil that our going to England might do. He said he did not think it would do any; for, said he, it is as bad as can be already. I have had remarkably kind invitations from one of the council within these few days; for what reason I know not. I have refused his kindness hitherto; perhaps it may do for something or other at some future time. He happens to be a courtier, and therefore not to be depended on. Our religious affairs have been full as well, if not better, than I expected. * * *

JOHN DAVIS."

The petition referred to in this letter seems to have been the following, which was addressed to the General Court in the fall of 1770.

"To the Honorable the Lieut. Governor, the Honorable his Majesty's Council, and the House of Representatives, in General Court assembled:

The petition of the Baptist Committee of Grievances, acting in the name and by the appointment of the Baptist churches met in association at Bellingham in this Province, the 11th, 12th and 13th days of September last, humbly sheweth:—

That although the Baptists have been repeatedly disappointed in their addresses to the General Court, and have not received that relief from their distresses which they humbly conceive all our people are entitled to, as men and Christians, and subjects of a free government; yet, very unwilling to leave any means untried, and hoping all things from this Court,—We, the committee aforesaid, with great earnestness and seriousness, do recommend ourselves to you, Gentlemen, whom we consider as the guardians of our rights and privileges, as well religious as civil; the protectors of the injured; the fathers of our common country; and beg leave to say that we are encouraged in this our address from the consideration of the rights of mankind having been so well defined in the votes of your honorable House, by which we are taught to think:—'That no taxation can be equitable where such restraints are laid upon the taxed as take from him the liberty of giving his own money freely.'

"This being true, permit us to ask, with what equity is our property taken from us, not only without our consent, but violently, contrary to our wills, and for such purposes as we cannot in faithfulness to that stewardship with which God hath entrusted us, favor. Permit us, therefore, to lay before this honorable Court the grievances of which we complain, and pray your friendly as well as legislative interposition, that our brethren may be saved from threatening ruin, who have suffered much in their persons and estates, to the great disquietude of their minds and distress of their small and chargeable families.

"And these evils have arisen from some of the laws of this Province, which are ecclesiastical in their nature, and bear hard upon us, and, as we think, deprive us of a charter privilege; especially one law, made in favor of the proprietors of the town of Ashfield in the county of Hampshire, which is contrary to, and in respect to that town, supersedes all acts of the General Court heretofore enacted and declared to be in favor of the Baptists. In consequence of which law, and by a power granted in the same to the proprietors of Ashfield aforesaid, three hundred and ninety-eight acres of our land have been sold to build and remove and repair when moved, a meeting-house in which we have no part, though our money helped to build it, and to settle and support a minister whom we cannot hear. The lands were valued at three hundred and sixty-three pounds thirteen shillings, lawful money, and were sold for nineteen pounds three shillings; so that our loss is three hundred and forty-four pounds fifteen shillings, lawful money. Part of the lands aforesaid belonged to the Rev. Ebenezer Smith, a regularly ordained Baptist minister, who, together with his father and others, their brethren, in the last Indian war, built at their own expense a fort and were a frontier; and this they did without any help from any quarter; for which we beg leave to say that they deserve, at least, the common privileges of the subjects of the crown of England. Part of said lands had been laid out for a burying-place, and they have taken from us our dead. They have also sold a dwelling-house and orchard, and pulled up our apple trees, and thrown down our fences, and made our fields waste places.

"Permit us further to add, that the act of the General Court, made with design to favor us, and for the same purpose hath been renewed from time to time, is attended with such difficulties as render it ineffectual in many instances, and by no means sufficient to answer the good purpose for which we are willing to believe the honorable Court intended it. The difficulties arising from this quarter, of which we complain, we are ready to lay before the House whenever it shall please them to call upon us.

"We must beg your indulgence while we recite one thing more, which we deem hard, and that is, a proviso in the above mentioned law or act of General Court, by which no Baptist can avail himself even of that law in new settled towns; and we are thereby virtually prevented from settling in such towns.

"Should we go through with an enumeration of all our grievances, we must take up too much of the time of this honorable Court, which we are unwilling to do. We therefore pray the General Court to relieve the following particulars, viz.:

"1. To repeal a law entitled 'an Act in addition to an Act for erecting the new plantation called Huntstown,' in the county of Hampshire, into a town by the name of Ashfield, and restore the lands which have been taken from them to support the ministers settled by law, and give them damages for the many and great injuries they have been made to suffer.

"2. To enable our brethren, in different parts of the Province, to recover damages for the losses they have been made to sustain on a religious account.

"3. To grant perpetual exemption to all Baptists and their congregations from all ministerial rates whatsoever, according to the full intent and meaning of the charter of the Province, that we may all enjoy full liberty of conscience as others his Majesty's subjects of this Province, and also to disannul all such rates heretofore laid on any of our people in the government. And your petitioners as in duty bound will ever pray.

Signed in behalf of the whole Committee. { SAMUEL STILLMAN. HEZEKIAH SMITH.. JOHN DAVIS.

An accurate narrative of the oppression in Ashfield, mentioned above, is given by Mr. Backus in the second volume of his History. We have inserted in the Appendix[1] one of the petitions offered to the General Court by the Baptists of this place and extracts from another.

The old certificate law had now expired, and near the close of this year 1770 a new one was made. By this new act the title *Anti-pedobaptists* was substituted for that of *Anabaptists* and the word *congregation* for that of *church*. The certificates were to be signed by three or more principal members and the minister, "if any there be." Parishes were moreover authorized, if they pleased, to free the Baptists by vote from the payment of ministerial rates without any certificates. It would be interesting to know whether such a vote was passed by any parishes in the Province; charity would lead us to hope that many were. "But in

[1] See Appendix E.

this law," says Mr. Backus, "the word *conscientiously* was still retained and the certificates were to be given annually to the assessors." Accordingly, no one could attend a Baptist meeting and give his support to the same, free from taxes to the standing order, unless he was known to be *conscientiously* of the Baptist persuasion. The term seems therefore to have been shrewdly inserted in order to prevent those who had not as yet fully embraced the views of any denomination from connecting themselves with the tolerated sect. As soon as this law was passed, Mr. Davis called together the committee, and it was voted unanimously not to accept the new act as satisfactory.

Meanwhile, an anonymous article, dated Cambridge, Oct. 22, 1770, and purporting to be written by a Baptist, had appeared in several public journals, pronouncing the complaints made by our brethren to be without the least foundation, throwing out the challenge: "If any have suffered let him appear," and defending the action of the civil authorities as altogether just and liberal. Mr. Davis was requested by the committee to answer this production. He did so by presenting a brief sketch of actual grievances complained of by his brethren. Such an appeal to facts ought to have called forth at least a respectful answer; but instead of this the only response which followed was an article replete with personal abuse. "There is a little upstart Gentleman," it said, "lately settled in town; * * the *Youth* discovers the most insufferable arrogance; * * I very much *suspect* he is one employed by the *enemies* of America to *defame* and blacken the Colonies," etc. Such were the weapons used by some to repel the arguments and importunities of a respectable body of Christians for religious equality!

To illustrate the way in which this law and others similar to it were made ineffectual the following instances may be given. In 1765 a Baptist church was organized in Montague, and the members of it gave in their certificates to the parish assessors according to law. Yet they were taxed for the support of the regular minister, and distress made upon them. At length Samuel Harvey sued the assessors for a cow and calf which had thus been taken from him. After the writ was served, a parish meeting was called and a vote was passed to sustain the assessors. The case was tried before Judge Williams, who, in his charge to the jury, said: "The law says the certificate shall be signed by three principal men in the Baptist church; the plaintiff is one of the signers, and he cannot certify for himself; therefore there are but two, and the law says there shall be three. The jury brought in a verdict in accordance with this charge. The plaintiff appealed to the superior court and the case was continued until September, 1770. It was then called up, and witnesses were produced, but were not allowed to testify, because they were Baptists. The trial was therefore again deferred; but in May of the next year the superior court reäffirmed the opinion of Judge Williams and rejected the plaintiff's claim. Distress was then fearlessly made by the parish upon the Committee. A yoke of oxen was taken from Mr. Harvey, and a cow from Mr. Sawyer, etc.

A Baptist church was constituted in Chelmsford, in October, 1771. In the following March the town voted to raise a sum of money to pay the town charges and to support their minister. The taxes were made during the same month, and were assessed upon the Baptists as well as others. The money was, moreover, ordered to be immediately collected. Although the Baptists had carried in certificates according to law, the collector said they were a praying people, and he would put them all into jail together, where they would have nothing else to do but pray. This he began to do on the sixth of January, 1773. When he came to the house of Mr. Nathan Crosby, with a large number of assistants, a woman who lived in another part of the house told him that Mr. Crosby was sick and not able to go to prison. But one of the company declared that if he were sick and in bed, and if they took him out and he died in their hands, nobody would hurt them. Mr. Crosby entreated the collector to let him remain till he should be better, which the latter seemed inclined to do. But one of the assistants, who had given the collector a dollar to induce him to carry Crosby to jail that very day, insisted that it should be done. The warrant was then served, and he was ordered to get ready. The collector, however, allowed him to ride with himself, on his horse; but as he left his wife and children in tears, some of the company told them he would be put in a room without fire, where he would freeze to death. The collector next took Gershom Proctor, who was about eighty-two years of age; then his son Henry Proctor, both of whom had carried in certificates. Henry left a wife and seven small children, with no one to assist them but a young man who was then sick. They were all committed to the Concord jail. By the advice of a lawyer, they paid their taxes, and then commenced a suit for damages. The trial was delayed a long time. Moreover, both collector and assessors were put into the writ by the lawyer; and when the case of Mr. Crosby was tried, the jury condemned the assessors, but cleared the collector; so that the plaintiff was allowed three pounds for damages and costs, but was obliged to pay the collector for carrying him to prison! Mr. Crosby never *received* anything; and the other cases were not tried.

Another instance of oppression may be given in the language of the sufferer.

"Mr. Backus: — I understand that you are collecting materials for a Baptist history, in which you propose to let the public know how the Baptists have been oppressed in Massachusetts Bay. This is to let you know that in the year 1768, in a very cold night in the winter, about nine or ten o'clock in the evening, I was taken prisoner and carried, by the collector in the town where I live, from my family, consisting of three small children, in order to be put into jail. It being a severe cold night, I concluded, by advice, while I was detained at a tavern in the way to jail some hours, to pay the sum of $\frac{4}{8}$ L. M.,[1] for which I was made a prisoner, it being for the ministerial rate. The reason why I refused paying it before, was because I was a Baptist, and belonged to the Baptist society in Haverhill, and had carried in a certificate to the assessors, as I suppose, according to law. Thus they dealt with a poor widow woman in Bradford, the relict of Solomon Kimball, late of said town; — at whose house the Rev. Hezekiah Smith was shamefully treated by many of the people in Bradford, who came, headed by the sheriff, Amos Mullikin, at a time when Mr. Smith was to preach a sermon in our house, at the request of my husband, and warmly contended with him, and threatened him if he did preach. Mr. Smith went to begin service by singing, notwithstanding the noise, clamor and threats of the people. But one of their number snatched the chair, behind which Mr. Smith stood, from before him. Upon which my husband desired Mr. Smith to tarry a little, till he had quelled the tumult; but all his endeavors to silence them were in

[1] i. e. Legal Money.

vain. Upon which my husband desired Mr. Smith to begin public service; which accordingly he did, and went through, then, without further molestation.

MARTHA KIMBALL.

BRADFORD, SEPT. 2, 1774.

"N. B. The above I can attest to. It may be observed, that the tavern whither they took me is about two miles from my house. After I had paid what they demanded, then I had to return to my poor fatherless children, through the snow, on foot, in the dead of the night, exposed to the severity of the cold."

Such events as those now recited by way of example, were obviously fitted to enlist the sympathy and awaken the indignation of all those who agreed in belief with the suffering parties. They were likely also to render more deep and intense the conviction that civil government has no right to intermeddle with the worship of God; no right to determine what Christianity is, and then support it by the power of the sword; no right to bring that kingdom which is not of this world, and whose weapons are only spiritual, into formal union with the powers that be, whose weapons are carnal; no right to intermingle and identify the claims of Cæsar and of God, employing one officer to enforce them both.

Whatever may be said of others, the head and the heart of Mr. Backus were fully enlisted for the cause of soul liberty. Before the next meeting of the General Assembly, which took place near the close of March, 1771, he had written a letter to a gentleman of that body, "concerning taxes to support religious worship." In this manly production he replies at some length to the usual arguments in defence of a religious establishment supported by law, and then shows the actual disabilities and sufferings to which those of his own persuasion had been thus far subject; and in conclusion urges that the authorities of Massachusetts, in order to be consistent with themselves, in their present complaints against England, should cease taxing men for the support of religious worship.

"If it be oppression," he remarks, "to take away from a people the right of *giving* their money, either by themselves or their representatives, to support civil government where force belongs, as I believe it is, what must it be to deprive them of a right that never can be conveyed to any representative? For unless a man could constitute another to answer for him at the bar of God, it is impossible for him to convey to another a right to compel him or others to attend or support any worship contrary to their consciences." The next sentence is sharper. "What then shall we think of those men who often accuse their neighbors of *covetousness*, only because they plead, with Moses, for liberty to carry their substance with them, to help support the worship they believe to be right, while these accusers act the part of Pharaoh, who, when he could no longer hold their persons, yet said, 'Let your flocks and your herds be stayed!'"

It is quite obvious that such a letter, at once truly bold and truly patriotic, touching the question at issue by every word, from beginning to end, cannot have been lost upon the people whose views it expressed, whatever may have been its effect upon those in power. By enunciating, clearly and concisely, the claims of his brethren, and by advocating those claims with undeniable ability, Mr. Backus strengthened their conviction of the righteousness of their cause, and prepared them for more decisive action in its defence. His letter must also have been very inspiriting to Mr. Davis, whose vigorous and prominent efforts, as agent for the Baptists, had exposed him to much vituperation. His labors, however, were soon terminated. In the early part of 1772, his health began to decline, and in July he was obliged to relinquish his pastoral charge, and seek a milder climate. The next year, while travelling on the banks of the Ohio, with a single companion, for the purpose of recruiting his health, he was suddenly taken away from this life.

Mr. Davis was graduated at the University of Pennsylvania, and is said to have been "a man of fine talents, and of a finished education;" also, "a truly pious man, and an excellent preacher." Mr. Backus calls him "the pious and learned Mr. John Davis," and always refers to his character and conduct with the utmost respect. During the brief period of his ministry, in a place remote from all his early friends, he so discharged the duties of his responsible office, as to win the esteem and love of his flock; and he so commended himself to his brethren throughout New England, as to be made their agent in affairs which they esteemed of vital interest. His task was soon done; but we have reason to believe it was well done.

CHAPTER XIV.

MR. BACKUS AS AGENT.

HIS APPOINTMENT. — CIRCULAR TO THE CHURCHES. — LETTER TO DR. STENNET, OF LONDON. — NOTICE OF MR. DAVIS. — MEETING OF THE ASSOCIATION. — ITS ACTION IN RESPECT TO GIVING CERTIFICATES. — APPEAL TO THE PUBLIC FOR RELIGIOUS LIBERTY. — LETTER TO SAMUEL ADAMS. — BAPTISTS OF WARWICK IMPRISONED. — PETITION FOR THEIR RELEASE. — EXTRACT FROM A LETTER TO BENJAMIN WALLIN.

When the Warren Association met, in September 1772, Mr. Backus was chosen agent, in place of Mr. Davis. This office he continued to fill, at the desire of his brethren, for ten successive years. It was no sinecure. A Committee of Grievances, consisting of eight members besides the agent, was likewise appointed. On the 5th of May, 1773, six members[1] of this committee met in Boston, and agreed to send the following circular to the churches, — a paper revealing the conclusions which Mr. Backus had reached, after long reflection, on a matter of great practical importance:

"Beloved Friends: — These lines are to acquaint you that five of our committee, appointed to care for and consult the general good of the Baptist churches in this country, especially as to their union and liberties, met

[1] Messrs. Backus, Stillman, Alden, Plimpton, and the two Freemans.

with me at Boston, on May 5, 1773, when we received accounts that several of our friends at Mendon have lately had their goods forcibly taken from them, for ministerial rates, and that three more of them at Chelmsford, (two of whom were members of the Baptist church there,) were seized for the same cause, last winter, and carried prisoners to Concord jail; so that liberty of conscience, the greatest and most important article of all liberty, is evidently not allowed, as it ought to be in this country, not even by the very men who are now making loud complaints of encroachments upon their own liberties. And as it appears to us clear that the root of all these difficulties, and that which has done amazing mischief in our land, is civil rulers assuming a power to make any laws to govern ecclesiastical affairs, or to use any force to support ministers; therefore, these are to desire you to consider whether it is not our duty to strike so directly at this root, as to refuse any conformity to their laws about such affairs, even so much as giving any certificates to their assessors. We are fully persuaded that if we were all united in bearing what others of our friends might, for a little while, suffer on this account, a less sum than has already been expended with lawyers and courts, on such accounts, would carry us through the trial, and, if we should be enabled to treat our oppressors with a christian temper, would make straining upon others, under pretence of supporting religion, appear so odious that they could not get along with it. We desire you would consider of these matters, and send in your mind to the assembly of our churches, which is to meet at Medfield, on the seventh of September next, when it will be proposed to have these matters, both as to principle and facts, as clearly stated as we can, and to see if all our churches cannot agree upon publishing our joint testimony for true liberty, and against the oppressions of the present day.

From yours, in gospel bonds,

ISAAC BACKUS, *Agent.*

By advice of the Committee."

"P. S. Our charter gives other denominations no more power to tax the Baptists, than it does the Baptists to tax others; and in the town of Boston, they have all along had this equality, so that there has not been any occasion for one society to give certificates to another; and why may not the country enjoy the same liberty?"

The following letter to the Rev. Dr. Stennett, of London, describes the immediate results of the circular just given:

"MIDDLEBORO', OCT. 9, 1773.

"REV. AND DEAR SIR: As our Association have chosen me to be their agent here, in the room of our beloved friend, Mr. John Davis, deceased, I am set down to write you some answer to yours of Aug. 6, 1772, addressed to him. The ill state of his health had induced him to return to Pennsylvania before it arrived at Boston; it was sent after him, but I suppose never reached him. For, with Mr. David Jones, he set out on a visit to the western Indians, but was taken sick near the Ohio, and after an illness of three weeks, died there, the 13th of last December, in the thirty-sixth year of his age. A very just character was given him from Philadelphia, in which are these words: 'He was an entertaining companion, possessed of uncommon calmness of temper. In preaching, he endeavored to reach the understanding of his audience.

Educated in the genuine principles of liberty, born under one of the happiest of civil constitutions, he felt with the keenest sensibility for the oppressed, and when his duty called, with a manly and virtuous boldness he defended them.' This is a true sketch of the character of that valuable friend we mourn the loss of.

"Pennsylvania, his native colony, enjoys that religious liberty which he soon found the want of here. Upon search, he found that our charter gives equal religious liberty as well as theirs, and that what is called the religious establishment in this Province stands only upon some laws made by the Congregationalists to support their way, which [laws] happened not to be timely discovered by the powers at home, but [which] are really in their nature contrary to our charter. And when they tried to call a Provincial Synod in 1725, an express was sent from the British court against it, in which it was declared that their way was not established here. Therefore Mr. Davis judged it to be our duty to strike more directly at the root of our oppressions than we had before done.

"And though he is taken from us, yet the cause remains the same; and last May our committee were called together at Boston, when we had late accounts of the sufferings of our brethren in sundry places and in violation of the Pedobaptists' own laws; upon which we wrote to all our churches to consider and to give their mind upon the affair. Accordingly, they sent in their thoughts to our association at Medfield, Tuesday, September 7th; and though we were agreed that our Legislature had no right to impose religious taxes upon us, yet some doubted the expediency of our now refusing any compliance with their laws in that respect; and since we were not all of a judgment in this case, they stood against our coming to any vote upon it, lest our want of union therein should give an advantage to our adversaries. Thus matters labored all day Wednesday, until many of the brethren became very uneasy about being thus held back. But on Thursday morning, Mr. Stillman, who had been against our coming to a vote, brought in the following paper, which was unanimously adopted:

1. That the mind of the association respecting giving or not giving certificates, be taken by written vote, in order to confine the difference which subsists among us on this matter, in the association.

2. That those churches that agree to neglect the law for the future, shall, in a spirit of meekness, plead as the reason, that they cannot, in conscience, countenance any human laws that interfere in the management of the kingdom of Christ, which is not of this world.

3. That the churches which think it expedient to give certificates for the present, be advised by letter how many are of a contrary mind, and be desired to consider the matter against the next association, and to unite with their brethren if possible.

4. That the churches allow each other entire liberty, without any hard thoughts one of another.

5. That all the churches which shall be called to suffer through the year, shall transmit an account of such sufferings to their agent, to be made use of by him as may be thought best to subserve the common cause.

6. That our true state, with what we have transacted at this association, be sent to our agents in England, and their opinion be requested by the next meeting of the churches.

7. That if any are called to suffer, their sister churches be applied to, to assist them in their trouble.

"When we came to act upon the first of these articles, there appeared thirty-four elders and brethren against giving any more certificates, six for it, and three at a loss how to act. Then it was voted by all that an appeal to the public, which I had read in part to them, should be examined by our committee and then published. And our association was dismissed in a very comfortable and happy manner, and all seemed well pleased with what was done. The following week our committee met at Boston and deliberately examined and approved of our appeal, a copy of which I now send you. We were privately encouraged in this attempt for religious liberty by several members of both houses of our great General Court; and the state of people's minds of various ranks through New England is such that I cannot but hope to obtain our freedom without a necessity of appealing to his Majesty. The use of force in religious affairs is become odious to great numbers besides our own denomination, and that is increasing very fast.

"Thus, dear sir, I have given you as concise and just an account of our state as I can; and we request the best advice from yourself, Dr. Slewalen and Mr. Wallin, that you can give us. We are greatly obliged to you all for the friendship and favors you have already shown us, especially concerning the case of Ashfield, for which we hope and pray that God may abundantly reward you.

"By the printed minutes I send you, it appears that we have one thousand one hundred and sixty-one church members in our association, and I suppose there are full as many more within the Provinces of Massachusetts and New Hampshire only; which are but two of the four governments of New England; and full two-thirds of all those have been baptized within these seventeen years; and the abundant evidence I have that the pure doctrines of grace set home by the power of the divine Spirit, have been the cause of it, affords me unspeakable satisfaction. Brother Hinds, who lives nine miles south of me, has been favored with a glorious visitation this year, and he has baptized four more since the meeting of the association. In such a new state and rapid increase of churches, you, sir, must be sensible that we stand in great need of the best assistance that can be had. I therefore hope for some from yourself and brethren to be communicated to

Your unworthy brother in gospel bonds,

ISAAC BACKUS."

The "appeal" mentioned in this letter was a pamphlet of sixty-two pages. After a preface designed to show that civil government is conducive and even necessary to individual freedom, it lays down the position "that God has appointed two kinds of government in the world, which are distinct in their nature and ought never to be confounded together; one of which is called civil, the other ecclesiastical government," and then proceeds in the first section to specify "some essential points of difference between them." The next section shows how "civil and ecclesiastical affairs are blended together among us, to the depriving of many of God's people of that liberty of conscience which he has given them." At the close of this section an injurious reproach is thus noticed: "Though many of us have expended ten or twenty times as much in setting up and supporting that worship which we believe to be right, as it would have cost us to have continued in the fashionable way, yet we are often accused of being covetous for dissenting from that way, and refusing to pay more money out of our little incomes, to uphold men from whom we receive no benefit but rather abuse." Section third gives a brief account of what the Baptists had suffered under the existing laws and of their reasons for refusing any active compliance with them. These reasons, directed chiefly against the giving of certificates, were substantially as follows: 1. "Because to give certificates implies an acknowledgment that civil rulers have a right to set up one religious sect above another; which they have not. 2. Because civil rulers are not representatives in religious matters, and therefore have no right to impose religious taxes. 3. Because such practice emboldens the actors therein to assume God's prerogative; and to judge the hearts of those who do not put into their mouths. 4. Because the church is to be presented as a chaste virgin to Christ; and to place her trust and love upon any other for temporal support, is playing the harlot, and so the way to destroy all religion.[1] 5. Because the practice tends to envy, hypocrisy, and confusion, and so to the ruin of civil society."

Among the sons of liberty in Massachusetts, no man was at this time more distinguished than Samuel Adams. Mr. Backus heartily approved the political views of this eminent patriot, and doubtless looked upon him as one who would be likely to encourage every suitable effort in behalf of greater religious freedom. He therefore, early in the year 1774, addressed to him the following letter:

"JANUARY 19, 1774.

"To Mr. Samuel Adams.

"HONORED SIR: As you have long exerted yourself and improved your abilities with great applause, for civil lib-

[1] Hosea 2: 5.

erty, I beg leave, though a stranger to your person, to address you upon the cause of religious freedom. I fully concur with your grand maxim — That it is essential to liberty that representation and taxation go together. Well then, since people do not vote for representatives in our Legislature, from ecclesiastical qualifications, but only by virtue of those which are of a civil and worldly nature, how can representatives thus chosen have any right to impose ecclesiastical taxes? Yet they have assumed and long exercised such a power. For they assumed a power to compel each town and parish in this Province to settle a minister, and have empowered the majority of the inhabitants to give away as much of their neighbors' estates as they please to their minister; and if they refuse to yield it to them, then to take it by force. And I am bold in it that taxes laid by the British Parliament upon America are not more contrary to civil freedom, than these taxes are to the very nature of liberty of conscience, which is an essential article in our charter. For certainly the discharge of a good conscience towards God, as much concerns the support of his worship, as it does the attendance upon it, though modern nations would confine it to the latter. Yes, many take away our money to support a way contrary to our consciences; and after they have got it, reflect upon us for not supporting our own way better. And though many pretend that the case is not as I have now represented, because acts from time to time have been made to exempt our denomination and others, from taxes to the established worship; yet if we examine we shall find that this exemption is just like the proceedings of the power at home in taking off some of the taxes which they had laid upon this country, while they still claim the power to tax us when they please. Two thousand dollars will not make good the damages that the Baptists in this Province have sustained within these ten years by being taxed to the other party, and by suing for their rights before judges and jurors who were of that party. * * * And now for no other crime than refusing last year to yield any further obedience to that taxing law, which is unjustly called an act to exempt our denomination from taxes; a number of people who have been my steady hearers for twenty years are, by Judge Oliver's direction, taxed to his minister. Our reasons for the above refusal I here send you in print. And as the act aforesaid, is now out of date, I hope, sir, that you will give proof both to the court and to the world, that you regard the religious as well as the civil rights of your countrymen; that so a large number of as peaceable people and as hearty friends to their country as any in the land, may not be forced to carry their complaints before those who would be glad to hear that the Legislature of Massachusetts deny to their fellow servants that liberty which they so earnestly insist upon for themselves. A word to the wise is sufficient. Therefore I add no more, but am

Your real friend and humble servant,

ISAAC BACKUS."

Less than a month after the date of this letter, Mr. Backus received notice, that eighteen men living in Warwick, and members of the Baptist society in Royalston, who had carried in their certificates according to law, had recently, February 8th, been shut up in the Northampton jail for declining to pay ministerial rates in support of the established worship. Without delay he sent the following petition to the General Court, then sitting in Boston.

"PROVINCE OF THE MASSACHUSETTS BAY.

"To his Excellency the Governor, to the Honorable his Majesty's Council, with the Honorable House of Representatives in General Court assembled at Boston, January 26, 1774.

"The Memorial and Petition of Isaac Backus, Agent for the Baptist churches in the province, humbly sheweth: That whereas, by the charter of this province, liberty of conscience is granted to our denomination, equally with other Protestants; and it was declared to the first General Court, after the charter was received, that the magistrate is most properly the officer of *human society*, and that a Christian, by non-conformity to this or that way of worship, does not break the terms on which he is to enjoy the benefits of human society, and that a man has a right unto his life, his estate, his liberty, and his family, notwithstanding such non-conformity; which declaration was then received with the thanks of the House of Representatives (Magnalia B. 7. p. 28, 29); yet it has been a common custom, ever since, to impose taxes upon the inhabitants in general, in every town and precinct in this province, to support Pedobaptist worship; and though there have been sundry temporary acts made to exempt our denomination from such taxes, yet great numbers of them have, from time to time, been taxed and despoiled of their rights; and I have direct information, that eighteen men of the inhabitants of Warwick, who belong to the Baptist society in Royalston, and had the same certified to the assessors of Warwick, last June, yet were seized, last week, for the minister's rate of that town, and carried prisoners to Northampton jail; by which they are deprived of their precious rights, and their dear families, in a new country, are exposed to suffering greatly, for want of their help:

"This is therefore to beseech your Excellency and Honors, as guardians of the rights of your people, immediately to order these men to be set at liberty, and that reparation be made of the damages they have sustained; and also to take some effectual methods, as in your wisdom you shall see fit, that for the future all persons within this province, who shall demean themselves as good members of civil society, may not be despoiled of the aforesaid rights, under a pretence of supporting religious worship; but that all persons, who shall presume thus to encroach upon the rights of their neighbors, may be punished according to the demerit of their crimes. And your petitioner, as in duty bound, shall ever pray.

ISAAC BACKUS.

MIDDLEBORO', FEB. 15, 1774."

The fate of this memorial, and some further particulars respecting the affair to which it related, are mentioned in the following extract from a letter to Rev. Benjamin Wallin, of London:

"I have been called to address our Legislature, in behalf of a number of our friends, who were seized the second week in February, and carried, in that extreme season, forty miles, and confined in jail, for a Pedobaptist minister's rate; though most of them had, for many years, been of the Baptist denomination, and had lately moved into that town. The President of His Majesty's council, and several other men of note of both Houses, gave their opinion in favor of the first article in the prayer of the petition; but the majority turned the case against it. Upon which, some friends in Boston sent to our friends in prison, to bail themselves out and sue for their rights in executive courts, which they did, after being confined fifteen days. Upon the other article of providing a more effectual remedy against such things for the future, the House of Representatives sent out a committee upon it, who conferred with Mr. Stillman and others of our committee in Boston; and they framed an act more favorable than they had done before, which passed both Houses. But in the contest about Judge Oliver, the Court was prorogued so abruptly, that it was not laid before the Governor; so that there is no act in force at all in the province, to exempt us from taxes to their ministers. But the more they stir about it, the more light gains; so that my hope of deliverance in due time increases."

CHAPTER XV.

VISIT TO PHILADELPHIA.

MEETING OF THE FIRST CONTINENTAL CONGRESS. — BACKUS' NOTE OF INTRODUCTION TO IT. — HIS JOURNEY TO PHILADELPHIA. — CONSULTATION WITH FRIENDS. — PHILADELPHIA ASSOCIATION APPOINTS A COMMITTEE OF GRIEVANCES. — MEETING AT CARPENTERS' HALL. — MEMORIAL OF THE BAPTISTS; 1. RELIGIOUS FREEDOM; 2 GRANTED TO ALL PROTESTANTS BY THE NEW CHARTER; 3. EXEMPTION LAWS UNSATISFACTORY; 4. THE LIBERTY DESIRED. — COLLOQUY; REMARKS OF JOHN ADAMS, SAMUEL ADAMS, R. T. PAINE, MR. CUSHING, AND MR. BACKUS. — ACTION OF THE PHILADELPHIA COMMITTEE. — PROMISE OF THE DELEGATES FROM MASSACHUSETTS.

As the year advanced, the spirit of resistance to the claims of England rose higher and higher, and it was at length determined, if possible, to unite the separate colonies in defence of their common rights. To effect this, delegates from twelve provinces met in Congress, at Philadelphia, on the fifth day of September, and entered upon their difficult and perilous service. It will be necessary for us to follow the subject of our narrative to this first Continental Congress. His own words will best describe the reasons and the object of his visit. "A Congress of delegates from our several colonies met in that city, September 5, 1774, to use their endeavors to preserve and defend our liberties, civil and religious, which were greatly threatened. Our elders, John Gano, of New York, and William Van Horne, of Southampton, in Pennsylvania, being at Commencement, at Providence, September 7th, they, with

Mr. Manning and Mr. Hezekiah Smith, of Haverhill, were earnest with me to go to Philadelphia, and to see if something might not be done to obtain and secure our religious liberties, beyond what we have as yet enjoyed. And in our association, at Medfield, September 14th, they were unanimous for my going, and contributed for it." The association gave him this certificate:

"To the honorable delegates of the several colonies in North America, met in a general congress at Philadelphia:

"HONORABLE GENTLEMEN: — As the Anti-pedobaptist churches in New England are most heartily concerned for the preservation and defence of the rights and privileges of this country, and are deeply affected by the encroachments upon the same, which have lately been made by the British Parliament, and are willing to unite with our dear countrymen, vigorously to pursue every prudent measure for relief; so we would beg leave to say that, as a distinct denomination of Protestants, we conceive that we have an equal claim to charter rights with the rest of our fellow-subjects; and yet have long been denied the free and full enjoyment of those rights, as to the support of religious worship. Therefore we, the elders and brethren of twenty Baptist churches, met in association at Medfield, twenty miles from Boston, September 14, 1774, have unanimously chosen and sent unto you the reverend and beloved Mr. Isaac Backus, as our agent, to lay our case, in these respects, befor you, or otherwise to use all the prudent means he can for our relief.

JOHN GANO, *Moderator*,
HEZ. SMITH, *Clerk*."

Mr. Backus began his journey to Philadelphia on the 26th of September. It occupied nearly a fortnight. At Providence he met with elders Gano and Van Horne, who went on with him by land. Old Mr. Chileab Smith joined them at Norwich, prepared to testify of the oppressions at Ashfield. On the eighth of October they arrived in Philadelphia, and Mr. Backus was kindly entertained at the house of Samuel Davis. On the morrow, it being the Lord's day, he preached three times in the pulpit of Rev. William Rogers. His diary indicates sufficiently the course of events during the next few days.

"Monday, Oct. 10th. Visited Robert Strettle Jones, Esq. in the forenoon, and Mr. Joseph Moulder in the afternoon, gentlemen who were desirous of knowing how our affairs were in New England, and who seem willing to exert themselves in our favor."

"Oct. 11th. Our elders Manning and Jones arrived with others; and we had a meeting at Esquire Jones', in the evening, where were Israel and James Pemberton, and Joseph Fox, principal men among the Quakers, with other gentlemen. I then laid open our condition in New England, and asked their advice, whether to lay the case before Congress or not. They advised us not to address Congress, as a body, at present, but to seek for a conference with the Massachusetts delegates, together with some other members who were known to be friendly to religious liberty. They also manifested a willingness to be helpful in our case."

"Oct. 12th. Spent the forenoon with Esquire Jones, in drawing up a memorial of our case, to lay before the conference. In the afternoon, the Philadelphia Baptist Association met in that city, continuing in session three days. Before closing, it "made choice," says Mr. Backus, "of a committee of grievances to correspond with ours in New England and to prosecute such measures for our relief as they should judge best."[1]

"Oct. 14th. In the evening there met at Carpenters' Hall, Thomas Cushing, Samuel Adams, John Adams, and Robert Treat Paine, Esqrs., delegates from Massachusetts; and there were also present James Kinzie of New Jersey, Stephen Hopkins and Samuel Ward of Rhode Island, Joseph Galloway and Thomas Miflin, Esqrs., of Pennsylvania, and other members of Congress. Mr. Rhodes, Mayor of the city of Philadelphia, Israel and James Pemberton, and Joseph Fox, Esqrs., of the Quakers and other gentlemen, also elders Manning, Gano, Jones, Rogers, Edwards, etc., were present. The conference was opened by Mr. Manning, who made a short speech, and then read the memorial which we had drawn up."

The memorial here referred to was as follows:

"It has been said by a celebrated writer in politics, that but two things were worth contending for, — Religion and Liberty. For the latter we are at present nobly exerting ourselves through all this extensive continent; and surely no one whose bosom feels the patriot glow in behalf of civil liberty, can remain torpid to the more ennobling flame of RELIGIOUS FREEDOM.

"The free exercise of private judgment, and the unalienable rights of conscience, are of too high a rank and dignity to be subjected to the decrees of councils, or the im-

[1] The names of the committee were: Mr. Samuel Davis, Mr. Stephen Shewell, Mr. Thomas Shields, Mr. George Westcott, Rev. William Rogers, Rev. Morgan Edwards, Rev. Wm. Van Horne, Rev. Samuel Jones, Benjamin Bartholomew, Esq., Alexander Edwards, Esq., Robert S. Jones, Esq., John Evans, Esq., John Mayhew, Esq., Edward Keasby, Esq., Samuel Miles, Esq., Abel Evans, Esq., Mr. Abraham Beakley, Mr. James Morgan, Mr. John Jarman.

perfect laws of fallible legislators. The merciful Father of mankind is the alone Lord of conscience. Establishments may be enabled to confer worldly distinctions and secular importance. They may make hypocrites, but cannot create Christians. They have been reared by craft or power, but liberty never flourished perfectly under their control. That liberty, virtue, and public happiness can be supported without them, this flourishing province[1] is a glorious testimony; and a view of it would be sufficient to invalidate all the most elaborate arguments ever adduced in support of them. Happy in the enjoyment of these undoubted rights, and conscious of their high import, every lover of mankind must be desirous, as far as opportunity offers, of extending and securing the enjoyment of these inestimable blessings.

"These reflections have arisen from considering the unhappy situation of our brethren, the Baptists, in the province of Massachusetts Bay, for whom we now appear as advocates; and from the important light in which liberty in general is now beheld, we trust our representation will be effectual. The province of the Massachusetts Bay, being settled by persons who fled from civil and religious oppression, it would be natural to imagine them deeply impressed with the value of liberty, and nobly scorning a domination over conscience. But such was the complexion of the times, they fell from the unhappy state of being oppressed, to the more deplorable and ignoble one of becoming oppressors.

"But these things being passed over, we intend to begin with the charter obtained at the happy restoration. This charter grants, 'that there shall be liberty of conscience allowed in the worship of God, to all Christians except

[1] Pennsylvania.

Papists, inhabiting or which shall inhabit or be resident within this province or territory;' or in the words of the late Governor Hutchinson, 'We find nothing in the new charter, of an ecclesiastical constitution. Liberty of conscience is granted to all except Papists.' The first General Court that met under this charter, returned their thanks for the following sentiments delivered before them:—'That the magistrate is most properly the officer of human society; that a Christian by non-conformity to this or that imposed way of worship, does not break the terms upon which he is to enjoy the benefits of human society; and that a man has a right to his estate, his liberty, and his family, notwithstanding his non-conformity.' And on this declaration the historian who mentions it, plumes himself, as if the whole future system of an impartial administration was to begin. By laws made during the first charter, such persons only were entitled to vote for civil rulers as were church-members. This might be thought by some to give a shadow of ecclesiastical power; but by the present [charter] 'Every freeholder of thirty pounds sterling per annum, and every other inhabitant who has forty pounds personal estate, are voters for representatives. So that here seems an evident foundation to presume they are only elected for the preservation of civil rights, and the management of temporal concernments. Nevertheless they soon began to assume the power of establishing Congregational worship, and taxed all the inhabitants towards its support; and no Act was passed to exempt other denominations from the year 1692 to 1727, when the Episcopalians were permitted to enjoy their rights.

"The first Act for the relief of the Baptists was in 1728, when their polls only were exempted from taxation, and not their estates; and then only of such as lived within five miles of a Baptist Meeting-house. The next year, 1729, thirty persons were apprehended and confined in Bristol jail; some churchmen, some friends, but most of the Baptist denomination. Roused by these oppressions, the Baptists and Quakers petitioned the General Court; being determined if they could not obtain redress, to apply to his Majesty in council. Wherefore the same year, a law was passed exempting their estates and polls; but clogged however with a limitation, for less than five years. At the expiration of this Act, in 1733, our brethren were obliged again to apply to the General Assembly; upon which a third Act was passed, 1734, exempting Baptists from paying ministerial taxes. This third Act was more clear, accurate and better drawn than any of the former; but for want of a penalty on the returning officer, badly executed, subjecting our brethren to many hardships and oppressions. This Act expired in 1740, and another was made for seven years; but still liable to the same defects. In 1747, the Baptists and friends, wearied with fruitless applications to the assemblies, once more proposed applying at home for relief, when the laws exempting them were reënacted for ten years, the longest space ever granted.

"To show what the liberty was that these unhappy people enjoyed, it will be necessary, though we aim as much as possible at brevity, just to mention that if at any time a Baptist sued a collector for the breach of these laws, any damages he recovered were laid on the town, and the Baptists residing therein were thereby obliged to pay their proportionable part towards his indemnification. At this time such an instance occurred in the case of Sturbridge, when Jonathan Perry sued the collector, Jonathan Mason, and the damages were sustained by the town, though the Baptists in town meeting dissented. And here it may not be improper to observe, that the judges and jury are under the strongest bias to determine for the defendants. In the beginning of the year 1753, an act was passed, breaking in upon the time limited, enacting that "no minister or member of an Anabaptist church shall be esteemed qualified to give certificates, other than such as shall have obtained, from three other churches commonly called Anabaptist, in this or the neighboring Provinces, a certificate from each respectively, that they esteem such church of their denomination, and that they conscientiously believe them to be Anabaptists.'

"But not to take too much of your time, we would here just observe that all the laws have been made temporary, and without any penalty on the collector or assessors for the breach of the law, and come more particularly to speak of the law passed at the . last June session; as it has been generally understood to be so framed as to take away complaint and establish a general liberty of conscience. This act is like all the others, temporary, and indeed limited to a shorter duration than most of them, being only for three years. It is without any penalty on the breach of it, and an additional trouble and expense is enjoined by recording the certificates every year, (though in some others obtaining one certificate during the existence of the law was sufficient,) and concludes thus: 'That nothing in this act shall be construed to exempt any proprietor of any new township from paying his part and portion with the major part of the other proprietors of such new township, in settling a minister and building a meeting-house, which hath been or shall be required as a condition of their grant.'

"And here we would just add a few words relative

to the affairs of Ashfield. On the 26th day of December next, three lots of land belonging to people of our denomination, will be exposed for sale; one of them for the payment of so small a sum as ten shillings eleven pence. Although we have given but two instances of oppression under the above laws, yet a great number can be produced, well attested, when called for.

"Upon this short statement of facts we would observe, that the charter must be looked upon by every impartial eye to be infringed, so soon as any law was passed for the establishment of any particular mode of worship. All Protestants are placed upon the same footing; and no law whatever could disannul so essential a part of a charter intended to communicate the blessings of a free government to his Majesty's subjects. Under the first charter, as was hinted, church-membership conferred the rights of a freeman; but by the second, the possession of property was the foundation. Therefore, how could it be supposed that the collective body of the people intended to confer any other power upon their representatives than that of making laws relative to property and the concerns of this life?

"Men unite in society, according to the great Mr. Locke, 'with an intention in every one the better to preserve himself, his liberty and property. The power of the society, or Legislature constituted by them, can never be supposed to extend any further than the common good, but is obliged to secure every one's property.' To give laws, to receive obedience, to compel with the sword, belong to none but the civil magistrate; and on this ground *we affirm* that the magistrate's power extends not to the establishing any articles of faith or forms of worship, by force of laws; for laws are of no force without penalties. The care of souls cannot belong to the civil magistrate, because his power consists only in outward force; but pure and saving religion consists in the inward persuasion of the mind, without which nothing can be acceptable to God.

"It is a just position, and cannot be too firmly established, that we can have no property in that which another may take, when he pleases, to himself; neither can we have the proper enjoyment of our religious liberties, (which must be acknowledged to be of greater value,) if held by the same unjust and capricious tenure; and this must appear to be the case when temporary laws pretend to grant relief so very inadequate.

"It may now be asked — *What is the liberty desired?* The answer is; as the kingdom of Christ is not of this world, and religion is a concern between God and the soul with which no human authority can intermeddle; consistently with the principles of Christianity, and according to the dictates of Protestantism, we claim and expect the liberty of worshipping God according to our consciences, not being obliged to support a ministry we cannot attend, whilst we demean ourselves as faithful subjects. These we have an undoubted right to, as men, as Christians, and by charter as inhabitants of Massachusetts Bay."

After Dr. Manning had taken his seat, Mr. Backus says: "The delegates from Massachusetts used all their arts to represent that we complained without reason. John Adams made a long speech, and Samuel Adams another; both of whom said, 'There is, indeed, an ecclesiastical establishment in our province; but a very slender one, hardly to be called an establishment.' When they would permit, we brought up facts, which they tried to explain away, but could not. Then they shifted their plea, and asserted that our General Court was clear of blame, and had always been ready to hear our complaints, and to grant all reasonable help, whatever might have been done by executive officers; and S. Adams and R. T. Paine spent near an hour more on this plea. When they stopped, I told them I was very sorry to have any accusations to bring against the government which I belonged to, and which I would gladly serve to the utmost of my power; but I must say that facts proved the contrary to their plea; and gave a short acccount of our Legislature's treatment of Ashfield, which was very puzzling to them. In their pleas, S. Adams tried to represent that *regular* Baptists were quite easy among us; and more than once insinuated that these complaints came from enthusiasts who made it a merit to suffer persecution; and also, that enemies to the Colonies had a hand therein. Paine said, 'There was nothing of conscience in the matter; it was only a contending about paying a little money; and also that we would not be neighborly, and let them know who we were, which was all they wanted, and they would readily exempt us?'

"In answer, I told them they might call it enthusiasm or what they pleased; but I freely own, before all these gentlemen, that it is absolutely a point of conscience with me; for I cannot give in the certificates they require, without implicitly acknowledging that power in man which I believe belongs only to God. This shocked them; and Cushing said: '*It quite altered the case;* for if it were a point of conscience, he had nothing to say to that.' And the conference, of about four hours' continuance, closed with their promising to do what they could for our relief; though, to deter us from thinking of their coming upon equal footing with us, as to religion, John Adams, at one time, said we might as well expect a change in the solar system, as to expect they would give up their establishment;[1] and, at another time, he said we might as soon expect they would submit to the Port Bill, the Regulating Bill, and the Murder Bill, as to give up that establishment, which he and his friend, in the beginning of their plea, called a very slender thing. Such absurdities does religious tyranny produce in great men."

The language and bearing of the delegates from Massachusetts, in this conference, were such as to diminish greatly the value of their closing promise. The committee appointed by the Philadelphia Association held a meeting the next evening, and in their records say, "we think it did appear that the delegates from Boston were determined to support the claim the Legislature make to a right to make penal laws in matters of religion." It was also resolved, "That the Committee, not being satisfied with the declaration made last evening by the delegates from Massachusetts Bay, are determined to pursue every prudent measure, to obtain a full and complete redress of all grievances, for our brethren in New England." Gentlemen were appointed to deliver to each of the delegates a copy of the memorial read by Dr. Manning, a copy of this resolve, and a copy of Mr. Backus' "Appeal to the Public."

According to the records of the Committee, the gentlemen to whom this service was assigned made report Oct. 22, 1774, that "they delivered to the delegates from Massachusetts Bay copies of the foregoing resolve," etc., "who said they would endeavor all in their power to obtain a

1 Compare Appendix F.

redress of grievances, and as the situation of the Baptists in Boston was satisfactory, they would endeavor to diffuse the same spirit to the remotest parts of the colony." It may be remarked that Mr. Backus had declared in the conference, that he would be satisfied if the Baptists in the country might have the same liberty which their brethren had in Boston.

CHAPTER XVI.

SHARP CONTROVERSY.

OBJECT OF BACKUS' VISIT TO PHILADELPHIA MISREPRESENTED. — ADDRESS TO THE CONGRESS OF MASSACHUSETTS; TAXATION AND REPRESENTATION; CHURCH AND STATE; COERCION FOR THE SUPPORT OF RELIGION; OBJECT OF BACKUS IN GOING TO PHILADELPHIA; OPPRESSION IN ASHFIELD, MONTAGUE, AND GORHAM; DEMANDS OF THE BAPTISTS. — LETTER OF DR. SMITH ON ITS RECEPTION. — RESOLVE OF THE CONGRESS. — LETTER FROM THE PHILADELPHIA COMMITTEE. — REPLY OF BACKUS. — MEMORIAL TO THE GENERAL COURT. — RECEPTION OF IT. — DR. FLETCHER'S LETTER. — ADDRESS TO CHRISTIANS.

WHETHER it was wise or unwise in the Baptists of New England to send their agent to Philadelphia, at this time, may perhaps be doubtful; but there can be no doubt of his hearty sympathy with the love of liberty which animated the members of the first Congress, and his strong desire for the union of the several colonies, in defence of their civil rights. He visited Philadelphia for a single purpose; but it was a purpose, as he conceived, in absolute harmony with the ultimate object of this Congress, namely, the vindication of natural or chartered rights. Yet, when the Congress was dissolved, Oct. 26th, and Mr. Paine, one of the Massachusetts delegation, had returned as far as Newport, Rhode Island, a report was spread from that place, "as coming from him," that Mr. Backus went to Philadelphia in order to prevent the colonies from uniting in defence of their liberties. The proceedings of the conference were also grossly misrepresented by this report. In a letter from President Manning, to one of his friends, dated December 2, 1774, he mentions the following assertions, made by Dr. Ezra Stiles, at Newport: "That the Baptists had made an application to the congress against the Massachusetts Bay; that the delegates of that province expected only a private interview with some of the Baptists, but instead of that, when they came, they found a house full, etc.; that they were attacked and treated in the most rude and abusive manner; that the Baptists pretended they were oppressed, but after all their endeavors, they could only complain of a poor four-pence; that they were ashamed of their errand, and gave up their point, except one or two impudent fellows, who, with Israel Pemberton, abused them in a most scandalous manner; that all the delegates present were surprised at and ashamed of them, and thought they complained without the least foundation," etc. Then Dr. Stiles added: "*When we have the power in our own hands, we will remember them.*"

Finding that such false and injurious reports were in circulation, and that the first parish in Middleboro' had voted to tax all the Baptists within its limits who did not give in certificates, Mr. Backus met the Committee of Grievances at Boston, December 31st, and they drew up the following address, and sent it to the Congress of Massachusetts, then in session:

"To the honorable Congress of the Massachusetts province, convened at Cambridge, Nov. 22, 1774.

"HONORED GENTLEMEN: At a time when all America are alarmed at the open and violent attempts that have been made against their liberties, it affords great cause of joy and thankfulness, to see the colonies so happily united to defend their rights; and particularly that their late Continental Congress have been directed into measures so wise and salutary for obtaining relief and securing our future liberties; and who have wisely extended their regards to the rights and freedom of the poor Africans. Since then the law of equity has prevailed so far, we hope that it will move this honorable assembly to pay a just regard to their English neighbors and brethren at home.

"It seems that the two main rights which all America are contending for at this day, are — Not to be taxed where they are not represented, and — To have their causes tried by unbiased judges. And the Baptist churches in this province as heartily unite with their countrymen in this cause, as any denomination in the land; and are as ready to exert all their abilities to defend it. Yet only because they have thought it to be their duty to claim an equal title to these rights with their neighbors, they have repeatedly been accused of evil attempts against the general welfare of the colony; therefore, we have thought it expedient to lay a brief statement of the case before this assembly.

"It is well known that a freehold of forty shillings sterling a year, or a personal estate of forty pounds, gives any inhabitant in this province a right to vote for representatives in our Legislature; and can constituents give their representatives any power which they never had themselves? If not, then they never were empowered to lay any taxes but what were of a civil and worldly nature; and to impose religious taxes is as much out of their jurisdiction, as it can be for Britian to tax America; yet how much of this has been done in this province. Indeed, many try to elude the force of this reasoning by saying that the taxes which our rulers impose for the support of ministers, are of a civil nature. But it is certain that they call themselves ministers of Christ; and the taxes now referred to are to support them under that name; and they either are such, or else they deceive the people. If they are Christ's ministers, he has made laws enough to support them; if they are not, where are the rulers who will dare to compel people to maintain men who call themselves Christ's ministers when they are not? Those who ministered about holy things and at God's altar in the Jewish church, partook of and lived upon the things which were freely offered there; *Even so hath the Lord ordained that they who preach the Gospel, should live of the Gospel.* And such communications are called *sacrifices to God* more than once in the New Testament.[1] And why may not civil rulers appoint and enforce with the sword, any other sacrifice as well as this?

"Although by an express law of God, Israel were required to give a tenth of all their increase to the Levites, etc., yet we are so far from finding that their civil rulers were ever allowed to use force to collect the same, that instead thereof, we find that they were *sons of Belial*, and persons *who perverted judgment and abhorred all equity*, who attempted any such thing.[2] Civil rulers ought undoubtedly to be nursing fathers to the church, by reproof, exhortation, and their own good and liberal example, as well as to protect and defend her against injustice and oppression; but the very notion of taxing all to support any religious denomination, tends to bias its professors against all such as dissent from it; and so to deprive them of having unbiased judges; for every man knows that so much money as he can get from a neighbor to support his minister, so

[1] 1 Cor. 9: 13, 14. Phil. 4: 18. Acts 13: 15—17.

[2] 1 Sam. 2: 12, 16. Mic. 3: 5—9.

much he saves to himself. As we are fully persuaded that there is not a man in this honorable assembly, but what if he had suffered a quarter so much as many Baptists have from interested judges, would think it high time to be in earnest to have this pernicious evil removed. Two thousand dollars will not make good the damages the Baptists in this province have suffered on this account, within these twelve years, as we can make appear by facts.

"Therefore, when our churches understood that the Congress at Philadelphia was designed, not only to seek present relief, but also to lay a foundation for the future welfare of our country, they desired me to repair to that city, and with the best advice I could obtain, to try if something could not be done to obtain and secure full religious liberty to our denomination with others. I proceeded accordingly, and with a number of gentlemen and friends, had a conference with the honored delegates of this province, upon this subject; but one of them repeatedly declared that he believed this attempt proceeded from the enemies of America; the injustice of which inflection, let facts declare.

"For although they then asserted, that if a society of Quakers or Baptists regularly settled a minister of their own persuasion in a new town, it answered the design of the last paragraph in the law our court made us last June; yet it is certain that after the Baptists of Ashfield had so settled a minister, a Pedobaptist minister was brought in, and the Baptists were taxed to him for five years; and then they petitioned our Legislature for relief, who gave them encouragement of it, yet in a few days made a law that cut them off from any liberty on that account at all; and they in time and money, spent fifty pounds lawful currency in petitioning for the removal of that burden, and could get no help. Then our united churches addressed the court upon it; but in a few days, a piece dated from the place where the court was sitting, was published in the Boston newspapers, insinuating that the Baptists had complained without any reason. And when the worthy Mr. Davis, (now at rest,) answered it by reciting the fact of Ashfield, he was accused in a succeeding paper, as we have now been, of being an enemy to the colonies. There being thus no hope of relief here, that Ashfield law was sent home, and was disannulled by his majesty in council. And from that and other evidence, we have reason to think that an ear was open there to hear our further complaints; but we have never sent any other, as we would not injure the general cause; and hoped that at last our countrymen would be brought to regard our rights. But alas! the very laws that have been made about us, have proved to many to be only a snare to get away our money.

"The Baptists at Montague took advice of a lawyer, and endeavored to comply with your law, according to his direction; yet they were taxed and strained upon; they sued for relief in your courts, which was so far from helping them that it took away one hundred and fifteen dollars more. The Baptists in Haverhill took the same method; but the case was turned against them, which cost them about three hundred dollars. A Baptist church was regularly formed at Gorham, in 1768, and Mr. Joseph Moody of Scarborough, a member of it, yearly had the same certified to the assessors of his town, yet still he has been taxed and strained upon; and when he petitioned our Legislature last winter for help, we are credibly informed that his petition was thrown out, because Mr. March, the representative from Scarborough, said,—*there was no Baptist church in Gorham.* The Baptists in Warwick complied with your law, yet were taxed to the parish minister; and for it eighteen of them were imprisoned about forty miles from home, in the extremity of last winter; and when our General Court were addressed upon it, they afforded no help. The Baptists in Chelmsford complied with your law, yet they were taxed; and three of them were imprisoned in January, 1773; and when they sued for recompense, their case was shifted off from court to court, till it has cost them above a hundred dollars; and when the Superior Court, at Charlestown, last April, were constrained to give Nathan Crosby his case, as having been taxed and imprisoned unlawfully, yet they gave him but three pounds damages and costs of court; and at the same time judged that the constable who carried him to prison should recover costs of Crosby for his so doing. If this is unbiased judgment, we know not what bias means. Must we be blamed for not lying still, and thus let our countrymen trample upon our rights, and deny us that very liberty that they are ready to take up arms to defend for themselves? You profess to exempt us from taxes to your worship, and yet tax us every year. Great complaints have been made about a tax which the British Parliament laid upon paper; but you require a paper tax of us annually.

"That which has made the greatest noise, is a tax of three pence a pound upon tea; but your law of last June laid a tax of the same sum every year upon the Baptists in each parish, as they would expect to defend themselves against a greater one. And only because the Baptists in Middleboro' have refused to pay that little tax, we hear that the first parish in said town have this fall voted to lay a greater tax upon us. All America are alarmed at the tea tax; though, if they please, they can avoid it by not buying the tea; but we have no such liberty. We must either pay the little tax, or else your people appear even in this time of extremity, determined to lay the great one upon us. But these lines are to let you know, that we are determined not to pay either of them; not only upon your principle of not being taxed where we are not represented, but also because we dare not render that homage to any earthly power, which I and many of my brethren are fully convinced belongs only to God. We cannot give in the certificates you require, without implicitly allowing to men that authority which we believe in our consciences belongs only to God. Here, therefore, we claim charter rights, liberty of conscience. And if any still deny it to us, they must answer it to Him who has said, 'With what measure ye mete, it shall be measured to you again.'

"If any ask what we would have, we answer: Only allow us freely to enjoy the religious liberty that they do in Boston, and we ask no more.

"We remain hearty friends to our country, and ready to do all in our power for its general welfare.

ISAAC BACKUS,
Agent for the Baptist Churches in this Province.
By advice of their Committee.

BOSTON, DEC. 2, 1774."

In a letter to President Manning, dated January 20, 1775, Dr. Hezekiah Smith, of Haverhill, thus describes the reception of this address.

"Will you believe that the old persecuting spirit remained in Massachusetts Bay? I know you will believe your old friend, if he asserts it. Mr. Joseph Haynes was one of the Provincial Congress, when Mr. Backus sent in a petition in behalf of the Baptists, to see if they would use their influence to free them from their oppressions, etc.; who gave me the following account in substance.— Mr. Hancock, the President, informed the House that Mr. Backus had sent in a petition to them in behalf of the Baptists, etc., and with a smile, asked them whether it should be read, or not? One answered: No; we are no ecclesiastical court, and have no business with it. Another, another and another agreed to the same. At last, one of the members got up and said;—This is very extraordinary, that we should pay no regard to a denomination who in the place where he lived were as good members of society as any, and were equally engaged with others in the defence of their civil liberties, and motioned to have it read. Another seconded the motion. Upon which it was read. Then it was proposed to know whether they should act upon it or not. It was generally agreed not to do anything about it, but throw it out; when Mr. Adams got up and said, he was apprehensive, if they threw it out, it might cause a division among the provinces; and it was his advice to do something with it. Upon which, they chose a committee to sit upon it; who reported that they were no ecclesiastical court, and had no business with it. If the Baptists were oppressed, they might apply to the General Court."

The resolution passed by this Congress in answer to the address given above, reads thus:

"IN PROVINCIAL CONGRESS, CAMBRIDGE, DEC. 9, 1774.

"On reading the memorial of the Reverend Isaac Backus, agent to the Baptist churches in this government:

"Resolved, That the establishment of civil and religious liberty to each denomination in the province, is the sincere wish of this Congress. But being by no means vested with powers of civil government, whereby they can redress the grievances of any person whatever, they therefore recommend to the Baptist churches, that when a General Assembly shall be convened in this colony, they lay the real grievances of said churches before the same, when and where this petition will most certainly meet with all that attention due to the memorial of a denomination of Christians so well disposed to the public weal of their country.

By order of the Congress.

JOHN HANCOCK, President.

A true extract from the minutes.

BENJAMIN LINCOLN, Secretary."

This resolution was forwarded to Mr. Backus in the following note.

"BOSTON, DEC. 14, 1744.

"REV. SIR:—In obedience to the direction of the Provincial Congress, I now transmit to you the enclosed Resolve. I hope the time will soon come when all our grievances shall be removed.

I am, Rev. Sir, your most humble servant,

BENJ. LINCOLN."

Meanwhile Mr. Backus had previously ascertained the doings of the Congress at Cambridge, and had written to the committee at Philadelphia. Early the next spring he received an answer from which we select the following passage.

"In our dispute about religious liberty, we must take into consideration, that it is against the interest of the people we apply to, to grant us any remedy. If we should be eased of the burden of contributing towards the support of Congregational ministers, the expense will fall the heavier on those who attend that worship; consequently great interest will be made to prevent any act, effectually to answer our wishes, from passing through the Legislature. If we fail in procuring redress here, our only resource will be to apply on the other side the Atlantic. This channel we ought ever to keep open, and not to preclude ourselves by our own conduct, from being heard there with that attention and favor that our case will require. Our conduct ought to be such as to prevent us, on the one hand, from being deemed *enemies to our country;* and to secure to us, on the other, a *favorable reception* at the throne, if it should be necessary to apply there at a future day. These two grand things we ought to have constantly in view; and I must differ in opinion from you about the propriety of addressing your Provincial Congress. They are and will be undoubtedly looked upon by government at home, as men who are illegally and in direct opposition to lawful authority, exercising legislative and executive powers of government; a procedure which must highly incense his Majesty against them, and against those who so publicly and avowedly recognize their authority as you have done in presenting to them your petition, and praying them to interpose their authority to relieve you from the mischievous effects of an act of the Legislature; thereby tacitly acknowledging their power to be equal to that constitutional body that passed the law. The same reasons will hold good, and the same mischief will attend applications made to any other constitutional body or congress, provincial or continental, that may be hereafter.

By order of the Committee,

R. Strettle Jones, *President.*

March 23, 1775."

It will be recollected that the colonies had not yet severed themselves from the mother country, and that the people of New Jersey and Pennsylvania were strongly disinclined to such a step. They looked forward to a change of policy at the British court, and desired still as heretofore to hold a provincial relation to England. At the same time they suspected the people of New England, and particularly of Massachusetts, of aiming at independence; little imagining how soon they themselves would catch the spirit of the eastern colonies and renounce their allegiance to the crown. The reply of Mr. Backus shows that he was not anticipating the necessity of an appeal to the throne, but was chiefly solicitous to be known in his true character as a friend to the liberties of his country as well as to religious liberty.

"MIDDLEBORO', Aug. 16, 1775.

"HONORED AND BELOVED: Your favor of March 23d I received, and soon wrote to appoint a meeting of our committee at Boston, in order that we might return you the best answer in our power. But alas! before the time came, Boston was shut up, our friends dispersed, and I know not where all our committee are, to this day, and those that I have intelligence of, the nearest is about thirty miles from me; and Mr. Smith, of Haverhill, is over seventy, so that we have done nothing as a committee since. Mr. Manning lately sent word to remind me of the advice of our congress, last December; I have therefore drawn up the enclosed memorial, which I send for your advice upon it; and shall not present it before our association meets at Warren, which is to be September 12th.

"Perhaps if you review our address to the congress, you will find that you went a little too far in calling it a *petition*, praying them to interpose their authority to relieve us. Sure I am that I did not understand it in that light. In your letter you well observe the importance of conducting so as not to be deemed enemies to our country. Now, Mr. Paine represented my errand to your city to be such, at Newport, on his return; and from him, Dr. Stiles and others had spread the slander to Providence and elsewhere, before I arrived there in November. And when I came home I heard that the Pedobaptists had determined to tax our people; which they have since done in Middleboro' and other places. Therefore I thought an address to our congress might stop the spread of such slander, might check their violence towards our friends, and also prevent their saying any more that they did not know that we pleaded conscience in not giving in certificates; and it has answered these ends. * * *

ISAAC BACKUS."

When the General Court met at Watertown, Sept. 20, 1775, Mr. Backus sent in a memorial which sketched with great plainness of speech the policy of Massachusetts from the first towards those who were not of the standing order, and insisted, as usual, upon the right of every man to freedom from legal control in the worship of God and in the support of that worship.

In a letter dated Oct. 4, 1775, Mr. Backus says this memorial was read in the Assembly last Saturday; whereupon Major Hawley rose, and among other things "told the Assembly that though the language of the memorial might not be so polished or polite as some others would have used, yet the matters it contained were weighty, and the Baptists had undoubtedly been injuriously treated; he desired that these things might be deliberately considered, that the petition might lie on the table for some time, and a future day be appointed to take it up. * * *

ISAAC BACKUS."

The Assembly agreed with this view of the case, and on Friday, Oct. 6, the memorial was taken up and read the second time. After some debate, it was referred to a committee of seven, three of whom were Baptists. The following letter to Mr. Backus, from Dr. Asaph Fletcher, one of these three Baptists, will continue our narrative:

"DEAR SIR: I think it not amiss to let you know, in some measure, the proceedings of the committee on your memorial, and the conduct of the House in consequence. The committee met four times upon the memorial before they reported, as we could not agree upon a bill of redress. In consequence of desire, I formed a bill to suit our purpose, but the majority of the committee did not, as above, agree with it. But, at length, the committee reported as follows, viz.: 'The committee on the memorial of Rev. Mr. Backus report to the House that the Baptists have leave to bring in a bill for the redress of grievances complained of in the said memorial.' The memorial was read last Friday and the report; but other important business prevented action upon it at that time. Yesterday it was acted upon. The same disposition appeared in some, as when you were present. The memorial was censured as casting reflections upon the House; and as calling in question their right to interpose in religious matters, etc. Major Hawley commended the memorial greatly, and told the Court that the established religion of this Colony was not worth a groat, and wished it might fall to the ground, or to that effect. Some said one thing and some another. At length, on a motion made, they voted the following, viz.: 'Ordered, that Dr. Fletcher have liberty to bring in a bill for the redress of such grievances as he apprehends the Baptists labor under.' This bill is to be brought in at the next session. After the vote passed, Mr. Gerry moved that the Baptists withdraw their memorial. Major Hawley opposed it; and said he would have it lay on the files, for it was worthy to lay there, and he hoped it would lay there till it had eaten out the present establishment, etc. And so it lays on the files. * * * Now, sir, I must leave all these things with the *Great Disposer* of events, not doubting but he will remove, ere long, all obstacles to gospel liberty.

"Wishing the divine assistance to be with you, and unerring wisdom to direct you in all things, I subscribe myself

Yours in the truth,

ASAPH FLETCHER.

WATERTOWN, 31st Oct., 1775."

Accordingly Dr. Fletcher brought in a bill which was read once; but the House never acted upon it.

The association which met this year, 1775, at Warren, 'agreed that our agent and committee be desired to draw up a letter to all the Baptist societies on this continent, stating the true nature and importance of religious liberty, and signifying that we think that a general meeting of delegates from our societies in every colony is expedient, as soon as may be, to consult upon the best means and methods of obtaining deliverance from various encroachments which have been made upon that liberty, and to promote the general welfare of our churches, and of all God's people throughout the land; and to desire that our friends in each Colony would communicate their sentiments concerning the design, and time and place of meeting, with all convenient speed.' In accordance with this direction the agent prepared an address, portions of which are subjoined:

"To all Christian people in the American Colonies, and especially to those who are of the Baptist denomination:—

"While the united inhabitants of this vast continent are appealing to heaven against the open attempts that have been made against their liberties, it is surely of great importance that we all regard that law of heaven: *Make straight paths for your feet.* And can we do so, if we are not as earnest for the removal of oppression from among ourselves, as we are to repel its encroachments from abroad? An ingenious author well observes,—'That the power of decreeing *rites* and *ceremonies* is a power absolutely indefinite, and of the very same kind with those claims which in things of a civil nature always give the greatest alarm. A tax of a penny is a trifle; but the power of imposing that tax, is never considered as a trifle, because it may imply absolute servitude in all who submit to it. Our ancestors, the old Puritans, had the same merit in opposing the imposition of the Surplice that Hampden had in opposing the levying of ship-money. In neither case was it the thing itself they objected to, so much as the authority that enjoined it, and the danger of the precedent. And it appears to us that the man who is as tenacious of his religious as he is of his civil liberty, will oppose them both with equal firmness."[1] And is not the power of levying money for religious ministers as dangerous to liberty, as the power of decreeing rites and

[1] Appendix to Blackstone's Commentaries.

ceremonies? Yea, more so; for they who can command the purse, either in Church or State, can usually carry the day in other affairs. * * * As the Baptist churches in the Massachusetts Colony have been brought to view things in this light, many of their elders and brethren at a meeting in Warren, September 13, 1776, desired us, the subscribers, to write to all the societies of our denomination in the American Colonies upon the subject of religious liberty, and to signify to them that a general meeting of delegates from our societies in each colony, we think, is very expedient, as soon as may be, to consult upon the best means and methods for obtaining and establishing full and equal religious liberty throughout this continent, and to promote the general welfare of all; so that truth and peace may prevail, and glory dwell in our land. And to request our friends in each colony to communicate their sentiments of the design and of the time and place of meeting, with all convenient speed. * * * Our Lord and Saviour has let us know as plainly as words can express, that his kingdom *is not of this world;* but that it is founded in and supported by *the truth.* And he says: 'Every one that is of the truth, heareth my voice.' Neither can anything be true religion that is not a *voluntary obedience to him.* The evident design of civil government is, to arm particular men with the sword, enforced by the power of the whole politic body, to restrain and punish such as violate the rules of justice and equity, to guard the civil peace; and so to be ministers of God for good to all the community. But for them to empower the majority of any town or place, to judge for their neighbors, who shall be teachers and guides to their souls, and to force those who do not choose them to support them, is going as much out of their jurisdiction as ever the Parliament of Britain did in taxing America. And how can we answer it, either to posterity or to our great and impartial Judge, if we do not exert ourselves as honestly and earnestly for the defence and establishment of religious liberty as we do for that which is only of a civil and worldly nature? We say, as *honestly* and *earnestly;* but not with the same weapons. For Jesus says: 'If my kingdom were of this world, my servants would *fight* that I should not be delivered to the Jews; but now is my kingdom not from hence. To this end was I born, and for this cause came I into the world, that I should bear witness unto the truth.'[1]

"That we may all in our stations bear our proper witness unto the truth, and against the corruptions and oppressions of the present day, is the hearty desire and prayer of your servants for Jesus' sake.

ISAAC BACKUS,
NATHAN PLIMPTON,
ASAPH FLETCHER.
Per Order."

[1] John 18: 36, 37.

CHAPTER XVII.

THE BILL OF RIGHTS.

ADDRESS TO THE PEOPLE OF NEW ENGLAND. — DRAFT OF A STATE CONSTITUTION. — PROTEST AGAINST THE SAME. — PAYSON'S SERMON. — BACKUS' PAPER ON RELIGIOUS LIBERTY; CHAUNCY AGAINST ESTABLISHMENTS; PRINCIPLES NOT PENCE; CHAUNCY FOR THE ESTABLISHMENT; INCONSISTENCY. — STILLMAN'S SERMON. — CONVENTION; PLEAS FOR THE THIRD ARTICLE OF THE BILL OF RIGHTS. — BACKUS' REPLY TO THEM. — COERCION IN BRIDGEWATER. — PROTEST AGAINST THE THIRD ARTICLE OF THE BILL OF RIGHTS. — CONSTITUTION ADOPTED. — CIRCULAR TO THE CHURCHES.

THE pen of Mr. Backus was not suffered to rest for any considerable length of time. In 1777 he read an "Address to the People of New England" on the subject of religious freedom, before the Warren Association, which was holding its annual meeting with the first Baptist church in Middleboro'. The address was adopted by the association and printed in the minutes as its circular letter. It urges nearly the same arguments in support of his view which are presented in other writings from his pen, and may therefore be passed over with this brief notice.

During this year the first volume of Mr. Backus' History of New England, with particular reference to the Baptists, was issued, and the facts which it narrated were of themselves an eloquent plea in favor of religious liberty. We shall speak in a subsequent chapter more fully of his labors as a historian.

The people of Massachusetts were now beginning to desire the establishment of a constitution as the basis of legislation. Accordingly a constitution was framed by the General Court for 1777, to be submitted to the next General Court for adoption or rejection. This constitution embraced no declaration of rights; but it had an article restoring some of the old ecclesiastical laws. The Baptists were alarmed, and their Committee of Grievances met in Boston, February 28, 1778. They drew up a protest against the insertion of those old laws in the constitution, and took measures to circulate a hundred copies of this protest among the Baptists of Massachusetts for their signatures. In the same paper which contained the protest, there was placed a petition that it might be a "fundamental principle of our government, that ministers shall be supported only by Christ's authority; and not at all by assessment and secular force, — which impartial liberty has long been claimed and enjoyed by the city of Boston."

Many persons, of different denominations, signed this protest and petition; but as the proposed constitution was rejected, they were never presented to the General Court. Yet the reception which they met evidently alarmed the friends of an establishment, and Mr. Payson of Chelsea, in his Election Sermon at Boston, May 27, 1778, warned the rulers against making any change in the authorized modes and usages of religion. "Let the restraints," he said, "of religion once be broken down, as they infallibly would be by leaving the subject of public worship to the humors of the multitude, and we might well defy all human wisdom and power to support and preserve order and government in the State."

When the Warren Association met in Leicester, October 8, 1778, Mr. Backus read before that body another paper on the subject of religious liberty, and "was unanimously requested to publish the same, with all convenient speed." Besides a brief discussion of the general question, this pamphlet contained strictures upon several statements in Mr. Payson's sermon and some accounts of recent oppression. We select the following paragraphs.

"Eleven years ago the Episcopal clergy appeared very earnest for having bishops established in America; which caused Dr. Chauncy of Boston to write an answer the next year, to what Dr. Chandler had published upon that subject. And as Chandler had declared, that all they wanted was only to have their church completely organized, without the least design of injuring others, the best reason that Chauncy could give why his request ought not to be granted was this: Says he, 'We are, in principle, against all civil establishments in religion. It does not appear to us that God has entrusted the State with a right to make religious establishments. If the state in England has this delegated authority, must it not be owned that the state in China, in Turkey, in Spain, has this authority likewise? What should make the difference in the eye of true reason? Hath the state of England been distinguished by heaven by any peculiar grant, beyond the state in other countries? If it has, let the grant be produced. If it has not, all states have, in common, the same authority in establishments conformable to their own sentiments in religion: what can the consequence be, but infinite damage to the cause of God and true religion! And such in fact has been the consequence of these establishments in all ages, and in all places. Should it be said, we claim liberty of conscience and fully enjoy it; and why should we confine this privlege to ourselves? Is it not as reasonable Episcopalians should both claim and enjoy it? It is readily allowed; and we are as willing they should possess and exercise religious liberty in its full extent as we desire to do it ourselves. But then let it be heedfully minded we claim *no right* to desire the interposition of the *State* to *establish* that mode of worship, government, or discipline, we apprehend is most agreeable to the mind of Christ. We desire no other liberty than to be left unrestrained in the exercise of our principles in so far as we are good members of society; and we are perfectly willing Episcopalians should enjoy this liberty to the full. If they think bishops, in their appropriate sense, were constituted by Christ or his apostles, we object not a word against their having as many of them as they please, if they will be content to have them with authority *altogether* derived from Christ. But they both claim and desire a great deal more. They want to be distinguished by having bishops upon the footing of a *state establishment.* The plain truth is, by the Gospel-charter, all professed Christians are vested with precisely the same rights; nor has one denomination any more a right to the interposition of the civil magistrate in their favor than another; and whenever this difference takes place, it is beside the rule of *Scripture*, and I may say also, the genuine dictates of *uncorrupted reason.*'

"* * * They [the members of the Standing Order] often declare that they allow us liberty of conscience, and also complain of injury if we recite former and latter acts of their party to prove the contrary. Just so has Dr. Chandler done with regard to bishops; and he declares they had now no design of taxing America to them; yet he says, 'Should a general tax be laid upon the country, and thereby a sum be raised sufficient for the purpose, I believe such a tax would not amount to more than four pence in a hundred pounds; and this would be no mighty hardship upon the country. He that could think much of giving the six-thousandth part of his income to any use which the Legislature of his country should assign, deserves not to be considered in the light of a good subject or member of society.'

But in answer hereto, Dr. Chauncy says: 'If the country might be taxed four pence in one hundred pounds, it might for the same reason and with as much justice, if it was thought the support of bishops called for it, be taxed four shillings, or four pounds, and so on.' All but Tories will allow this to be good reasoning; and why is it not as good in a Baptist as in a Presbyterian? He goes back one hundred and fifty years, and tells of the EPISCOPAL YOKE OF BONDAGE, which our forefathers came into this wilderness to avoid, and says: 'Shall it be declared in the face of the world, that this would be *no hardship* to their posterity, and that they would be neither good subjects nor good members of society, if they *thought much* of supporting that POWER which has been, and may again be TERRIBLY OPPRESSIVE!'

'True, doctor; there lies the difficulty. It is not the PENCE but the POWER, that alarms us. And since the Legislature of the State passed an act, no longer ago than last September, to continue a tax of FOUR PENCE a year upon the Baptists in every parish where they live, as an acknowledgment of the POWER that they have long assumed over us in religious affairs, which we know has often been TERRIBLY OPPRESSIVE, how can we be blamed for refusing to pay that acknowledgment; especially when it is considered, that it is evident to us that God never allowed any civil state upon earth to impose religious taxes; but that he declared his vengeance against those in Israel who presumed to use *force* in such affairs."[1]

Now, just before the publication of this pamphlet, the American army had been compelled, through fear of being surrounded by the British fleet, to relinquish its position on Rhode Island. It effected a retreat to the main land on the night of August 30, 1778. "Chauncy," says Mr. Backus, "imagined that this defeat might be turned to ministerial advantage; and therefore, at his next lecture, when many of our rulers were present, he delivered a discourse from the seventh of Joshua, wherein he represented that one of the *accursed things* which caused that defeat, was their neglect of *making a new law* to help ministers about their salaries, which the depreciation of our currency had greatly lessened. This sermon was soon printed and dispersed in the country. And in the 'Continental Journal,' of October 8th, it was highly commended and its author also; and then it was said: 'Although the General Assembly has now been sitting for some time, no motion (as I can learn) has as yet been made, or is likely to be made, for this purpose. Are the clergy then to submit to this treatment? Are they, as an order, and the only order of men in the community, to remain subjected to *injustice* and *fraud?*' Now it was so ordered that the above passages in the Baptist pamphlet were inserted in the 'Independent Chronicle' the *same day*, Oct. 8th, and in the same street in Boston. By which means the same author was declaring to the world in one paper that all religious establishments were of infinite damage to the cause of God and true religion; and in another that the want of

[1] 1 Sam. 2: 16, 34. Mic. 3: 5, 12.

further exertion in that way was an accursed thing which caused the defeat of our army! And what could be done in such a case? In the 'Boston Gazette,' of November 2d, it was declared that said Baptist pamphlet 'exhibited only a compound of *ignorance*, *impudence* and *abuse*.'"

In spite of opposition from a certain quarter, Dr. Stillman, pastor of the first Baptist church in Boston, was chosen to preach the next election sermon. He availed himself of the opportunity to set forth clearly the difference between church and state, and to show the importance of keeping them entirely distinct. This sermon was, as usual, printed and distributed through the state by order of authority.

Delegates from the several towns, elected for the purpose of framing a constitution, assembled at Cambridge on the first of September, 1779. They chose a large committee to prepare a draft for their consideration, and then adjourned. They reässembled October 28th, and heard the report of their committee. In the bill of rights laid before them the third article gave to civil rulers power in religious affairs, and led to much debate. At length it was referred to a special committee of seven. Five of these were distinguished politicians. A new draft was prepared, which, however, retained the obnoxious principle, and after warm debates was passed by a majority. To obtain this vote it was asserted that there had never been any persecution in the land, and also that the Baptists had sent their agent to Philadelphia in 1774, with a false memorial of grievances, in order to break the union of these colonies.

Hearing of these statements, Mr. Backus repaired to Boston and published, in the "Independent Chronicle," of December 2, 1779, a reply to the same. In this article he first states his objections to that portion of the bill of rights which gave to civil rulers, as such, power to act in religious affairs; he then recites the principal facts connected with his visit to Philadelphia; and lastly he refers to the recent debates, and closes with the following language: "Yet, after all this, I am informed by several members of the convention * * * that to obtain the above described power over us, Mr. John Adams and Mr. Paine brought up the above named accusation against us, and that Mr. Paine said he had reason to think that some things, mentioned in our memorial, never existed. This is therefore to give notice that I am ready to meet them before any proper judges, when called, to answer for every word therein, and to suffer deserved punishment if I am convicted of advancing any one accusation against my country, or against any person therein, that I cannot support. Yea, or if I have ever discovered the least degree of an inimical disposition towards my country in any part of this contest with great Britain. I am willing to make all the allowance in this case to forgetfulness and other human infirmities, that reason or religion calls for; but if those gentlemen should persist in their accusations against us without fairly supporting them, or in acting contrary to their promise at Philadelphia, the public will judge how far they will deserve regard for the future. * * *

ISAAC BACKUS,

Agent for the Baptist Churches in this State.

MIDDLEBORO', NOV. 16, 1779."

It may here be remarked that supporters of the established faith were not slow to avail themselves of these charges and insinuations against Mr. Backus as a sufficient pretext for taxing them afresh. We insert, by way of specimen, a single instance of the kind. Two members of the convention, who resided in the south parish of Bridgewater, were led by these false accusations to move the collector of their minister's salary to go with a constable and seize Lieut. Elijah Ames and his brother, Joseph Ames, Jr., members of the first Baptist church in Middleboro', for said minister's tax, which they declined paying. These officers commanded two regular hearers of Mr. Backus to assist them in carrying the recusant brothers to Plymouth jail; but they were promptly disobeyed. "Then," says Mr. Backus, "they went and took to themselves some lewd fellows of the baser sort, and came again with ropes to bind our brethren. And they did bind one of them, and carried them both a mile or two to a tavern, when one of that party paid the money and released the prisoners. * * * Before our said brethren were seized, they mildly labored to convince those officers that they had no right to do it. But the constable said: 'Our churches are built upon the law.' Lieut. Ames replied: 'I knew that before; but I thought you would be ashamed to own it.' It may be added that the assessors of the parish taxed these Baptists again for the support of their minister, and that they were fined for refusing to pay the tax.[1]

The convention met after a second adjournment, on the fifth of January, 1780, and continued in session until the second of March, when their work was finished. On the sixth of April, the Baptist committee was called together in Boston, and it was concluded to publish an Appeal to the People of the state against the third article noticed above. This Appeal was signed by Mr. Backus as Agent, and five hundred copies of it were sent out. It called forth several articles in the Boston papers, to which the

[1] See "Independent Chronicle," December, 1779.

Agent with his usual energy and promptitude replied. And when the association met at Royalston, in September, "it was unanimously agreed to circulate for subscribers, and then send the following protest to the General Court, by whose power the Constitution was to be ratified or rejected.

"To the General Court of the Massachusetts, assembled at Boston, October, 1780.

"We, whose names are hereunto subscribed, inhabitants of this state, who are twenty-one years of age and above, of various religious denominations, enter our PROTEST against the power claimed in the Third Article of the declaration of rights in the new plan of government introduced among us; — for the reasons following, viz.:

"1. Because it asserts a right in the people to give away a power they never had themselves; for no man has a right to judge for others in religious matters; yet this Article would give the majority of each town and parish the exclusive right of covenanting for the rest with religious teachers, and so of excluding the minority from the liberty of choosing for themselves in that respect.

"2. Because this power is given entirely into the hands of men who vote only by virtue of *money* qualifications, without any regard to the church of Christ.

"3. Because said Article contradicts itself; for it promises *equal* protection of all sects, with an exemption from any subordination of one religious denomination to another; when it is impossible for the majority of any community to govern in any affair, unless the minority are in subordination to them in that affair.

"4. Because by this Article the civil power is called to judge whether persons can conveniently and conscientiously attend upon any teacher within their reach, and oblige each one to support such teachers as may be contrary to his conscience; which is subversive of the unalienable rights of conscience.

"5. Because, as the convention say, 'power without any restraint is tyranny;' which they explain as meaning the union of the legislative, executive and judicial powers of government in the same hands; and it is evident that these powers are all united in the Legislature, who by this Article are empowered to compel both civil and religious societies to make what they shall judge to be *suitable provision* for religious teachers 'in all cases where such provision shall not be made voluntarily.'"

The General Court met October 25, 1780, and notwithstanding the above protest, adopted the new constitution. In view of this action, the Warren Association, at its next meeting in September, 1781, directed their agent and committee to address the Baptists of this Commonwealth through the public papers. Upon meeting, however, the committee concluded to send out the following circular.

"Dearly Beloved:—Inasmuch as the Association at their last meeting desired their agent and committee to present our address to the public, upon the commencement of our new plan of government, concerning religious liberty; we have taken the matter into serious and deliberate consideration; and are of opinion that a publication of that nature, in a newspaper, at this time would be inexpedient. We therefore have rather concluded to address you on that matter in a circular.

"It is evident that our strength consists in union and perseverance in opposition to the unjust claims of our enemies. The last shift which they have made, is to plead that those claims are a matter of conscience with them; and so have set their liberty of conscience against ours. But this plea is easily confuted. For no man is allowed to have a seat in any Legislature, till he solemnly declares: —'I believe the christian religion, and have a firm persuasion of its truth! And as surely as it (i. e. the christian religion), is true, we have but one Law-giver in all religious affairs, who forbids our calling any man Master upon earth, and commands us to stand fast in the liberty wherewith he hath made us free.[1] As the name *Christian* is derived from Christ, it is essential to a christian society that it be constituted and governed by his laws; and they are as express concerning the choice and support of his ministers, as on any other point of christian practice. And nothing is more contrary thereto, than the empowering of some to give away others' money to soul-guides whom they never chose, and to imprison their persons if they refuse to pay it. And where is the man upon earth who will come up plainly and plead conscience for so doing.' Oh, brethren, face them down boldly upon this point and they cannot stand. And the best way to attain and enjoy true boldness herein, is a near approach to God through Jesus Christ; and a faithful discharge of all the duties of our several stations and relations according to his directions. Look to the great Captain of our salvation, who will not fail nor be discouraged till he has set judgment in the earth, and the isles shall wait for his law.

"A free communication to our brethren who have suffered in the cause, and the promotion of oneness and union therein, is of great importance, and we trust will finally prevail to our deliverance and happiness. And for

[1] James 4: 12. Matt. 23: 3–12. Gal. 5: 1.

the encouragement of any who may be called to suffer in any towns or parishes for refusing to give certificates, or to pay their money for the support of a ministry from which they conscientiously dissent,'— We, the Agent and Committee of the Baptist churches, will endeavor that the expenses which may fall upon any individuals for such refusal, shall be made equal, by collecting money for said purpose among the churches.

Isaac Backus, Agent,

By the advice and direction of the Committee.

Boston, Oct. 5, 1781."

CHAPTER XVIII.

LIBERTY SECURED AT LAST.

DECISION AT TAUNTON, THE OLD LAWS NO LONGER IN FORCE. — LETTER TO A BROTHER IN LONDON. — CASE OF WEST CAMBRIDGE. — PROPRIETY OF RECOGNIZING CIVIL AUTHORITY IN RELIGIOUS AFFAIRS. — A NEW LAW, RETROGRADE. — LETTER TO GEORGE WASHINGTON. — LETTER TO MR. RIPPON; DEATH OF PRESIDENT MANNING; PARTIAL HISTORY; RELIGIOUS PROSPERITY. — LETTER TO MRS. DRAPER; PROGRESS OF BAPTIST PRINCIPLES; HUMAN WICKEDNESS; HOPE IN GOD. — LETTER TO WILLIAM RICHARDS. — INSTANCES OF OPPRESSION. — CHANGE OF PUBLIC SENTIMENT. — FREEDOM SECURED AT LAST.

But while the new constitution gave to the Legislature power to make "suitable provision" for christian teachers in case this was not done by the several towns, it also declared that "no subordination of one sect or denomination to another shall ever be established by law." It was therefore deemed important to ascertain whether the old laws in respect to certificates, etc., were now constitutional. An opportunity to do this presently occurred; for the east parish of Attleboro' taxed several persons in 1781 for the support of worship in said parish, although they attended elsewhere. One of them, Mr. Elijah Balkom, being seized for his tax, sued the assessors for damages before a justice of the peace in Norton. Judgment was given against him, but he appealed to the county court at Taunton.

On the fifteenth of March, 1782, Robert Treat Paine, Attorney General for the Commonwealth, moved to have this case taken out of court and referred to particular men. Mr. Backus and his friends consulted with John Daggett, Esq., and others, who owned that referees were not tied up to points of law as a jury were, and "therefore," says Mr. Backus, "we could not consent to a reference, because our aim was to know how the judges understood the present laws in these matters." Accordingly, the case was tried before the honorable Walter Spooner, Thomas Durfee, Benjamin Williams, and William Baylies, Esquires. After the cause had been plead in a "learned and elegant" manner by William Bradford and James M. Varnum for the appellant, and Robert T. Paine for the parish, the judges unanimously agreed to give the appellant damages and costs." "This judgment not only settled the controversy in Attleboro', but was extensively beneficial elsewhere."

The following letter of Mr. Backus to a brother minister in London, will be read with special interest by those who have accompanied us thus far in our narrative.

"MAY 28, 1783.

"DEAR SIR: * * * * You are doubtless sensible that different circumstances alter cases; so that some may be called of God to do things which their brethren in other places are not there called to do. When I had an interview with our brethren, Shakspear and Mackennesse, at Providence, they were very desirous that I and others here, should act as neuters in the contest between your country and ours. I know not but that in their circumstances, such a conduct might be excusable, if not justifiable; but in me it would have been criminal. The claims of the British court over the persons and property of this country were such, that for sixteen years past, in my nearest approaches to God, I could not hesitate about them for one hour; though at the same time, I had no better opinion of many leaders here in the opposition to those claims, than of those who made them there.

"I should have fainted long ago, had I not believed that wherein men dealt proudly God was above them. And he fixed a persuasion on my soul that if we faithfully improved the advantage he gave us, rulers would be forced to give up their tyrannical power over the church of God and the consciences of men. A large part of my good friends here, rather wished than believed we should obtain so great a blessing; and, therefore, have often been clogs instead of helps, in this great work. And my mistakes and imperfections in acting therein have been so many and great, that instead of wondering at others' fears at my attempts for liberty, I may well wonder that I was not confounded long ago. To think that one who knew so little should write so much, and that he should now propose to expose more of his writings even in foreign countries, is a consideration almost sufficient to put a stop to any further proceedings in that way. I speak before Him who will judge all; if a persuasion of duty has not been my greatest motive, I know not what has. Oh, that mine was more single therein!

"But shall we faint at the threshold of deliverance? On the tenth instant, one of the most politic adversaries which we have ever had in our Legislature, sued for our favor. One who, when our House of Representatives had chosen Mr. Stillman to preach the next election sermon, in 1779, was so opposed thereto that he would give them no rest till they had reconsidered that vote, (though in the second trial our friend had many more votes than before,) one who was an attorney for Hingham rioters, and treated brother Lee very abusively last January; yet now on said day, he paid a complaisant visit to brother Stillman, with a request that the Baptists would present a memorial to the Legislature which is to meet at Boston, the twenty-eighth, (whereof he is a member,) for equal religious liberty to be established, and was forward to promise his influence in favor of it. The reasons whereof we take to be these: First, To save their own honor in appearing to grant what they cannot keep from us. Second, To keep the laboring oar still in our hands. But as God has given us liberty contrary to their designs, we choose things should appear as they are, and to stand fast therein according to his command. * * * *"

From a passage in this letter it appears that the bold and unyielding course advocated by Mr. Backus, was not approved by all his brethren. Some of them at length became disheartened, and were ready for the sake of peace to make the best of existing laws without subjecting themselves to yet further and seemingly profitless toil or expense. The following narrative will illustrate our statement.

In 1781 a Baptist church was organized in the town of Cambridge, (now West Cambridge,) but no pastor was settled over it until 1783. And when this was done they were all taxed for the support of the Congregational ministry. Distraint was made upon the property of Gershom Cutler and two others for the payment of this tax. Believing the tax unconstitutional, they sued the assessors for damages, and after much delay the case was decided in their favor by the county court at Concord, September 1784; "but at the Superior Court at Cambridge, October 26, Judge Sargeant declared that their old laws were still in force, and that they knew no societies in this Commonwealth but corporate bodies. With him Judge Sewall concurred; the other judges said little on the point; and the next day the jury turned the case against the Baptists." The latter were now informed by a distinguished lawyer, "that if they would give in certificates to the ruling sect that they belonged to said Baptist society, and desired their money to go to the minister thereof, he (the minister) might sue the money out of the hands of those who took it."

On the thirty-first of October, 1785, Mr. Backus went to Boston for the purpose of consulting with the Committee of Grievances in respect to this affair. "Our committee," he says, "when now met, concluded that, if they (the Congregationalists) would go on and take away the money of our people, our ministers should demand it again, according to the recent interpretation of the third article in our bill of rights — all but myself; for I could not concur therewith. Accordingly the Baptists in Cambridge complied with legal advice, and their minister sued the money out of the hands of their oppressors, from time to time, until they left off collecting such money; and the like was done in various parts of the country."

Now it will be remembered that Mr. Backus regarded the giving of these certificates as a voluntary submission to the civil power, when this power was breaking over its proper limits and usurping the authority of Christ. For many years in public and in private he had solemnly protested against this submission, and had urged his brethren to suffer their property to be all confiscated rather than to recognize the validity of human laws in the domain of religion. Whether his views were correct or erroneous, they were the result of protracted examination, were endorsed by his conscience, and were maintained with christian fidelity to the last. His was not the spirit to falter and turn back at the prospect of danger. There was moral heroism in his soul, and he was ready for the severest conflict. To find his brethren prepared to relinquish in discouragement their high position and plant themselves on lower ground, was therefore a sore trial to his patience and charity; but so far as we can ascertain, he was enabled to bear this trial, if not without complaint, yet without bitterness of feeling. Had his brethren throughout the State refused at this time to give in certificates and cheerfully taken the consequences, it is at least probable that Mr. Backus would have been permitted to welcome in his own day that complete separation of church and state for which he longed. As it was, he died in faith, not having seen the blessing which he desired for the churches of Christ.

In March, 1786, a new law was made "which confounded ministerial and civil taxes together, and empowered every man in each town who pays two thirds more in one tax than a poll tax, to vote in such affairs." The act says, "The freeholders and other inhabitants of each respective town, qualified as aforesaid at the annual meeting for the choice of town officers or at any other town meeting regularly warned, may grant and vote such sums of money as they shall judge necessary, for the settlement, maintenance and support of the ministry, schools, the poor, and other necessary charges arising within the same town; to be assessed upon the polls and property within the same as by law provided." This certainly was a retrograde movement, adapted to fill the minds of all who differed conscientiously from the Standing Order with alarm. The following letters will reveal in some measure the feelings of Mr. Backus during the next few years.

"To George Washington, Esq., President of the United States.

SIR: Among the many addresses to your Excellency since your advancement to the highest seat of government in America, I suppose you have received none from any community of Baptists in the State of Massachusetts. Not because they have not as hearty a regard for your Excellency as any denomination therein, but for want of a convenient opportunity when you were in these parts. But an obscure individual begs your acceptance of a private token of love, which may be of more real service than many flattering public addresses. Indeed, if elegance of style and composition were necessary to render any book acceptable to your Excellency, the author would not have presumed to send such a present as his History of New England. But believing that the knowledge of principles and facts, and of their influence on mankind through various changes, is of great importance in your view, he hopes that this work will not be unacceptable. Much of it was taken from original records and papers which were never before published; and none of them have ever since been disputed in any newspaper among us. The Quakers were so much affected with my first volume, published in 1777, that one of them wrote a considerable volume against it; but when he came to lay it before their committee, they thought it better to apply to me for corrections; and a committee of theirs met with me in Providence, in December, 1780, and after two days' labor we agreed upon the corrections which are in the end of the second volume, which agreement was signed by me, and by * * * their committee. If any others would have favored me with their corrections, as they might have done and concealed their names if they pleased, it might have been of public benefit. But no such favor hath been granted me.

"The continuance of tax and compulsion for religious ministers in New England, while it is abolished in Virginia, is a clear demonstration of the narrow selfishness of mankind. The continuance of it here for Congregationalists, and the abolishing of it there for Episcopalians, are both commended by Dr. Gordon in his History of the American Revolution, in which is much impartiality about civil and military affairs. But religious ministers, when supported by force, are the most dangerous men upon earth; while no men are more necessary and useful to human society than faithful teachers. Of this further evidence is given in two late pieces which I here send you.

"That your Excellency may still be guided and preserved in your exalted and difficult station until righteous government shall be well established in this land; that your latter days may be peaceful and happy, and your end be eternal life, is the earnest prayer of

Your humble servant,

ISAAC BACKUS.

NOVEMBER 15, 1790."

"AUGUST 19, 1791.

"DEAR SIR: More than a year has elapsed since I received a line from you; and the unfaithfulness which generally prevails renders it exceedingly difficult to keep up a distant correspondence, which perhaps has prevented the arrival of letters which you may have sent me. Be that as it may, yet I shall now attempt to inform you of our affairs; especially as one of our most useful ministers has gone the way of all the earth. I was with President Manning two days in June past, and when I parted with him the eighth of that month, I had as little thought of its being the last parting for time, as at any parting we ever had. But near night on July 29th, I received a line from Providence informing me of his decease at four o'clock that morning. I went there the first instant and met the College Corporation the next day, who have thought of Dr. Jones for his successor, if he can be obtained; but we have no idea of obtaining any man who will equal President Manning in all respects, at least soon. His extensive knowledge, fervent piety, constant study to be perfectly serviceable to mankind; his easy access to every class of people, with his gift of governing so as to be feared and loved by all, where keen envy did not prevail, — rendered him the most accomplished man for that station of any one I ever saw. Yet, in the midst of his usefulness, he is gone, as universally lamented as any man that I have known. A loud call to us all, to be always ready.

His beloved consort, whose tender mind could scarcely tell how to look over his papers, yet kindly put into my hands a number of letters, one of which was yours to Dr. Manning last spring; and either in that or one before, your proposals for printing an annual Baptist Register, which I had heard of before, but had not seen the plan till then. The proposal I like well, and hope the work will be extremely useful. As my health has failed more this year than ever before, I cannot expect to be here long, either to be helpful in that work or to partake of its benefits. But I have seen and felt so much of the evil effects of ignorance and prejudice caused by *partial history* and *invented stories* about the Baptists that I am still desirous of doing all I can towards removing those evils out of the way of posterity. For that end I was willing to comply with the earnest request of our brethren in Virginia to assist them in publishing a history of the Baptists in that State; in which hath been the greatest revolution about baptism and religious liberty that ever I heard of in any government upon earth. And the May before last I had the promise, by letter, of having many historical materials sent me soon, but have never had a line from them on that subject since. True and impartial history, especially of our own times, is one of the most difficult services in the world.

Dr. Gordon has published a valuable history of the American Revolution; and yet a man might read through his two thousand pages, and not learn from the whole work that there was one Baptist in all New England or in Virginia; although no denomination in our country was more unanimous and hearty in the cause of liberty than they; and in Virginia they were the main instruments of its salvation. Gordon is the minister referred to in page 331 of my second volume, who accused me of giving up the cause for which I was agent. But the prejudices of natural affection, education and honor, gain and self-righteousness, have all conspired together against believers' baptism and against having the church of Christ governed wholly by his laws. And as tax and compulsion, for the support of religious ministers, are still continued in New Hampshire, Massachusetts and Connecticut, it not only causeth much envy and oppression in Congregationalists and Presbyterians, but it hath such influence upon the Baptists, that I know not of one of our churches especially in Massachusetts, which is entirely free of the evil of giving in a list of their society to their oppressors; which draws covetous men among us, whose influence with others hath cruelly withheld reasonable support from many of our ministers, a number of whom have been dismissed from their people, and equity is amazingly shut out from among us.

"Yet, in the midst of the flames, the bush is so far from being consumed, that believers' baptism gains ground very fast, and our cause was never so openly honored by men of the greatest note in the land as in a year past. And although the work of conviction and conversion is abated in Providence, yet it has been the most powerful in Boston during the year past that it has ever been since 1742. And a brother was with me yesterday from above Casco Bay, who informs me of a powerful revival of religion now going on in various towns in the county of Cumberland; and I have, in other ways, heard of the like far down our eastern coasts, as also westward into the State of New York, where one of our ministers has travelled by special request this summer, even an hundred miles beyond Albany.

In a word, the folly of all the inventions of men, and the infinite excellency of Divine revelation, appear more and more to open every day. My thoughts, which I have published on these subjects lately, I shall endeavor to send you. In the mean time, dearly beloved, I remain yours in the kingdom and patience of Jesus Christ,

ISAAC BACKUS.

MR. RIPPON."

We interrupt the series of letters written by Mr. Backus, to insert a letter from the Committee of Grievances. It is, we presume, a fair specimen of the appeals made by this committee to parishes which persisted in taxing the Baptists:

"GENTLEMEN: The Baptist church in Barnstable belongs to the association of regular churches, and as such claims the advice and protection of the whole body, so far as their case requires it, and they have power to afford it.

"By the Warren Association, at their meeting in September last, we were appointed a Standing Committee, to which all churches of our denomination in this commonwealth are to apply for advice and assistance, when oppressed on a religious account. Having therefore received a well attested account from Barnstable, that some of the members of our society have been repeatedly taxed, and their property taken from them to support the Congregational minister of that place, from whom they conscientiously dissent, and though they have a minister of their own to maintain; we, the committee of the Baptist churches, think it our duty to say, that in an age and country as much enlightened as this is, such acts of injustice were not to be expected; and in all companies in which the affair has been mentioned, it has been a matter of astonishment.

"As a denomination of Christians, we stand on an equal footing with any in the commonwealth, and this equality we mean to maintain, by every proper method in our power. If the parish refuse to return the monies taken from our society, and continue to tax them to the support of the Congregational minister of Barnstable, we shall be reduced to the disagreeable necessity of publishing the whole to the world, and of taking such other steps as shall appear to be necessary.

"It is our most sincere wish, that the different denominations of Christians throughout the commonwealth may live together in love and friendship, agreeable to the spirit of the gospel.

We are, with sentiments of respect, yours, etc.,

SAMUEL STILLMAN,
ISAAC BACKUS,
THOMAS BALDWIN,
THOMAS GREEN,
JOSEPH GRAFTON,
} *Committee.*

BOSTON, JAN. 24, 1791.

"P. S. We enclose you the minutes of the Warren Association, for your perusal.

"To the gentlemen, the Committee of the First Parish in Barnstable."

MIDDLEBORO', AUG. 16, 1793."

"To Mrs. Margaret Draper,
London:

"As your Aunt Starr has shown me several of your letters to her, and has desired me to write to you, I am now set down to answer her request. The ideas you have communicated to her, concerning vital and practical religion, agree with what I trust God taught me above fifty years ago. And he hath undoubtedly revived that religion in many parts of America, in a few years past. At the earnest request of brethren at the Southward, I sailed from Newport, January 2, 1789, and landed on the tenth, in North Carolina; and betwixt then and May 27th, I travelled above two hundred miles in that State, and a thousand miles in Virginia, and preached one hundred and seventeen sermons, to very attentive audiences, who had shown but little regard to religion but a few years before; and in Portsmouth, opposite to Norfolk, in Virginia, when I sailed from thence, May 27, 1789, there was no Baptist church nor settled minister of any other denomination; and yet, in two years after, there was a Baptist church of one hundred and fifty members, with a settled minister. And in the north-eastern part of New England, not a tenth part of their towns had any settled ministers, and but very few churches, until a revival of religion began upon Kennebec River, ten years ago; and it has prevailed so as to form about fifteen Baptist churches in the counties of Cumberland, Lincoln and Hancock; and above half of them in two years past, and the work still prevailed when I was there in June. A like blessing has been granted in many other parts of our land. Even in the places where much blood was shed, when General Burgoyne's army was defeated, in 1777, there were two hundred and ninety-three members added to only two churches, at Saratoga and Stillwater, in 1791.

"Yet we have great cause to be ashamed of ourselves, for our behavior under these unspeakable mercies; for the greater light men have, if the heart is not changed, the more artful they grow in deceiving each other, and in hardening their hearts against the truth. And I am fully persuaded that these evils are now carried as far, in America and elsewhere, as ever they were in any period since Adam fell. Cruel superstitions prevailed amazingly in former ages, as they do now where gospel light does not shine; but infidelity, under the name of liberty and charity, has come in, like a flood, upon countries which were favored with the light of the gospel. The injustice which you complain of in Boston, which holds you at such a cruel distance from your native country, came from infidelity, though under the name of patriotism, liberty, religion, and government. And I had fainted long ago, unless I had believed that the infinitely wise God, who has said the heart is deceitful above all things, is now trying the hearts of all men, in order to the future display of his justice, mercy and faithfulness, and of the *blessedness* of each man *who trusteth in him.*[1] In this light of revelation, the darkest providences appear worthy of him who worketh all things after the counsel of his own will. The darkest time that the church of God was ever in, was when his Son was crucified, and lay in the tomb until the third day. But he said unto his church: This is as the waters of Noah unto me; for as I have sworn that the waters of Noah shall no more go over the earth, so have I sworn that I will not be wroth with thee nor rebuke thee. All thy children shall be taught of the Lord, and great shall be the peace of thy children;[2] which prophecy is applied to the christian church by our Lord and by the apostle Paul.[3] And as a rainbow is round about the throne of God, and his covenant as sure to his church as ever it was, all believers may well say, 'Thou art worthy, O Lord, to receive glory, and honor, and power; for thou hast created all things, and for thy pleasure they are and were created.[4]

And my dear friend, that we may all learn to believe and obey God, through all changes, so as finally to join in the heavenly songs, is the earnest prayer of

Yours, for Jesus' sake,

I. BACKUS."

"MAY 28. 1796.

"To William Richards.

DEAR SIR: Yours of March 5, 1793, I answered the Fall after, and then sent a copy of a long letter which Roger Williams wrote in 1670, lately come to light; and

1 Jer. 17:1—10. 2 Is. 54:1, 9, 13.
3 John 6:45; Gal. 4:26, 27. 4 Rev. 4:3, 11.

also Governor Winthrop's printed journal, which gives much light about Williams. If you should finally fail of receiving them, the third volume of my history, which I hope you will soon receive, will give you some further light about him. And if my life should be spared, and I hear that you still want those materials, I will make a further attempt to help you in that affair. In the mean time, I would take this opportunity to give you a concise view of the present state of America.

The war in Europe has called away much of the produce of America; in return for which, money has flowed through the country beyond what it ever did before, and provisions, live stock, and labor have been nearly double what they were in 1791, and bread has been much more than double. And because the powers of Great Britain have taken many American vessels, the public papers throughout the country have been filled, the year past, with inflammatory pieces against our highest rulers, because they have not made reprisals upon them, and at length have openly pleaded for war with them. But, after long debates, our Congress concluded, about a month ago, to carry the treaty into execution, which prescribes a way of compensation without a war. Thus we see how men are inclined to wax wanton in prosperity, and to abuse their liberty as an occasion to the flesh, and as a cloak of maliciousness.

But *Infinite Wisdom* is carrying on great designs, wherein he takes the wise in their own craftiness, and makes their wrath to praise him. For at the return of peace, both in 1763 and 1783, the folly of the people in running into debt, and the craft of men in power in seizing their estates at home, caused many to remove into the wilderness, and to enlarge the cultivation of our country, beyond what all the wisdom of men could possibly have done. And in the year 1795, the showers and shines of heaven caused it to be a very fruitful season in New Hampshire and Vermont, while they had such a severe drought in Canada, as to force them to have recourse to these States, for food to keep them alive; and many of their cattle and horses were driven into these States, and sold for a small matter, being almost starved. Of these things we have undoubted evidence. And though the teachers and rulers of the uppermost party in Massachusetts, Connecticut, New Hampshire and Vermont are as earnest as ever Pharaoh was, to hold the church of Christ under the taxing power of the world, to support religious ministers, yet that power is daily consuming by the Spirit of God's mouth, and the brightness of his coming.[1] Very few of them now dare to make distress upon any who refuse to pay minister's taxes; and the credit of Baptist churches and ministers is daily rising, in all parts of our country. And the gospel, enforced upon the souls of men by the Spirit of God, has been the evident cause of it; for before the work of his Spirit in the county of Hampshire, under the ministry of Edwards and others, in and after 1734, there were but six Baptist churches in all the governments of Massachusetts and Connecticut, and none in New Hampshire; Vermont was not then begun. Yet in these four States there are now two hundred and eighty-five Baptist churches, and they are increasing fast, against all the powers of the world. I have received accounts of some Baptist churches, since my history was in press, more than are inserted therein; and these show that not less than twenty-eight such churches have been formed in the counties of Cumberland, Lincoln, and Han-

[1] 2 Thess. 2:8.

cock, in the District of Maine; besides a number more which are not in fellowship with those churches.

Yet, in the midst of all these wonders, there are many thousands in America, who are willing to own the Baptist name, who require their ministers to go a warfare at their own charges; and they, and multitudes of other denominations, pay no more regard to the law of Christ, about the government of his church and the support of his ministers, than dead men do to the voice of the living. And these things make me often think of what God says of his witnesses in the street of the great city.[1] And if they are now slain, we may hope for glorious times as near at hand. Be that as it may, our Lord says: Behold, I come as a thief. Blessed is he that watcheth and keepeth his garments, lest he walk naked, and they see his shame.[2] Dear brother, that we may duly regard this rule from heaven, is the earnest prayer of

Yours, in gospel bonds,

ISAAC BACKUS."

But we must bring this record of injustice to a close. Petitions were originated, from time to time, in the Warren Association, and presented to the General Court, praying for an act exempting the Baptists from the payment of rates to other denominations. These petitions were generally called for by fresh instances of oppression. We subjoin a specimen.

The minutes of the Warren Association, for 1797, after stating that Dr. Stillman, Dr. Smith, Mr. Backus, Mr. Baldwin and Mr. Grafton were chosen a committee to whom any persons taxed to religious teachers of another denomination might apply for advice, contain the follow-

1 Rev. 3: 1; 11: 18; Isa. 59: 14. 2 Rev. 16: 15.

ing paragraph: "Whereas the Baptist church and society in the South Parish of Harwich have been taxed, for several years past, to the support of the Congregational minister, to the amount of several hundred dollars, and very considerable sums of it have been actually distrained from them, and in attempting to recover it by law, they have expended near five hundred dollars more: It is therefore earnestly recommended to the several churches, to have a contribution for the said society, in order to assist them in supporting their just rights, and that the money be brought forward to the next association."

Meanwhile, the public sentiment was becoming gradually more favorable to the principles of religious liberty and equality. The arguments and appeals which had been spread abroad in the community were slowly and silently effecting the change desired by their authors. The use of coercion in obtaining support for the ministry was resorted to with increasing reluctance, as an unpopular, if not an unchristian measure. And so great was the change in this direction, during the first twenty years of the present century, that when a convention was called to amend the Constitution, in 1820, it was confidently hoped, by a large body of the people, that legislative interference, for the support of religion, would be at length prohibited, and Christianity be left, as in the beginning, to the hearts and consciences of men.[1] But, although strenuous efforts

[1] John Adams was elected a member of this convention, and thus alludes to the subject before us, in a letter to Henry Channing: "The *cantilena sacerdotis* will be sung as long as priesthood shall exist. I mean not by this, however, to condemn the article in our Declaration of Rights. I mean to keep my mind open to conviction upon this subject, until I shall be called upon to give a vote. An abolition of this law would have so great an effect, in this State, that it seems hazardous to touch it. However, I am not about to discuss the question at present. In Rhode Island,

were made in the convention to accomplish this result, they proved to be unavailing. Not until 1833 was the third article of the Bill of Rights so amended, that Church and State were separated in the Commonwealth of Massachusetts, and soul-liberty, as maintained by Roger Williams and the Baptists of every age, finally and perfectly secured.

I am informed, public preaching is supported by three or four wealthy men in the parish, who either have, or appear to have, a regard for religion, while all others sneak away and avoid payment of anything. And such, I believe, would be the effect in this State, almost universally; yet this, I own, is not a decisive argument in favor of the law. *Sub judice lis est.* The feelings of the people will have pomp and parade of some sort or another, in the State, as well as in the Church. In the Church, they have risen from the parson's band and the communion plate, up to the church of St. Peters and the Vatican library."

CHAPTER XIX.

MINISTERIAL AND HISTORICAL LABORS.

BACKUS' USEFULNESS AS A PASTOR.—REVIVAL IN 1780.—EXTRACTS FROM MR. BACKUS' JOURNAL.—RESTRICTED COMMUNION.—ITINERANT PREACHING.—JOURNEY TO VIRGINIA; REFLECTIONS AT SEA; A PIOUS NEGRO; QUERIES PROPOSED TO A BAPTIST ASSOCIATION IN VIRGINIA.—TREATMENT OF THEM.—BACKUS AS A COUNSELLOR.—ANECDOTE BY REV. SILAS HALL.—HISTORY OF THE SOUTH BRIMFIELD CHURCH; BACKUS' LETTER TO THIS CHURCH.—HIS LABORS AS A HISTORIAN.

HAVING traced the course of Mr. Backus, as an advocate of religious liberty, to its close, we must now return and speak of his labors as a pastor, an evangelist, a counsellor, and a historian.

He was a diligent and faithful pastor, at home among his people, their friend as well as their teacher, taking heed to the flock over which the Holy Ghost had made him overseer. He not only addressed them from the pulpit on the Lord's day, but also from house to house during the week. Until quite advanced in life, he preached, on an average, about two hundred sermons each year, and one half of them in private houses. He longed earnestly for the salvation of those entrusted by the Great Shepherd and Bishop of souls, to his charge, and he labored patiently and persistently to win them to Christ. By the record of his baptisms "at home," it appears that his efforts were not altogether fruitless, during any considerable period. One after another, two or three in a year even in times of declension, those who listened to his preaching were convicted of sin and led to cry out, 'What must we do to be saved?' But the days were evil. There were wars and rumors of wars in the land. Every thing seemed unfavorable to religious prosperity. Yet there were occasionally times of refreshing from the presence of the Lord. One of these occurred in the midst of the war of the Revolution. During the year 1780, God was pleased to remember his people, and visit them in a remarkable degree by his spirit. Since the Great Awakening, there had not been so extensive and deep a work of grace in New England. Though most powerful in 1780, it began the previous year and continued in various places until about the close of 1782. Mr. Backus baptized upwards of seventy-five persons "at home," who were converted during this revival. We subjoin a few notices which he gives of this blessed work in different parts of New England.

"Sept. 12, 1780. Our Association met at the town meeting-house in Royalston. The most remarkable accounts were received of an extensive work of conviction and conversion in various parts of this land that has been known therein for these thirty-seven years."

"Dec. 30th. We [Mr. Backus and Mr. Hunt] had a pleasant passage over to Martha's Vineyard, and I preached in the evening at Jonathan Manter's, where elder Lewis and brother Samuel Parker met us. A glorious work of God has lately taken place here. It began in the following manner. David Butler, his cousin Rebecca Butler, and Abigail Pease, on the east side of Holmes' Hole, and Ebenezer Daggett's wife, on the west side, were brought under soul concern a year ago; the latter by the loss of a son, another by means of a transient preacher; and after great distress of soul were converted in April and May. These were instrumental of awakening many others. And the last of June, David Butler came over and was baptized by elder Lewis; who went to the Island in July and baptized Peter Norton, Esq., High Sheriff of the county, and seven more. He went over again in August and a third time in October. Elder Hunt went there in November, and such a blessing was granted upon their labors that they sent a request to each of us to come over at this time to assist in forming a church among them."

"Dec. 31st. In the year which is now closed, I have travelled nineteen hundred and eighteen miles, and preached two hundred and forty-eight times, with as little weariness of body and with as much liberty of soul as I ever was favored with in my life. The work of conviction and conversion has prevailed more extensively in New England than it has done since the year 1742; and not less than three quarters of the subjects of the work have embraced believers' baptism; so that ten new Baptist churches have been formed in this State, besides what have been formed in others. Very large additions have also been made to our old churches."

"Jan. 14, 1781. Preached once, and baptized six men; the power of God was with us."

"March 3d. My own vileness and insufficiency, and the greatness of my work of watching for souls as one that must give account, were impressed with uncommon weight upon my mind during the last week."

"July 15th. Preached twice in Barnstable, and administered the supper. Isaac Case, of Rehoboth, met me at Baxter's and is still with me. He was converted in December, 1779, aged 19, was called to preach in July, 1780, and was instrumental last winter of a number of conversions here and at Harwich. The church in Barnstable has about doubled her members."

"July 23d, (Pembroke). I find a great change in Mr. Hobart's children since I preached here last year. On Tuesday I went to Marshfield and preached at brother Thomas Joyce's; also again on Wednesday, and twice at David Howard's. A precious number have been converted here in the year past, and they discover a good temper now."

"Sept. 11th. Proceeded from Charlton to South Brimfield, where thirty churches met in association. We had a most agreeable interview, and much business was despatched with great harmony, till our meeting was dissolved Wednesday night. On Thursday, I came and heard Thomas Green preach at Sturbridge in the evening. On Friday I preached there, and also at elder Green's meeting-house in Charlton, where a glorious work has prevailed during the year past."

"Dec. 30th. Another year is now closed, wherein I have been enabled to preach two hundred and fifty sermons, and to journey fourteen hundred and four miles, with health of body and freedom of mind. The work of conviction and conversion has abated in most parts of the country, though we have still great spiritual favors. In South Brimfield the work is lately revived, and it begins to spread in Sandwich, formerly a very ignorant and stupid place. In June a powerful work began in Woodstock, Windsor, Newport and other towns, in or near the State of Vermont; and it reached to Dartmouth College.

The old continental money passed, from July to February, at seventy-five dollars for one of silver; it then depreciated fast till it stopped passing, about May 25th, by reason of news from Philadelphia. On the 26th of May a man at Norwich gave one thousand dollars for a felt hat."

"April 7, 1782. Barnabas Perkins of Hanover in New Hampshire, informs me of a glorious work of divine grace, which began last June in Newport in that state, and which has spread into twenty towns or more. In Dresden and Hanover it has risen to a most happy degree."

"April 21st. (Canterbury.) Preached three times in the centre of the town, where a remarkable revival of religion began on January 20th, so that they had meetings nearly every night for above a month, and fifteen or twenty souls were hopefully converted. After sundry conferences they began, the fifteenth instant, to rebuild their church, each one telling his own experience, and so covenanting together; but the old party, who are for building on human laws, try to counter-work them."

"September 10th. Went to Providence to the meeting of the Warren Association, which was large and remarkably harmonious. Very agreeable accounts were received of a powerful work of grace now going on in Putney, Westminster, Fullum, and towns adjacent, in Vermont; and at Saratoga and Stillwater, above Albany."

The following item in his journal reminds us of an earlier period of his life. "August 20, 1783. Went with my daughter Eunice to Braintree; lodged at my old friend Linfield's; and saw a paper, dated April 25, 1783, attested by John Porter, pastor, which debarred their sister, Hannah Linfield, from communion in that church, for being rebaptized, which implied that infant baptism was a nullity, and so that the church were unbaptized. Thus those who call us very rigid, debarred a sister from communion for no other crime than answering a good conscience in baptism."

The blessed revial of 1780, was followed in Titicut by a long period of relative declension; and not until the labors of Mr. Backus were almost finished, was there another season of extraordinary attention to religion. For upwards of twenty years he continued his work of faith in the patience of hope. One by one a few of those under his care were brought to repentance, but the many appeared to have chosen the world for their portion. Still his ministry was not without a blessing. He endeavored under Christ to keep those who had been committed to his charge and to feed them with the sincere milk of the word. He esteemed it no inconsiderable part of his work to confirm the weak, to comfort the sorrowful, to restore the wandering, to instruct the ignorant, in a word, to edify the body of Christ; and in this department of labor he was successful even when the ungodly refused to hear and be saved. Thus, not without many trials and discouragements, but with many supports and tokens of usefulness, did he remain at his post and preach the Word to his own people until the Lord took him up.

Yet the preaching of Mr. Backus was not confined within the limits of his own parish. Having begun his ministry in the glow of youthful zeal as an evangelist, he seems to have retained through life a great interest in this species of christian effort. He loved to seek out districts which were comparatively destitute of the means of grace, and there preach the gospel to the poor. And when at length churches were planted in these places, he watched their progress with all a father's anxiety. He was acquainted with their leading members, was aware of the obstacles which they had to surmount in carrying forward the work, and rejoiced in their honor and usefulness more than if they were his kindred according to the flesh. Mr. Backus was not, to be sure, singular in this respect. Many of his brethren were accustomed to make excursions in the same way for the purpose of carrying the gospel to all. To mention the names of Hezekiah Smith, Thomas Baldwin, Joseph Grafton, Isaac Case, Stephen Gano, John Leland, and many others of similar spirit, is enough to prove that Baptist pastors of a former age went everywhere preaching the Word. But no one of these, we think, went forth so often and so far to give the Word of life to the destitute as did Mr. Backus. This may have been due in part to the smallness of his church, and to the pecuniary resources which he possessed; but it was chiefly due to the early and deep interest which he felt in this kind of ministerial activity. Without making any particular reference to the numerous visits which he paid to places in New England, it will be sufficient for our purpose in this narrative to furnish a brief account of his journey to the South.

In 1788, the Warren Association held its annual meeting in Sturbridge, on the ninth and tenth of September. At this meeting a letter was received from Virginia, giving some account of a remarkable work of God in that State, and earnestly requesting ministerial aid from the North. By the general voice of his brethren, Mr. Backus was selected to visit Virginia, and Mr. Hunt was requested to accompany him and assist in the work. "This," says Mr. Backus, "was entirely unexpected; but I agreed to take it into consideration and to act as light should be given." He finally decided to go; but Mr. Hunt was unable to accompany him. He sailed from Newport January 2, 1789, and after a rough voyage landed at Washington, in Beaufort County, North Carolina, about noon of the 10th. "While we were tossed," he says, "with the winds and waves, so that the seamen had many fears, I was led to review my life and carefully to search into the motives of this voyage and designed journey, and I had the testimony of my conscience that they were desires to be obedient to the will of God in doing good to the souls of men, and a conviction that this was the way of my duty in that respect." In the town of Washington, where he landed, Mr. Backus found a few brethren, and began without delay to proclaim the gospel. Obtaining a horse, he set forth on his journey, preaching as he went. Almost every day he found opportunity to discourse upon the vital doctrines of Christianity, in meeting-houses, court-houses, or dwelling-houses. Between January tenth and May twenty-seventh, he travelled on horseback twelve hundred and fifty-one miles in North Carolina and Virginia, and preached one hundred and seventeen sermons. The people generally were anxious to hear, and there is reason to believe his labor was not in vain in the Lord. Yet the notices of his diary are very brief, giving for the most part scarcely more than the names of places where he preached, and of persons with whom he became acquainted. We copy the following passages:

"March 27th. Mr. Templeman told me that overhearing a christian negro of his expressing his sense of the evil of his master's selling liquor on the Sabbath, provoked him so that he got a stick next morning with an intent to scourge him for it; but as soon as the negro saw his master come into the stable where he was, he very humbly asked liberty to speak; which being obtained, he gave a relation of his experience, which was followed with such an exhortation to his master as not only made him forget his cruel design, but also proved a means of his conversion."

"May 11th. We [the members of the association] met early, and three sermons were preached out under the trees, while the association went through their business in the meeting-house. Advice was asked in various cases; as whether a man might be an elder at large who was ordained over a small church and then dismissed? Whether all elders were equal in office? What should be done when a man slave was owned by one master and his wife by another, and one was carried to such a distance as never to be likely to see the other in this world? Whether they must continue single or not? Also, whether a master or mistress had a right to correct servants who were members of the same church, for family disobedience? In these and other cases, at their request, I gave the best light I had; and there appeared such a willingness to learn and to do the will of God, and our interview before had been so agreeable, and withal likely to be the last in this world, that our parting was much like that recorded in Acts 20 : 36–38."

"May 16th. Came through part of Surry and Southampton counties to elder Barrows' meeting-house in Isle of Wight county, to an association of churches, partly of Virginia and partly of North Carolina. This association was held amongst the small remains of an Arminian Baptist church which was gathered by Elder Norden, who came from London, 1714; the first Baptist church in Virginia, I suppose. They were reduced almost to nothing, when Elder Glamore and others came and preached sovereign grace among them, and a great reformation has taken place in these parts."

Besides accomplishing the direct object of his mission, Mr. Backus in this journey made himself acquainted with the history and condition of the churches which he visited; so far, at least, as this could be done in a brief period by inquiries upon the spot. The memoranda which he took at the time were not, however, of such a nature as to interest the general reader. Names and dates may be invaluable to the historian, but they convey little instruction to the mind of him who glances his eye rapidly over them and passes on.

It should also be remarked that Mr. Backus was often called to assist by his counsel in the settlement of ecclesiastical difficulties. In the collection of his manuscripts there is still a bundle of papers — the sheets being no larger than the palm of a man's hand — which describe in plain and simple language the journeys made by him during a series of years. From these papers we have made several extracts in a previous chapter to illustrate his spirit and success as an Evangelist. They show, however, not only the frequency and extent of his travels to preach the Word, but likewise, incidentally, the confidence felt by the churches in his wisdom and impartiality. For although in many instances he was led to go from place to place solely by his desire to proclaim the gospel and win men to Christ, it is made but too certain by these artless records that he was often called to sit in council with his brethren for the settlement of difficulties. Indeed, it is obvious from the papers to which I have referred, and from other sources of information, that the second half of the last century was a period of religious no less than of political agitation. It was a period of inquiry, discussion, action, transition. Laws, usages and opinions were fearlessly called in question. Men were earnest and energetic rather than amiable and wise. In the Baptist churches there were many restless spirits to be guided, and many difficult problems to be solved. Their members were for the most part zealous, independent and conscientious, but not always intelligent, liberal and far sighted. Hence it was not a strange thing for their pastors to suffer want and to charge their people with neglect. Hence, too, there were differences of opinion as to the course which ought to be pursued when the civil government trespassed on the territory of religion. And hence, likewise, whatever may have been the proximate causes, there were more frequent differences between brethren of the same church than we observe at the present day.

Mr. Backus was thoroughly versed in the principles of church polity laid down in the New Testament. His opinions were carefully drawn from this sacred fountain, and were, it is believed, intelligible, consistent and well-grounded. If we add to this the fact that he was personally known to a great part of the Baptists in Massachusetts, Connecticut and Rhode Island, it will be readily understood why he was present at so many ecclesiastical councils, and why he was so useful in reconciling dissensions. For obvious reasons we shall refer to but one or two instances in illustrating this part of his work as a servant of Christ.

"The following anecdote," says Rev. Silas Hall, "is sometimes related by the aged Christians in this region. An unpleasant rupture took place between Rev. Mr. Alden, late of Bellingham, and a certain Mr. Mann, a member of his church. All attempts for a reconciliation were in vain. At length a number of ministers were called together for consultation and advice; among them were Stillman of Boston, Manning of Providence, and Backus of Middleboro'. The conference was held at the house of Rev. W. Williams in Wrentham, and they spent the afternoon and almost all the following night in their pious efforts; but the parties were unyielding, and there was not the least prospect of a settlement. For a long time Mr. Backus had sat with his head bowed down, and appeared to be sleeping. A little before break of day (which is said to be the darkest time) Mr. Backus rose up, saying, 'Let us look to the throne of grace once more;' and then kneeling down, he prayed. The spirit and tone of his prayer were such as to make every one feel that the heart-searching God had come down among them. The result was, the contending parties began immediately to melt, and the rising sun saw the rupture healed and closed up forever."

We give another specimen of the labors of Mr. Backus as a counsellor, for two reasons; first, because it will acquaint the reader with the principal, if not the only instance in which the Baptists were justly charged with having endorsed the principles of the Standing Order as to the support of ministers; and secondly, because it will illustrate the way in which Mr. Backus always treated questions of church polity.

A small Baptist church was organized at South Brimfield on the fourth of October, 1736. Mr. Ebenezer Moulton was ordained pastor of this church on the fourth of November, 1741. Soon after, during the great awakening, Mr. Moulton and a number of his church were convinced of being still in an unregenerate state and were presently brought into God's marvellous light. This led to bitter dissensions in the church, until in the winter or spring of 1748, Mr. Moulton and ten or eleven of the old church gave an account of their experiences to one another, and having prepared and signed articles of faith and covenant, left the rest of the church, without letters of dismission, and proceeded to administer the ordinances by themselves. Affairs remained in this posture several years; but at length Moulton removed to Nova Scotia, and Mr. James Mellen of Framingham was chosen his successor. He was ordained on the eleventh of September, 1765. But Dr. Lawrence and some other Pedobaptists, being displeased with the settlement of a minister of their own denomination, the same week in the other part of the town, persuaded Mr. Mellen that they would get a parish set off there, and would make rates for him. He and some of his people were so unwise as to listen to this proposal. Accordingly, application was made to the General Court, and the winter following they were set off as a parish by themselves and made rates one year for Mr. Mellen. But a considerable part of the Baptists did not unite in this movement. And now the Pedobaptists moved to have a large meeting-house, which the Baptists had previously built, made over by vote to the parish; and because the Baptists would not consent to this they declined paying their rates in the following year to Mr. Mellen. The collector, wishing to be impartial, strained upon one Baptist and one Pedobaptist, and sold their goods at vendue. The matter was brought before a legal tribunal, which determined that Mr. Mellen was not such a minister as their law was made to support. Hence no more rates were made for him. Soon after, on the eleventh of June, 1770, the church took the following action: "After supplication to God under our destitute circumstances, it was *unanimously* agreed upon to send this confession abroad amongst our Baptist brethren, viz.: That the method of supporting the ministry by a rate some part of the time of Elder James Mellen's ministry amongst us was not opposed by us as it ought to have been; and for the future

[we] propose it shall be supported by a free contribution; asking forgiveness of God and our brethren; asking your prayers to God for us, that for the future we may conduct as becomes a church of Christ.

Signed by JOSEPH HOVEY, BENJAMIN JOHNSON, } *Deacons*,
In behalf of the church."

Mr. Backus visited South Brimfield, Oct. 18, 1770. By examining the church records, and by conversing with the most intelligent members, he made himself acquainted with the history and condition of the church, and then gave them his advice, in the following letter:

"SOUTH BRIMFIELD, OCT. 22, 1770.

"DEARLY BELOVED: I heartily sympathize with you in your trying circumstances; and my thoughts, this morning, were turned upon those words of the apostle: 'No chastening for the present seemeth to be joyous, but grievous; nevertheless, afterward, it yieldeth the peaceable fruit of righteousness unto them which are exercised thereby: wherefore lift up the hands which hang down, and the feeble knees; and make straight paths for your feet, lest that which is lame be turned out of the way, but let it rather be healed.'[1] These words contain both encouragement and direction, which appear to me suitable to your case; encouragement, though your trials are many, and direction how to proceed in order for relief. And if I might contribute anything towards it, it would add to my joy.

"In order to answer your request of my advice in your case, I would observe that in the next words we are com-

[1] Heb. 12:11—13.

manded to 'follow peace with all men, and holiness, without which no man shall see the Lord,' which words may be explained by those of the prophet, 'Love the truth and peace,'[1] and by those of the apostle, 'The wisdom that is from above is first pure, then peaceable;'[2] which plainly shows that a peace without holiness is to be avoided; but that peace, so far as it consists with truth and purity, is to be followed with all men. And as to church affairs, it is plain that moral evils, such as fornication, covetousness, idolatry, railing, drunkenness, and extortion, exclude persons from a right to communion therein.[3] So does the perverting of gospel doctrines; for of those who did this in the churches of Galatia, the apostle observes the same as he does of these moral evils, namely, that 'a little leaven leaveneth the whole lump,' and says he would that such were *cut off*, that is, excluded from their communion.[4] Also from such as have the form, but deny the power of godliness, we are commanded to turn away.[5] From whence it appears that moral evils, corruption in doctrine, or opposition to the power of true religion, are just bars of communion.

"In the next place, I would observe that the Scripture makes a plain difference between the action of a church and the acting of particular members, with regard to such things. To the church it says: 'What have I to do to judge them that are without? Do not ye judge them that are within? Put away from among yourselves that wicked person.'[6] But when the body of a church have become corrupt and can't be reclaimed, the saints are commanded to come out from among them, and be separate: 'Come out of her, my people, that ye be not partakers of

[1] Zech. 8:19. [2] James 3:17. [3] 1 Cor. 5:11.
[4] Gal. 5:9, 12. [5] 2 Tim. 3:5. [6] 1 Cor. 5:12, 13.

her sins, and that ye receive not of her plagues.[1] Here take notice, that if those who are truly God's people are the minor part, they are not to assume the power of the body, but to come out and separate themselves from it.

"And now to come to your case; I think it is agreed, on all hands, that those who told their experiences and signed the articles and covenant, with elder Moulton, in 1748, were the minor part of the church in Brookfield; therefore they could not properly be said to be the church which the elder first took the charge of. And though I am of the mind that they had just grounds to withdraw from the church, and have no disposition to condemn any past acting among you, in worship and ordinances, which was done with an upright heart,—though those who acted might have been as much wanting in a fruitful understanding of divine rule, as those in Hezekiah's time,[2]—yet I can't see any other way for you now to make straight paths for your feet, but to leave the things which are behind, and begin anew, by freely declaring what God has done for your souls, and so to join in covenant together, and go on to build the old wastes, etc.[3] And if you see light to proceed thus, it will naturally give opportunity of having the case of that sister, which has occasioned such difficulty among you, fairly tried and settled.

"This is the clearest light concerning your case which at present is afforded to your brother and servant in the gospel,

ISAAC BACKUS."

It will also be proper for us to say a few words, in this place, respecting his labors as a historian. These were commenced before the year 1770, and were continued till

[1] 2 Cor. 6:17; Rev. 18:4. [2] Chron. 30:18—20. [3] Is. 61:4.

near the close of his life. They engrossed a large share of his attention. They led him to make many journeys, for the purpose of consulting original papers; and they greatly increased the number of his correspondents. He doubtless composed rapidly, never seeking to adorn his pages with the graces of rhetoric; but, after making all due allowance on this score, it is evident, nevertheless, that a very considerable part of his time must have been consumed in writing. He ascertained most of the events narrated in the second and third volumes of his history, by visiting the localities where they took place, and searching the records on the spot, or taking the testimony of eye-witnesses. Hence it is that the materials of his valuable history may be found, to a considerable extent, in his diary and other manuscripts. From these records, which he was making wherever he went, and into which he compressed a vast amount of facts, he drew out the pages of his history. Had his literary culture been more thorough in early life, he would have made his narrative more attractive to the general reader; but it may be doubted whether he would have been able to give a more truthful account of his own age. His volumes are a full storehouse of events, indispensable to every one who would understand the true history of New England. But to those of his own religious faith, they are specially interesting; for they furnish almost the only memorials which have come down to us, of the piety, consistency, and sometimes heroism of brethren who lived in a darker period, and suffered long to obtain the freedom we now enjoy.

CHAPTER XX.

LETTERS FROM CORRESPONDENTS.

CHARACTER OF THESE LETTERS. — 1. FROM JOB MACOMBER, DESCRIBING A PREACHING TOUR IN MAINE. — 2. FROM JEDEDIAH HEBBARD, COMMENDING MR. BURROUGHS, OF HANOVER, N. H. — 3. FROM THE SAME; EXTRACT, NOTICING THE PERPLEXITY OF SOME AS TO THE CHURCH RELATION OF BAPTIZED CHILDREN. — 4. FROM THOMAS BALDWIN, REFERRING TO THE DOUBTS OF SOME, IN RESPECT TO THE GROUND OF CHRISTIAN FELLOWSHIP. — 5. FROM JOB SEAMANS, DESCRIBING A REVIVAL IN NEW LONDON, N. H. — 6. FROM ELEAZAR CLAY, SPEAKING OF RELIGIOUS LIBERTY IN VIRGINIA. — 7. FROM WILLIAM ROGERS, ON OPPRESSION IN MASSACHUSETTS, ETC. — 8. FROM HENRY TOLAR, ON THE GREAT REVIVAL IN THE MISSISSIPPI VALLEY. — 9. FROM JOSHUA BRADLEY, ON THE RELIGIOUS INTEREST IN NEWPORT, R. I. — 10. FROM JOSEPH CORNELL, ON A REVIVAL IN PROVIDENCE. — 11. FROM JOHN BOLLES, CONCERNING THE GROWTH OF THE BAPTIST DENOMINATION. — EXTRACTS FROM BACKUS' JOURNAL, AT THE CLOSE, RESPECTIVELY, OF 1782, '83, '84, '85, '89, '90, '91, '92, '93, '94, '97, '99, 1800, 1801, '2, '3, '4.

THE historical and other public labors of Mr. Backus gave rise to an extensive correspondence. His own letters have mostly perished; but a large collection of those which he received is in the hands of the writer. Some of them describe journeys, on foot or on horseback, for the purpose of preaching the gospel; some of them local revivals of special interest; some of them, the general state of religion throughout large sections of the country, north or south; some of them, the progress of Baptist sentiments; some of them, the spread of novel and erroneous opinions; and some of them, instances of oppression by the standing order. We present a few specimens of this correspondence, in order to assist the reader in forming an estimate of the men and the times with which Mr. Backus was connected.

Job Macomber, the writer of the following letter, was, at the time, a member of Mr. Backus' church, and a licensed preacher of the gospel. In 1782, he visited New Gloucester, Me., where a small Baptist church had been constituted the year previous. On turning to the journal of Mr. Backus, we find this record:

"Oct. 2, 1782. Elder Nelson and Jeremiah Basset, from Taunton church, and elder Job Seamans and Jacob Newland, from Attleboro' met here with our church, to consider a request from the Baptist church in New Gloucester, that we would ordain brother Job Macomber as a gospel minister. Upon mature deliberation, we found that their request was not to ordain him as their pastor, and we had not clearness in ordaining him as a minister at large, and so did not do it."

Mr. Macomber continued his labors for a time in New Gloucester, but soon after the letter which follows was written, he took up his residence in Bowdoinham, where he was ordained pastor of a Baptist church, in August, 1784, and discharged the duties of his office twenty-six years.

"New Gloucester, Me., Jan. 7, 1783.

"Dear Friend: These are to inform you that I and so many of my family as are in these parts are well, and, through the tender mercy of God, we are well provided for. My wife is in a better state of health than she has been for some years.

As for religion in this town, it is at present very low, although there are a number of very agreeable Christians, well established in the faith. But I must inform you that on the third day of December, Capt. Woodman and I set out on a journey east. On the same day I preached at Major Browne's in North Yarmouth; and the fifth day we arrived at Parker's Island, near the mouth of the Kennebec river. I preached the same day. We found there had been a great and marvellous work begun about a year and a half before; and no Baptist minister being nearer than Nathaniel Lord, hearing of them he went to see them and baptized a large number. I cannot now give you the particulars, but they informed me that about sixty had been baptized on this island and on another some eight miles from them. They appeared to be very serious Christians — not the least appearance of any wild disorder among them as in many places in this part of the country. December sixth, I preached on said neighboring island; the seventh, at the town of Wolley; and the eighth, on Parker's Island again — three meetings in the same day. We there heard of a wonderful work in Potterstown,[1] which is about eight miles from Brunswick. We set out for the town and arrived there on the tenth. We found the work had begun about eigthteen months previous, and had been so wonderful among men, women and children, that as they told us, there were none left in the town to oppose them; they were opposed by those out of town, but not by the residents. We had five meetings in the town, and they told us of a town about seven miles distant, called Smithsfield, where a work was newly begun. We went there and found it was a township newly settled; and as we passed by their cabins and log houses, we could hear their language in christian conversation. In passing this way we had two meetings in the town. At one of the meetings in Potterstown, though a new town, Capt. Wood-

1 Now Bowdoin.

man judged there were above two hundred people on a very cold day. One James Potter in said town met with a change about eighteen months ago, being near forty years old; and as there was no preacher in the place he told me he had spent fifteen months of the eighteen in going from house to house warning the people of their danger in a state of sin. Before he met with his change he was pursuing the world greedily, and obtained a great estate; but now he says that he had rather throw this estate all away than to have his mind entangled with it. His greatest gift appears to be in prayer and conversation. In discoursing with little children and with young converts his labors have been much blessed; and it seems to be no cross for him to go from house to house and exhort men, women and children. He told me that he had been a week from his family in a town called Bowdoinham, where there were signs of a great work, some in almost every family being under deep concern for their souls.

"On the sixteenth we left the town, and Mr. Potter went with us as far as a place called Little River, where there had been indications about three weeks before of a spiritual moving in the minds of a large number. Mr. Potter told us they had been a very secure, unconcerned people. We held a meeting there in the evening; and on the eighteenth we arrived home in New Gloucester, having been absent fifteen days, and having held eighteen meetings.

"Before we took this journey, Capt. Woodman had been very worldly minded for some time, but after he got home he spent two or three days in going from house to house and discoursing with his neighbors concerning their souls. As for my own part, I can tell you that I never had so great satisfaction in any visit or journey in all my life, nor so great freedom in preaching. These words were often in my mind: "The wilderness shall blossom as the rose."

"The people at Potterstown were brought up with the common denomination, and had never heard a Baptist preacher more than once before. In that case, Mr. Nathaniel Lord preached as he was coming from the islands where the work first began; and they said they had never before heard such a sermon as he delivered. Before going to visit them we had heard that they were of the common denomination; but when we came to discourse with them, it appeared that the greatest part of them had been led by the Word and Spirit of God, into believers' baptism, and were waiting for an opportunity to be baptized. * * *

"I desire you would send me a few lines by the bearer, to let me know how you and our brethren do. So I conclude, wishing you heaven's blessing.

From your friend and brother,

JOB MACOMBER."

Our knowledge of Mr. Hebbard, writer of the letter given below, is derived entirely from his correspondence with Mr. Backus. He was baptized by the latter, June 6, 1771, and is described as "a sensible and gifted brother." He was pastor of a small Baptist church in Lebanon, N. H., and several of his letters evince much intellectual vigor, as well as soundness of doctrinal belief and active piety.

"LEBANON, [N. H.], OCT. 11, 1784.

"DEAR BROTHER:—In general it is a time of declension in religion; but we have reason to rejoice in God, for he is carrying on a glorious work at the creek towards

Lake Champlain.[1] The last I heard was that sixteen towns were wonderfully visited with the outpouring of God's spirit.

"And the Lord has visited C——, so that there have been very lately between twenty and thirty hopeful converts; the work has also reached the next town. These are neighboring towns, and there is some appearance of conviction in our town. Dear brother, let us rejoice in God and his work.

"In these parts there is a great struggle about church discipline, and some have got on so far that men of the world call them distracted and say they will turn the world upside down; but they do n't consider that then it will be right side up. Mr. Burroughs, of Hanover, a town adjoining Lebanon, has written a piece holding forth the spirit of the churches and of discipline. I desire you to write me your thoughts upon it. I can say I think it an alarm from the walls of Jerusalem; and with these lines I send you a copy. Last Thursday night I lodged with Mr. Burroughs, and told him I intended to send you one of his books. He desired that you would write a letter to him, and condemn without flattery whatever you discover in the piece that is not agreeable to truth; but if you think it is according to truth, to signify the same in your letter.

"Mr. Burroughs has a very clear understanding of the doctrine of the cross, and seems to be willing to take it up. He has fellowship with the Baptists, and has exchanged with elder Baldwin, of Canaan, on the Sabbath. The reason, as he tells me, is because the Baptists in their discipline, honor Christ's laws, and do not, in so daring a manner, trample on Christ's authority. Desiring your

[1] Probably Otter Creek, Vt.

prayers for us, and wishing that grace, mercy and peace may be multiplied to the churches, I rest your brother in gospel bonds,

JEDEDIAH HEBBARD.

Elder Isaac Backus."

We select part of another letter from the same hand. "Our Congregational ministers in this region are forming an Association now. They can't agree with the Presbyterian Association lately formed here; for the latter hold that children sprinkled are in the church and under its authoritative care and watch, and the former do not. It seems they are at a loss to know whereabouts baptized children — so called — are, as to their relation to the visible church of God, or what their standing is; and this will always be the case when men, or societies of men, proceed without divine warrant in building or disciplining churches. Their language will be confounded. Sir, can you tell how many languages those that are building the Babel of infant baptism speak in that particular? But I acknowledge they are rather to be pitied and prayed for, than reproached; and I believe many are honest and sincere Christians, and are come to Mount Zion, the city of the living God.

"If you observe anything too hard in the above observations, impute it to my infirmity, and be so kind as to admonish me as a brother therefor; for I hold many of other denominations in charity, and am willing to walk together so far as we are agreed. I heartily wish a unity of spirit among Christians of different denominations might be secured; for it would not only be for the increase of love, charity and other christian graces, but also of greater freedom of thought. * * Sir, I have a desire to know whether our denomination in your State is like to obtain their religious liberty, or whether there has anything new turned up since the last association. I desist, begging your prayers for me, and the prayers of the saints with you, that I may know my duty, and have grace to do the same.

The Lord be with you, — from your friend,

JEDEDIAH HEBBARD.

LEBANON, MARCH 27, 1781."

Our readers will need no introduction to Thomas Baldwin, for so many years pastor of the second Baptist church in Boston. His letters to Mr. Backus were generally brief, owing, perhaps, to the amount of labor required of him as a preacher of the gospel. We present one which was written soon after he entered the ministry, while doing the work of his Master in a rugged and obscure town of New Hampshire.

"CANAAN, (N. H.), SEPT. 3, 1787.

"VERY DEAR SIR: — I received yours of July 9th, but have since had no opportunity to write till the present moment, which I gladly embrace. Nothing very special among us at present in respect to religion, at least no general awakening. Two of a city and one of a family are taken and brought to Zion. There is a measure of peace in our churches, although there are some trials respecting the new ideas of the atonement. These were treated somewhat in our association, as you doubtless will see by the minutes, and may be further informed of by elder Fletcher, who was present and heard the debate. * *

"I hear that there is a glorious work of reformation in many towns in Connecticut, particularly in Stonington, Groton, New London and Lyme. We also hear that the savages near the Ohio are submitting to the authority of truth.

"Many minds in these parts are perplexed respecting the ground of christian fellowship. Those that prefer communion with all Christians, plead for their practice chiefly, Rom. 15: 7. I wish your thoughts on that passage. Our association has requested me to write upon the subject against the next meeting. I hope to hear from you before long. My unfeigned desires are to the head of the church that this innocent cause may prosper, and I hope that you may be continued in your usefulness for a great while to come, that you may lean your head on Jesus' breast, and bring forth much fruit in old age. * * Please remember me to your dear consort, and permit me to subscribe myself.

Your brother in tribulation,

THOS. BALDWIN.

ELDER ISAAC BACKUS."

Job Seamans was for several years pastor of the Baptist church in Attleboro', Mass. But he removed at length to New London, N. H., where he labored faithfully and usefully about forty years, until the close of his life. His influence has not ceased to be felt in the place; Baptist sentiments have prevailed to an unusual extent, and to this day the only church in town is the Baptist church. A more intelligent and virtuous community can hardly be found than grew up around this devoted pastor, and transmitted its virtues to the present generation.

"NEW LONDON, Jan. 29, 1793.

"SIR: You may remember that when I saw you at Rowley, I was under trials in my mind, whether I had not stepped out of my lot in Zion, in coming to this town. No created being but myself knows what I have gone through on that account. Indeed, it appears to me that I should have fainted under, and been quite overpowered by, my trials, had it not been for that one single text of Scripture, Habakkuk 2: 3. Not that this was the only supporting scripture; but it was the *great* prop. I trust I shall have cause to bless God for it forever. And now, that you may bless the Lord with me, and that we may exalt his name together, I will give you some account of my deliverance.

"Last election day I preached a lecture to our young people from Mark 10: 21, '*One thing thou lackest.*' Ever after this our people came more generally to meeting, and gave much better attention than usual; but nothing special appeared, until I went to Hopkinton to supply the Baptist church there, Lord's day, August 19th, where I administered both ordinances. Here a good work has been going on since June. As I returned home, my mind was greatly exercised; the above quoted text, with Psalm 27: 4, and 126: 5, 6, Revelation 3: 12, sq., came into my mind, and my meditations on them were sweet. Now I felt great peace in my mind. I saw, to my great satisfaction, that there was a blessing for this people. Now, and never till now, could I give up Attleboro'; and as soon as I gave up Attleboro', I took New London; since which I have been at peace.

"The next Lord's day following, I preached in the forenoon from Exodus 14: 12. The next Monday week a youngerly married man, (excellent in nature,) came to see me to converse about the great concerns of his soul. I found him under heavy conviction, and that he got his wound from that sermon. He informed me that he thought his wife was more distressed than he. Both of them are now rejoicing in Christ. From that time to this, I hope I have preached but few sermons in vain.

"Lord's day, Sept. 23d, was very powerful. Two middle-aged men were struck under deep soul concern, who, with their wives, have been brought out and have joined the church. I can give you no further particular account; for by this time the town was pretty generally alarmed, and there are but few, if any, families amongst us that have not had a share.

"This town consists of about fifty families; and I hope that between forty and fifty souls in it have been translated out of darkness into God's marvellous light, besides a number in Sutton and Fishersfield, who congregate with us. They are aged, middle-aged, youth, and children. Fifteen have been baptized and have joined the church. A number more, I expect, will come forward in a short time; indeed I know of no one of them who is not likely to submit to gospel order; nor is there one person in the town, to my knowledge, who stands in any considerable opposition. As to the work itself, I know not of a dog to move his tongue in this town.

"We have lectures or conferences almost every day or evening in the week. Our very children meet together and converse and pray with each other. And I believe I may safely say, that our young people never were one-quarter so much engaged in frolicking, as they are now in the great things which concern their souls and eternity. The work still continues; though I believe there are not quite so many under heavy conviction as there were some time back. Some things in this work exceed anything I ever saw before. Their conviction has usually been very clear and powerful; so that industrious men and women have had neither inclination nor strength to follow their business as usual. They freely acknowledge the justice and sovereignty of God. I have put these questions to some of them: 'Is God just in casting you off forever?' Ans. 'O, yes!'—'Would God be just in damning you, though he should save another sinner just as bad as you?'—Ans. 'O yes! he has a right to do what he will with his own.' Some have been in such distress that they thought they should live but a few minutes, and those who were with them have been afraid they were dying. When they are delivered, they usually go into travails of soul for sinners—females as well as males, children as well as grown people, have this exercise, and some to such a degree that it has racked and weakened their bodies greatly. Also, they have desire , beyond what I have ever known, for a universal out-pouring of the Spirit.

"Perhaps my long broken letter will weary you; but I have only given you a sketch. I shall only add, that through superabounding grace to the vilest, I must say that, for the most part, my mind is comfortable and much encouraged; and I, with my wife, have abundant reason to bless God that we hope our oldest child (Sally) is brought into the kingdom; and our oldest son (Charles) has been under amazing distress of mind—I shall never forget his groans; but although he is relieved of his burden he is not clear in his own mind. Others of our children are thoughtful.

"I hope, sir, that you enjoy much divine consolation in the last stage of your journey; as, I doubt not, you will have many seals of your ministry, which will be stars in your crown forever. * * With sentiments of esteem and friendship, I subscribe myself your brother in the faith and fellowship of the gospel.

JOB SEAMANS.

REV. ISAAC BACKUS."

During his visit to the South, Mr. Backus became acquainted with the Rev. Eleazar Clay, who resided in Chesterfield county, Virginia, and who is characterized by him as a "wealthy and most agreeable Christian." Mr. Clay was a prominent and useful minister of the Baptist persuasion, and the acquaintance then formed was kept up by frequent correspondence.

"MARCH 29, 1799.

"AGED AND REVEREND BROTHER: * * In the church which I serve we have a great calm. Are not such times more to be dreaded, than when the billows are near bursting over our heads? Or has not God set one over against the other, that we may learn to fear him, who worketh all things after the counsel of his own will? In some of the churches of our district God has granted precious revivals; to wit, in the churches of brother Saunders and brother Flowers. Other ingatherings are small,—iniquity abounds, deism prevails, and the spirit of the world comes in like a flood on every side. * * * God has at last touched the hearts of our rulers, and they have listened to our memorial, doing away all we asked for. * * * So that all the clouds which threatened religious liberty with us are blown over. The Lord grant, that neither we nor our posterity may forget his favors, bestowed so freely on us. * * * From your history, you were not then free from the hand of power; may God grant you your request, after all your labors and toils, and an abundant entrance into his heavenly kingdom,—is the prayer of your unworthy friend and Christ's servant in the Gospel,

ELEAZAR CLAY."

The Rev. William Rogers, D. D., with whom Mr. Backus held correspondence for many years, was pastor of the first

Baptist church in Philadelphia, and Professor of Belles-Lettres in the University of Pennsylvania. He was a man of liberal culture, an active Christian, and a zealous friend of religious liberty.

"PHILADELPHIA, DECEMBER 20, 1799.

"DEAR SIR: * * * Our metropolis is now all pensiveness on account of the death of the venerable Washington. The United Sates have most assuredly lost a friend and a uniform patriot!

"I hope this will find you restored to health, and that your valuable life may be protracted many years to come, as a blessing to our Baptist Israel and to the church of God generally. The revivals of religion which you speak of are peculiarly illustrative of the glorious doctrines of grace,—"the wind bloweth where it listeth." Oh for the outpourings of the same Spirit in this city, where spiritual deadness is preëminently apparent and extreme wickedness boldly triumphant! Brother Baldwin transmitted me his printed details of the many revivals; verily, if God works, none can let!

"Of our associated connection, the New Britain church and one or two more, are at this time under similar visitations of kindness from the Almighty, though not to so great a degree. We will give thanks even for the day of small things.

"You will see by the enclosed *Aurora*, that I have made some use of that part of your excellent letter which relates to the shameful oppression of our brethren in Massachusetts. The introductory remarks are by the editor of the *Aurora* himself. In one or two instances, in the extract itself, I took the liberty of altering the phraseology only —strictly adhering to the sense. I trust this publication at the seat of government and in these middle states, will, if no other good be produced thereby, cause a relaxation of some sort to take place in the system of New England despotism! * * *

Very affectionately your friend and brother,

WILLIAM ROGERS."

In the following letter, from the Rev. Henry Tolar of Virginia, reference is made to the great revival in the valley of the Mississippi. In this revival, which was shared by the Presbyterians and Methodists, the Baptist churches, in Kentucky and Tennessee only, received by baptism more than ten thousand converts in four years. It may truly be said, that the wilderness was made to bud and blossom like the rose.[1]

"WESTMORELAND, VIRGINIA, AUGUST 8, 1801.

"BELOVED BROTHER: Two years ago you gave me a pleasing account of the work of God in various parts of New England. I could say in return, that, it would seem a greater work has appeared in Kentucky, but will only observe that two thousand five hundred had been baptized there since the beginning of last August, when we received the information last spring. There have been great revivals in some churches in this State within a year or two, particularly on James River. But alas, we have very little prospect of a great revival here. However, we may say, I trust, the Lord is with us. We have many visits of late by ministering brethren. I baptized nine persons last month, and have a few more to baptize now, and it seems that a serious inquiry has overtaken a few.

1 See an interesting account of this revival, by J. M. Peck, in the Christian Review of October, 1852.

"I cannot flatter myself that we shall see you here again, but wish we could. I have sometimes an inclination to visit your country, but I know not what God intends with me. May we each wait in the place and service we ought to be in! May the many revivals begun in different States of this Union, spread, till the earth shall be full of the knowledge of the Lord! And may the Lord be with you, and make your last your best days! * * * is the prayer of your very unworthy fellow-laborer in Christ's vineyard,

H. TOLAR."

It will be inferred from the first sentence of the following letter, that the writer, Joshua Bradley, pastor of the Baptist church in Newport, Rhode Island, was in some sense an agent for the sale of Mr. Backus' works. While omitting the subsequent details, we have retained this sentence for the purpose of calling attention to the fact, that Mr. Backus seems to have taken the pecuniary responsibility of his published works in general, and also to the fact that his brethren in the ministry made special efforts to increase their circulation. Many of his brethren obtained subscribers for his history, distributed the work and forwarded to him the pay.

"NEWPORT, [RHODE ISLAND] FEBRUARY 13, 1805.

"DEAR SIR: I am sorry that I have been disappointed in not receiving the money for your books which I sent into Connecticut. Brother West informed me last October that he would exert himself to send it before winter. * * * Concerning the good work among us, I have the happiness to observe that, in my opinion, it is increasing. I have baptized thirty-five since I saw you at Warren, and there are about fifteen more who profess to hope in Christ of late. Many of them, I think, will soon put on Christ and walk in the footsteps of the flock. The Lord was pleased to bless brother Kendall's preaching here, while I was at Kingston, to the awakening of some. Oh, pray for us, and especially for such a worthless sinner as I am. The more I study the holy Scriptures and see the glory of God shine around me, so much the more I am led to see the need of the Spirit to assist me, and of the righteousness of Christ to stand as the only sure ground of my acceptance before God. I can say from my heart, I do abhor self and am determined to deny it, take up my cross and follow Jesus.

Affectionately yours,

JOSHUA BRADLEY.

REV. I. BACKUS."

We add two letters more, one from Joseph Cornell, pastor of the Second Baptist Church in Providence, and the other from John Bolles, pastor of the Baptist church in Hartford. They were written at a very interesting period in the history of Zion.

"DEAR SIR: Your heart would rejoice, were you in Providence; for the Lord has come down like rain on the mown grass. The groans of the wounded and the songs of the delivered are heard almost continually. Twenty-four were baptized, and nineteen joined with the Baptist church on Lord's day, and many more are brought into liberty. The work is still going on in various parts of the town; our assemblies have increased, till our meeting-houses are full, and in some instances there is not room enough to receive them. The ears of the people are open to hear, and we hope the Lord will yet do greater things for us all, though we are most unworthy. The blessed Jesus must needs come through Providence, and make our hearts sing for joy; for which we would forever praise his most holy name. Pray for us, that, whilst we have left our wide field of the West and North, with the many tender plants of Christ's plantation in the wilderness, to come to this old town, we may not do anything against the truth, but for the truth. My unfeigned regards to all the family and church. God be thanked, we are all well. From yours, in Christ our Lord,

JOSEPH CORNELL.

PROVIDENCE, April 8, 1805."

HARTFORD [CT.], Nov. 9, 1805.

"MUCH RESPECTED AND DEAR ELDER: I thank the Lord that your useful life is yet continued; and I thank you for remembering your unworthy friend, and for the very friendly and interesting letter which you wrote me on the nineteenth of August last. The agreeable facts therein stated, showing the great increase of Zion's cause in our happy land and among our acquaintance, rejoice my poor, tried, unbelieving heart. When I look back on the fathers of our day and think what conflicts they have had with spiritual wickedness in high places, and now see the great deliverance which God has wrought for his gospel church, and then take a view forward to the still more glorious day when Jerusalem shall be made a praise through the earth; with what pleasing prospects may the faithful fathers yield up their missions with their breath into the hands of Jesus, who has called them and enabled them to be faithful to the death! My prayer to Almighty God is, that your active life may not stop at the advanced age of eighty-two years, but that you may yet live to see the increase of the Redeemer's kingdom, so that you may longer rejoice in hope of the glory of God. * * *

I remain, as ever, your friend
and unworthy brother in the truth,
JOHN BOLLES."

"P. S. After writing the above, I thought to mention some of the wonderful works of God's grace in parts of this State. In the town of Suffield, eighteen miles from Hartford, there has been the year past a marvellous shower of divine grace. One new Baptist church in the east part of the town, in fellowship with Elder Hastings' church, has been constituted; and the members that have been added to both are more than one hundred. In Lebanon there has been an extraordinary work. A large meeting-house was built by the Presbyterian people in a contention among themselves; and after it was done, on account of some dislike to the party that built, the Presbyterian ministers refused to preach in it, and the committee applied to the Baptist Association for preaching. The Lord was pleased to bless the labors of his servants, and last September there was a Baptist church constituted in gospel order, under the pastoral care of Elder Nehemiah Dodge. Since that time numbers have been added to the church; and the Baptist interest is gaining foot in that region, and in various places of this State, where our principles and people have been and still are spoken all manner of evil of. There is great attention to the word spoken, and many precious souls are hopefully brought to love the Lord Jesus, are willing to own his despised cause and follow his humiliating example. Thus the Lord is carrying on his work, raising up and sending forth faithful laborers into his glorious harvest. Ride on, ride on, O thou Prince

Immanuel, till the whole world shall crown thee Lord of all! I might continue such information; but concluding the good news from your old State has reached your ears before now, I shall forbear, — wishing you the pleasure of seeing Zion arise among your own dear people. J. B."

But while Mr. Backus, during the last thirty years of his ministry, was often cheered by tidings from different places where God was reviving his work and enlarging the borders of Zion, he was also reminded, by a thousand signs, of the general indifference to religion and devotion to worldly pursuits, which were characteristic of this period. Universalism began to prevail; novel views of the Atonement and of the higher nature of Christ were spread before the public by means of the press, and were tacitly endorsed by many of the standing order; and pride, extravagance and injustice were doing their strange work throughout the land. It is necessary for us to bear in mind these darker features of the times, in order to appreciate the language which Mr. Backus so frequently used in his diary at the close of another and another year. With a few extracts from this language we shall complete our survey of the last period of his life.

At the close of 1782 he says: "The doctrine of salvation for all men had spread so far in our country, that I thought it my duty to write against it — which [writing] was published at Providence on the fourth of June. In August, a pamphlet in favor of that heresy was published at Boston; in which Dr. Chauncy is judged to have a leading hand, and most of the ministers in Boston appear to favor it. In August also a second edition of Relly was published at Providence. These things have helped to shake down religious establishments by human laws."

"1783. Great indeed have been the events of this year. The British court gave up her claims of power over the American States, November 30, 1782. Preliminaries for peace were signed at Paris on the twentieth of January, 1783, and the peace was settled there on the third of September following. In the mean time, the *great men of the earth* crowded in their fine wares upon us, which all ranks of people in America were fond of buying, to an unspeakable damage in the sinking of public credit and the most extravagant gratification of pride, intemperance, fraud and cruel oppression."[1]

"1784. In our parts, and through most of the country, a sort of dead sleep has seized the minds of the people, so that public worship has been more neglected than ever before since New England was planted. Intemperance, profaneness and cruel oppression, have also greatly prevailed."

1785. "Considerable revivals of religion have been granted on our eastern coasts, in New York, in portions of New Jersey, and in some other places; but through most of New England, profaneness, intemperance, cruel oppression, damnable heresies, and a dead sleep about religion, have prevailed beyond what I never knew before."

Similar remarks occur in his review of the next four years.

"1789. Such a revival has been granted in the towns of Swansey, Rehoboth, Warren and Dighton, that about two hundred and fifty persons have been baptized. In the fall of 1788 a like revival began in our western borders, so as to gather a new Baptist church in Conway, and another in Buckland. In Hampshire and Berkshire not less than four hundred and fifty have been baptized; and

1 Rev. 18: 23.

many also in our northern and eastern counties. Yet in most parts of New England, a careless neglect of religious worship, and a spirit of fraud, oppression and sensuality, have prevailed to an amazing degree."

"1790. God hath visited many places by the converting influences of his Holy Spirit, public confidence in our continental government hath been considerably revived, and the fear of the people is a greater check to the lusts of officers, than in any government ever before erected by man. Yet the authority of the holy scriptures seems to lie as a dead body in our streets; but I hope for a glorious resurrection soon."

"1791. In several parts of the country, religion has been revived. Six new Baptist churches have been formed in our state. But a narrow selfishness hath prevailed so far about the support of Baptist ministers, that petitions from several societies have been carried to our Legislature for incorporation. * * * Fraud seems to have reached its height. But Zion's God reigneth; glory to his name!"

"1792. Wonders of the grace of God have appeared in many places."

"1793. A few have been awakened in our society, and one hopefully converted, though she hath not had strength to come forward and join the church. But such a glorious visitation hath been granted to the third Baptist society in our town, that about forty have been baptized, and a number in Carver. A great blessing also hath been granted in Barnstable and Harwich as well as Plymouth. Elder Case informs me that in two years past, fourteen Baptist churches have been gathered in the counties of Cumberland, Lincoln and Hancock. Many other places have likewise enjoyed heavenly showers, while amazing stupidity and extravagance generally prevail."

"1794. The grace of God has been gloriously displayed in various parts of our country, especially in the district of Maine and in New Hampshire."

"1797. Stupidity and infidelity are as visible in our land as ever they were since Christianity was planted therein. Yet several places have been happily visited in the year past. The Baptist church at Montville, under the care of elder Reuben Palmer, has had sixty members added to it; and the church in Groton, where elder Wightman died in November, 1796, had twenty-eight added before October 1797, when the work was still going on. The same number was also added to the church in Shutesbury between April and September, where more were expected soon. A like work was granted at Norwich and Thetford in Vermont, and at Lyme in New Hampshire. Last summer a work began at Buckland and Ashfield, which spread into Conway in the fall with great power; also into Colerain; and the two churches in Ashfield were happily united again."

"1799. Though great coldness about religion prevails in most of our country, yet it has been lately revived in more places than for eighteen years before. In the year closing with last June, two hundred and fifty-nine persons were added to the three Baptist churches in Shaftsbury, while not one member died in either of them during the year; seventy-six were added to the church in Sandisfield; above fifty to brother Nelson's church in Hartford; above eighty to elder Lee's in Lyme; eighty-two to elder Hall's in Cushing, county of Lincoln."

"1800. The revivals of religion in different parts of our land have been wonderful!"

"1801. Although stupidity has greatly prevailed in our land, yet religion has been revived in many places.

Thirty-three have been added to the two Baptist churches in Boston; thirty-four to that in Wrentham; thirty-three, to the first in Attleboro'; thirty-eight, to Woodstock; twenty-nine, to Harvard; sixty-two, to elder Hick's in Rehoboth; one hundred, to that in Dighton; and the like in many other places. In a letter from Georgia, dated Nov. 17, 1801, it is said: "According to the best accounts from Kentucky, there have been added to the Baptist churches since last March nearly six thousand, while multudes were joining the Methodists and Presbyterians."

"1802. Our religious privileges are still very great, and a powerful work of grace is going on in Newport, in Somerset near Swanzea, and in several towns of New Hampshire and Vermont."

"1803. We hear joyful news from several places. Religion is revived in the south part of our town and in many southern towns. In Boston there is the greatest work going on which they have ever known there. A measure of it prevails in Charlestown, Malden, Woburn, Reading, Salem, and more distant places."

"1804. During the past year, nineteen persons have been received into our church, and more are expected soon. Elder Kendall has baptized twenty-four at Carver and ten at Kingston within three months; and there has been the greatest work ever known in Boston within the last two years. Two hundred and eleven persons have been baptized the year past in both churches, making six hundred and seventy-five in the two churches, and the work is still going on there and in other places."

Thus did the present century, the era of modern missions, begin with a signal outpouring of the Holy Spirit; and even while we write, a no less extraordinary work of God is in progress. Now, as then, multitudes are flocking to Jesus, and men who have grown gray in his service, exclaim with grateful joy, What hath God wrought! May we not hope for the return of these times of refreshing from the presence of the Lord with greater and still greater frequency, until one shall overtake and unite with another, and the life of the church be a constant revival, an uninterrupted and victorious progress?

CHAPTER XXI.

CHARACTER OF BACKUS.

MR. BACKUS'S FAMILY.—DEATH OF HIS WIFE.—DEATH OF HIS DAUGHTER SIBEL.—HIS OWN DEATH.—EPITAPH.—TESTIMONY OF DR. BALDWIN.—BACKUS' REMARKABLE DILIGENCE.—HIS STERLING SENSE.—HIS ARDENT PIETY—HIS POSITION AND INFLUENCE.

VERY little has been said, in the progress of our narrative, of the domestic life of Mr. Backus; not, however, because it was less noble or happy than his public life, but because the sources of information respecting it are scanty, and the events which they preserve, in no way remarkable. Yet it would be unsuitable to close this narrative without noticing briefly the family circle, in which were passed the sweetest moments of his life, and speaking of his character in the tender relations of husband and father.

In a previous chapter, we have described his marriage to Miss Susanna Mason, and have cited the testimony which he bore in old age to her excellence. All the references made to her in his papers, perfectly agree with that testimony. She appears to have possessed, in large measure, those womanly virtues which make home peaceful and attractive. She was frugal, looking well to the ways of her own household. She was thoughtful and affectionate, seeking not only the domestic comfort of her husband, but also sympathizing with him in his religious opinions, and desires, and labors. She was devout, training up her children in the nurture and admonition of the Lord. His union with her continued fifty years, until her death. In his journal for November 24, 1800, we find this record:—

"A heavy day. My wife said but little about dying. Elder Rathbun was here on the twelfth, and prayed with her; and when he asked what she would have him pray for, she said: 'I am not so much concerned about living or dying, as to have my will swallowed up in the will of God.' And on the seventeenth she said much the same to Elder Cornell, who prayed with her. For many weeks she could take no hearty food, and rarely took any drink without vomiting after it. She had much inward pain, but bore it with great patience, and never expressed any fear of death. Thus she wasted away, until about six o'clock this morning, when she expired without any great struggle." Two days later "a large assembly met at eleven; Elder Samuel Nelson prayed; Elder Rathbun preached from Matthew 24: 44, and Mr. Gurney made the last prayer: after which, the remains of my dear consort were interred in our usual burying place. My daughter Nelson and a son, daughter Fobes, with her husband and children, with my children in the house, attended. May this great stroke be sanctified to us all."

Mr. Backus was no stranger to affliction. The death of his mother, whom he tenderly loved, many years before, and the death of his youngest daughter, more recently, had tried his submission to the will of God, and had illustrated in him the power of christian faith. But now a heavier blow had fallen upon him, and he was again called to prove the words: "As thy days, so shall thy strength be; the eternal God is thy refuge, and underneath are the everlasting arms." At the close of this year, he writes:—"The change in my family is unspeakably great; yet my mind has been upheld by God, beyond expectation."

They had nine children,[1] all of whom lived to grow up and gladden the hearts of their parents by dutiful and affectionate conduct. The youngest, however, was taken away at the age of twenty, after a lingering illness. "My daughter Sibel," says Mr. Backus, under date of March 20, 1788, "hath gradually declined, until she was scarce able to sit up to-day. She wasted away very fast, with ulcers in the stomach, which caused much pain; yet we never heard a murmuring word from her mouth. She had a very deep sense of sin upon her mind, and distressing fears that she had not true convictions, because her heart was so vile and hard. She once requested us to pray that she might have such a clear sight of God's righteousness, as to give up her all into his hands. At another time, I asked her if she had such a view of a righteous and gracious God, as to be willing to give up her soul and all into his hands? Her answer was: 'I think I have.' And she gave a like answer to a like question, a few hours before her death, March 23d, at about half-past four o'clock, P. M. I preached twice, and then came and saw my dear daughter pass through the dark valley without such a manifestation of light as I longed for; which grieved my heart. But God is wise and righteous, and hath done us no wrong. So far from it, he hath given us, for twenty years, her life, and for

1 Hannah, born Nov. 8, 1750, died Nov. 24, 1827. Nathan, born June 18, 1752, died March 24, 1814. Isaac, born Feb. 21, 1754, died April 16, 1814. Eunice, born Oct. 23, 1755, died Sept. 16, 1815. Susanna, born Oct 13, 1758, died Sept. 19, 1805. Lois, born Aug. 3, 1760, died Jan. 23, 1853. Lucy, born April 13, 1763, died March 4, 1837. Simon, born March 7, 1766, died July 20, 1833. Sibel, born Feb. 17, 1768, died March 23, 1788.

the most part of that time, her useful labors, in such an obedient manner as scarce ever to need a reproof from us."

Thus, for the first time, was the destroyer permitted to enter the pastor's family and bear away a beloved member. Twice more he came before the father was called, taking first his faithful companion, and then a second daughter. This last affliction preceded by a single year his own death.

On the 10th of September, 1805, Mr. Backus met at Warren, for the thirty-fifth and last time, with the Warren Association. He preached on the evening of the eleventh, and returning home the next day, found his daughter Susanna sick. Under date of September 20th, we find the following language in his journal: "When we came home from Warren, and found my daughter sick, we did not look upon her condition as very dangerous, until the seventeenth; yet she wasted fast away, till she expired, a little after one on the morning of the nineteenth, and was buried to-day. Oh, how sudden and great is this breach in my family!"

But he had little time remaining to deplore his loss. Turning once more to his journal we read, under date of Lord's day, March 9, 1806, this short but characteristic sentence: "I was favored with uncommon freedom in preaching." Within less than a fortnight, he lost the use of his right hand by reason of paralysis: yet he appeared before the people of his charge once more, at the Annual Fast, on the 3d of April, and uttered in their hearing his last public testimony for Christ. On the twenty-third of this month his speech failed; but he lingered along, confined to his bed, until the 20th of November, when he entered into rest.

"The grave of this good man," says Rev. Silas Hall,

"is in the burying-ground near the Congregational meeting-house in Titicut; at the head of which stands a plain stone, with this inscription:

"HERE LIE DEPOSITED, THE REMAINS

OF THE

REV. ISAAC BACKUS, A. M.,

WHO DEPARTED THIS LIFE NOVEMBER 20, 1806,

AGED 82 YEARS AND 10 MONTHS,

IN THE SIXTY-FIRST YEAR OF HIS MINISTRY.

As a Christian and Minister, the character of this man was truly conspicuous. As the pastor of a church in this town, for fifty-eight years, he was eminently useful and beloved. His domestic and relative duties, as a husband and parent, were discharged with fidelity, tenderness, and affection. His zeal and persevering industry in the cause of civil and religious liberty, through a long, laborious life, is still manifest in his writings, as an Historian of the Baptist denomination, and defender of the truths of the doctrine of Christ. Having uniformly borne testimony in his life, conversation, and ministry, of his ardent love to his Divine Master, and the doctrine of the Cross, in an advanced age he was called from his beloved charge and numerous christian friends and brethren, to sleep in Jesus, and his spirit into the garner of his heavenly Father, as a shock of corn fully ripe.

'God was his portion and his guide, through this dark wilderness,
And now his flesh is laid aside, his soul has endless rest.'"

With this record may properly be associated the language of Dr. Thomas Baldwin, his intimate friend, respecting his personal appearance, his manner in the pulpit, and his consistent life. "Mr. Backus' personal appearance was very grave and venerable. He was not far from six feet in stature; and in the latter part of his life considerably corpulent. He was naturally modest and diffident; which probably led him into a habit which he continued to the day of his death, of shutting his eyes when conversing or preaching on important subjects. His voice was clear and distinct, but rather sharp than pleasant.

In both praying and preaching, he often appeared to be favored with such a degree of Divine unction, as to render it manifest to all, that God was with him. Few men have more uniformly lived and acted up to their profession, than Mr. Backus. It may be truly said of him, that *he was a burning and shining light;* and, though dead, he left behind him the *good name which is better than precious ointment.*"

The estimate which we have formed of Mr. Backus, by a somewhat careful study of his life, accords with the testimonies thus given. We shall, however, be permitted, in closing this narrative, to isolate and place in the foreground, a few of his leading characteristics.

Mr. Backus was remarkable for his *diligence.* Accustomed from youth to manual labor, he was able, in the midst of his days, not only to superintend the cultivation of a farm, by which his large family was in part supported, but also, during his early ministry, to aid with his own hands in sowing the seed and gathering in the harvest. But as he advanced in years, and the weight of his public responsibilities increased, he was compelled to desist almost entirely from this kind of service. Not so, however, with his journeys. These were frequent and laborious until the end of life. Over the hills, across the valleys, and beside the streams of New England, he pursued his rugged and toilsome way, and accomplished his useful mission, — whether that mission was to preach the gospel to the poor, to plead the cause of the oppressed, to assist the people of God by his counsels, or to examine the simple records of their history. Once he was thrown from his horse and severely injured; at another time[1] he

[1] "February 1, 1785. Set off early [from Braintree] but the cold north winds so affected my head, that for some miles before I got into Boston,

was near losing his life by the cold; and very often he rode from morning till night in the chill and drenching rain.

He was also a faithful student. Giving little attention to poetry, or any other form of polite literature, he applied himself with deep earnestness to the study of God's Word, with the best helps accessible, and examined with great care the chief works in his own language upon systematic theology, ecclesiastical history, and church polity. He keenly watched the shifting forms of error, and assiduously qualified himself to withstand their approaches. Believing that a minister of Christ should understand the spiritual wants of his own age[1] and prove himself a watchman ever ready to give the alarm, and a champion ever willing to encounter the foe, he strove with uncommon zeal to illustrate this belief by his conduct. Hence he was compelled to read, not only standard works, but the fugitive writings of the day. Besides, he was himself a prolific author.[2] His published writings, including

I cannot recall one idea of any thing that passed, until I found myself by Mr. Freeman's fire in town." The danger incurred by this exposure to cold, is said to have induced Mr. Backus to procure the enormous wig which he wore in his later years.

1 See his Discourse on the "Nature and Necessity of an Internal Call," etc.

2 List of his published writings. — A Discourse on the Internal Call to Preach the Gospel, 1754. A Sermon on Gal. 4: 31, 1756. A Sermon on Acts 13: 27, 1763. A Letter to Mr. Lord, 1764. A Sermon on Prayer, 1766. A Discourse on Faith, 1767. An Answer to Mr. Fish, 1768. A Sermon on his Mother's Death, 1769. A Second Edition of his Sermon on Gal. 4: 31, with an Answer to Mr. Frothingham, 1770. A Plea for Liberty of Conscience, 1770. Sovereign Grace vindicated, 1771. A Sermon at the Ordination of Mr. Hunt, 1772. A Reply to Mr. Holly, 1772. A Reply to Mr. Fish, 1773. A Letter on the Decrees, 1773. A History of the Baptists, vol. I., 1777. Government and Liberty described, 1778. A Piece upon Baptism, 1779. True Policy requires Equal Religious Liberty, 1779. An Appeal to the People of Massachusetts against Arbitrary Power, 1780. Truth is Great, and will Prevail, 1781. The Doctrine of Universal

pamphlets, would make not less than eight volumes equal in size to this memoir; and the addition of his unpublished memoranda and correspondence, would more than double that number. And although he sought perspicuity and accuracy of statement, rather than elegance or force of expression, so that the mere work of composition was less with him than it is with many, it must nevertheless be granted, that he performed a great amount of labor with the pen. This was his constant companion at home and abroad; and a considerable part of his time for thirty years, was spent in arranging the facts or principles which he had obtained, and transferring them to paper.

If, now, we add to all this his labors in the pulpit, and his visits from house to house, among the people of his charge, some idea may be formed of his diligence. He was obedient to the apostolic charge, "Preach the word; be instant in season, out of season; reprove, rebuke, exhort with all long-suffering and doctrine." He preached on an average, during a considerable part of his ministry, about three hundred sermons each year. He visited the sick; administered consolation to the bereaved; restored the wandering; and conversed with

Salvation examined and refuted, 1782. A Door opened for Christian Liberty, 1783. A History of the Baptists, vol. II., 1784. Godliness excludes Slavery, in answer to John Cleaveland, 1785. The Testimony of the Two Witnesses, 1786. An Address to New England, 1787. An Answer to Remmele on the Atonement, 1787. A Piece on Discipline, 1787. An Answer to Wesley on Election and Perseverance, 1789. On the Support of Gospel Ministers, 1790. An Essay on the Kingdom of God, 1792. A History of the Baptists, vol. III., 1796. A Second Edition of his Sermon on the Death of his Mother; to which was added, A Short Account of his Wife, who died in 1800. Published 1803. An Abridgment of the Church History of New England, 1804. A Great Faith described, 1805.

the young at their homes, by the way-side, and in the paths of the fields, telling them of Christ, and urging them to flee from the wrath to come. He was an economist of time; was ever about his Master's business; and was therefore of greater service to mankind than many a pastor of more shining talents.

Mr. Backus was also a man of *sterling sense.* Nothing is more evident, from a study of his life, than that he was esteemed a wise counsellor. No man, of his generation, appears to have been oftener called to give advice in the settlement of difficulties, the gathering of churches, or the ordination of ministers. He possessed little imagination, and no fancy; but his habits of observation were careful, his memory was retentive, his love of right was strong, and the decisions of his understanding were clear and just. So far, at least, as we can ascertain from existing records, the confidence felt by his brethren in the soundness of his judgment, and in his practical wisdom, was not misplaced.

His good sense was no less conspicuous in the estimate which he formed of different writers, and the remarks which he made on their chief productions. Rarely, indeed, if ever, does he refer to an author's style; a silence which doubtless sprang from two sources, — a want of interest in this matter, as compared with the principles advocated, and a feeling of incompetency to undertake the work of literary criticism; but he often reviews the sentiments and arguments of a writer, sometimes for the purpose of commending them, and at others for the purpose of condemning and refuting them. He was a particular admirer of Jonathan Edwards, a man whose intellectual and spiritual vision has not perhaps been equalled since the apostolic age. He speaks of him as " our excellent Edwards," "one of the best men in our land," "an eminent minister," and the author of "an incomparable treatise on the liberty of the will," "which opened its true nature beyond anything that ever was published in latter ages." The estimate which he put upon the writings of other eminent theologians was just and discriminating. This might indeed have been expected; for one who could assign to Jonathan Edwards his true place among his contemporaries, would not be likely to fail in his judgment of others.

But was not Mr. Backus opposed to an educated ministry? Did he not call in question the importance of liberal study, to prepare one for the work of preaching Christ? Was not his mind warped at this point by prejudice, and blind, in a measure, to the advantages of learning? Did he not even cherish a fanatical opinion as to the direct assistance which a minister of Christ is authorized to expect from the Holy Ghost, in conceiving and delivering his message? In reply to these questions, it is to be admitted that he sometimes uses very strong language in favor of "lowly preaching," and perhaps equally strong language in disparagement of the "learned ministry" of his own day. But it is to be remembered, at the same time, that the unlearned ministers of that period were generally men of deep piety, who felt themselves to be called by the Spirit and providence of God, to preach his Word, while many of the educated clergy had, or were thought to have, scarcely any other qualification for their work but learning. Between an unlearned believer and a learned unbeliever, Mr. Backus could not hesitate; the former might be called of God to serve in the ministry of reconciliation, the latter could not have received that divine call; the former might teach the essentials of christian truth, and plead with lost men to believe in Christ; the latter were strangers to renewing grace, and must preach an "unfelt religion," or none at all.

But Mr. Backus was nevertheless a friend to ministerial education. He cherished a lively interest, from the first, in Brown University. He was, for many years, a trustee of the education fund, which was established for the purpose of aiding pious but indigent young men in preparing for the ministry. In his reply to Mr. Fish, he was careful to justify the Separates from the charge of despising learning, and as a Baptist, he was no less careful to recognize the value of liberal culture to the minister of Jesus. He rejoiced in the munificent donations of Hollis to Harvard College, and regretted that his brethren were so generally prevented, by the spirit of the standing order, from sending their sons to that school. And he distinctly specifies learning as a desirable qualification for the ministry. To answer the inquiry, "Who are the true preachers of the gospel?" he says: "In the *first* place, they are all *taught of God*, without which no man can come to his Son. If any man have not the Spirit of Christ, he is none of his. Without it he is not a Christian, but a blind leader of the blind. In the *second* place, all true ministers of Christ receive special gifts from him, for the great work to which they are called. A good natural capacity for teaching, and human learning and accomplishments, especially a good acquaintance with language, and with the best methods of conveying our ideas to others, are of great importance in these affairs."[1]

But he lived in an evil day, when learning was made, by some, the only indispensable qualification for the ministry; and this error was, in his opinion, so radical, so

1 Backus, On the Support of Gospel Ministers, p. 6.

exactly opposed to the will of Christ, that he could not too frequently or too earnestly assail it. His feelings on this subject may have been deeper than those of his brethren, who had enjoyed the benefits of classical study, but his judgment was at one with theirs. Said President Manning, in an address to the graduates of Rhode Island College, September 2, 1789, "Should the christian ministry with any of you become an object, reflect on the absurdity of intruding into it while strangers to experimental religion. See that yourselves have been taught of God, before you attempt to teach godliness to others. To place in the professional chairs of our universities the most illiterate of mankind, would be an absurdity by far less glaring, than to call an unconverted man to exercise the ministerial function. This is to expose our holy religion to the scoffs of infidels, and to furnish to their hands the most deadly weapons. I omit to insist on the account such must render in the great tremendous day!" We recollect no stronger protest than this in the writings of Mr. Backus, and submit the opinion that his usual good sense did not desert him on the subject of ministerial education.

It has also been said, we are informed, that Mr. Backus gave his influence against the payment of salaries to ministers; and his course in this matter has been deplored as unwise and disastrous. In reply to this charge, it may be well to cite his own words. "Again, Paul's foregoing his right of temporal communications from some of his hearers, for particular reasons that he gives, 1 Cor. ix., some have improved, as an argument, that hearers are under no obligation to communicate to any on account of their teaching, but only on account of poverty; and if they are not poor, then not at all; though there is not a plainer command in the Bible for ministers to preach the gospel, than there is for "him that is taught in the Word to communicate unto him that teacheth in all good things.'[1] I trust it has been sufficiently proved, that the authority of King George does not extend to this case; but shall that make us to disregard the authority of King Jesus?"[2] So, in another work, "As the gospel is a pure revelation from God, living of the gospel cannot mean a living by the laws of men, enforced by the sword. Neither can it mean that the bodies of ministers should live upon spiritual food. To communicate unto them in all *good things*, cannot mean only *good words* and *fair speeches;* neither can a *reward for labor* mean *alms to the poor*. Yet the world is full of these absurd imaginations."[3]

"The church is the only house of God upon earth; and it should ever be governed wholly by the revealed *will of God.* And in all expenses, both to the poor and to support gospel ministers, we should communicate *freely*, out of love to the Son of God, who, though he was rich, yet for our sakes became poor, that we through his poverty might be rich. And there ought to be an *equality* in the church, as there was in the church of Israel, when they knew that their bread came from heaven every day."[3] Again, "It is real *robbery* to neglect the *ordinances* of God, as it is to force people to support teachers who will not trust his influence for a temporal living. * * * * Let the *elders* that rule well be counted worthy of double honor, especially they who *labor* in the word and doctrine; for the *laborer* is worthy of his *reward.* Honesty requires a reward for labor, as much as charity does alms for the

1 Gal. 6:6. 2 Reply to Fish, p. 77.

3 "The Liberal Support of Gospel Ministers opened and inculcated," pp. 10, 11, 34, 35.

poor; and it is Babylonian confusion to hold them to be one and the same thing."[1]

Mr. Backus was also distinguished for *earnest piety*. This was the crowning excellence of his character, the source of his energy and his influence. To those who knew him best he appeared to be a man of God, holding daily communion with the Father of lights, a servant of Christ, working ever as "in the eye of his great Task-master."

To be more specific, his piety was evinced by his prayerfulness. Not only did he perform with regularity and solemnity the duty of praying in his family, but so far as we can learn, he was equally faithful in the closet. Our readers have doubtless been reminded of this by many of the extracts which have been made from his journal in the preceding narrative. He was accustomed to ask counsel of God, not only when about to enter upon new and great enterprises, but also when making his plans for the ordinary business of life. He seemed to bear in mind continually the words of Jesus: "Without me, ye can do nothing." And many times he felt himself to be guided in his course by the special influences of the Holy Spirit. It is not therefore surprising that his prayers in public were earnest and appropriate. Says one who is still living: "I have often heard that good man pray. The efficacy of his prayers did not consist in length, nor gaudy dress; but it seemed that he and his God loved one another, and that he was at home before the throne of grace."

His piety was also evinced by a reverent and successful study of the Scriptures. For only the renewed heart is

1 "The Liberal Support of Gospel Ministers opened and inculcated," pp. 10, 11, 32, 35.

completely docile and childlike, ready in all things to be taught of God. Mr. Backus was prepared to understand the Sacred Record by a rich experience of divine grace. The work of the law in revealing sin and slaying the transgressor had been prolonged and thorough in his heart, so that when the cross appeared and deliverance came, the change was like that of passing from darkness to light. "Everywhere," says Augustine, "the greater joy is ushered in by the greater pain." Speaking of himself in the third person, Mr. Backus thus describes his conversion: "In May, 1741, his eyes were opened to see that time was not at his command, and that eternity was directly before him, into which he might justly be called the next moment. Then he knew what it was to *work for his life for three months;* until, on August 24th, as he was alone in the field, it was demonstrated to his mind and conscience, that he had done his utmost to make himself better, without obtaining any such thing; but that he was a *guilty sinner*, in the hands of a *holy God*, who had a right to do with him as seemed good in his sight." No wonder that such a "law-work" as this was followed by a view of divine justice, shining with lustre, in the bestowment of free mercy! nor that God's glory engaged his attention, the burden of his guilt rolling off! nor that he was able thenceforth to comprehend the reasoning of Paul, and behold the cross of Christ, radiant with light and hope for lost men! Such an experience seems, at times, an almost divine interpreter of the gospel. It clears one's spiritual vision, and places him at the right point of observation to see the King in his beauty. Hence, while we believe that a knowledge of the original text would have been of great service to such a man as Backus, in preventing minor mistakes, and disclosing more fully the riches of living truth in God's Word, we would, nevertheless, with sincere gratitude, make mention of the divine goodness, as displayed in giving him a sound mind, and training that mind in the school of experience.

Again, his earnest piety revealed itself in social intercourse. He loved to converse with the friends of Christ, and especially upon experimental religion. He was in the habit of ascertaining, if possible, the spiritual condition of those whom he met at home or abroad. His journal alludes, very often, to conversations, even with strangers, on the subject of personal piety, and contains, no less frequently, notices of men, which presuppose a knowledge of their religious history, obtained from themselves. In one place, we read as follows: "January 10, 1790. Elder Robinson and James Maxcy, A. M., a tutor in Providence College, came here last night. Maxcy gives a clear account of how he was converted, on the twenty-first of last October, *after no more than eleven days' conviction.* When he was alone in his chamber, under a clear sense of the justice of God in his condemnation, such light and love shone into his soul, as struck his body to the floor, and he cried out, 'Glory, glory to God for his free love!' He was soon after baptized by elder Manning, and now talks excellently."[1] And pages might readily be filled with similar memoranda from his various papers.

His fervent piety revealed itself likewise in the pulpit. It was the chief source of his power over an audience. Men were convinced that he "did not preach an unfelt religion," and when he testified of the grace of God, and warned them, in the name of Christ, to flee from the wrath to come, his message made its way to the heart and conscience. Owing to a lack of mental discipline in early

[1] See Appendix G.

life, and to the habit of preaching, oftentimes, without careful preparation, he never became an able sermonizer; —never excelled in the orderly and logical presentation of truth, and rarely unfolded, in his discourses, the relation, coherence and harmony of the various doctrines which he taught. Nor did he rivet attention by vividness of description, beauty of language, or sweetness of voice. All these were wanting. It could never have been said to him, with literal propriety, "Lo, thou art unto them as a very lovely song of one that hath a pleasant voice and can play well on an instrument." And if, in the absence of all these qualities in his preaching, he was able to interest and persuade those whom he addressed, there is but one explanation of the fact. They saw that he was speaking from the heart; they felt that he was bearing witness for God; they perceived the impulses of a divine life in the simplicity, solemnity and fervor of his appeals; they recognized the ambassador of a king when he repeated the words of his master. This was the secret of his usefulness in the pulpit.

Again, his piety revealed itself in a firm adhesion to principle. No apprehension of loss, of reproach, or of danger, caused him to swerve from the path of duty. To all these he was exposed; his character was traduced, his property was seized, and his life was threatened; yet he obeyed the voice of conscience without the slightest apparent hesitation, and remained firm even when others wavered. He seems to have lived with a felt assurance that God is higher than the highest, and that he presides over the affairs of time. And however strange the statement may appear to some of the present age, his political opinions were matured in the closet and often reviewed at the throne of grace. He took part with the colonies in their separation from the British crown, because, "in his nearest approaches to God," he found them to be right. He obtained strength to persevere in his protracted and disheartening labors for soul-liberty, by remembering that it was the cause of his master which he advocated, and by seeking help from that master. "O brethren," said he, in one of his circulars on the subject of religious oppression, "face them down *boldly* upon this point, and they cannot stand. And the best way to attain and enjoy true boldness herein, is a *near approach* to God through Jesus Christ, and a faithful discharge of all the duties of our several stations and relations according to his direction."

Moreover, his piety was evinced by a true charity. Though he strenuously opposed the errors of his time, his productions are free from bitterness and railing. The sharpest language which he employs seems to us but the utterance of a just indignation. His writings contain no bitter taunts, malicious disclosures or dark insinuations. He was a frank and fair opponent, as prompt to correct a mistake of his own as to insist upon justice from others. He was averse to oral discussions, because of their tendency to inflame partisan zeal and call forth intemperate language. Once only, so far as we can learn, did he engage in a public debate, after becoming a Baptist; and then he took the place of another, who was necessarily absent.[1] More than this, he was a lover of good men, whatever might be their denominational affinities. He

[1] Among the arguments used by his opponent in favor of infant baptism, was the gender of the noun *τέκνοις*, *children*, in Acts 2: 39. "For this being a neuter noun," he said, "must signify *infants*, since these are more like inanimate objects, than children of a larger growth." We trust this ingenious argument will not be suffered to perish; though it inclines a little toward the development theory, and reminds one of the "Vestiges of Creation."

honored the piety of those from whom he differed widely in belief. Evidence of love to Christ was a sure passport to his affection. He may have cherished a special attachment to those of his own communion; for they were in a peculiar sense his brethren and companions in tribulation as well as in the kingdom and patience of Christ; but his charity was comprehensive enough to embrace all whose hearts had been renewed by the grace of God. He surrendered with great reluctance his belief that Baptists and Pedobaptists could "build together" harmoniously as a church, and to the end of life he retained a particular regard for many of the New-Lights who defended infant baptism.

It was these qualities—remarkable diligence, sterling sense, and ardent piety—which made Mr. Backus the friend and peer of James Manning and Hezekiah Smith, John Davis and William Rogers, Samuel Stillman and Thomas Baldwin, Stephen Gano and Jonathan Maxcy; men of singular ability and worth, raised up by the providence of God to accomplish a great work; men who would have been distinguished in any age or nation; men who were all nobly endowed by their Creator, and who enjoyed for the most part the advantages of liberal study in early life. To say that the subject of this narrative, without the aid of genius or learning or position, was yet the equal of such men in substantial worth, and stood side by side with them in council and in effort, is, we believe, no more than his just praise. He sympathized with their highest aims and shared in their gravest deliberations. He was not a whit behind the chiefest of them in courage, integrity, enterprise, liberality and devotion to Christ. He was at once conservative and progressive, a friend of order and a friend of zeal, maintaining the importance of creeds and the necessity of free investigation, and believing in human agency, though not at the expense of the Divine sovereignty.

And when we consider the length of his ministry, the amount and timeliness of his labors, and the whole influence of his life-work upon the character and progress of the Baptist denomination in New England, as well as less directly upon other denominations, it is impossible for us to hesitate in assigning him a high place among those servants whom the King of Zion has delighted to honor. He came to the grave in hoary age, as the sheaf is gathered in, in its season; and the record of his life will serve, we trust, to encourage not only his successors in the ministry of reconciliation, but all the friends of Christ who may peruse it as well.

APPENDIXES.

APPENDIX A.

OPPRESSION IN STURBRIDGE.

FROM the testimony of Henry Fisk we learn that a New-Light Church was organized in Sturbridge on the tenth of November, 1747. The next year John Blunt was ordained pastor. A petition to be exempted from taxes to support the "regular minister," was laid before the town by the members of this church, but their request was denied. On the twenty-sixth of May, 1748, "a great part of the town got together, and laying hold of two brethren that came from other places, drew them in a hostile manner out of town. About this time some others were seized for rates, paid them privately, and were set at liberty. As they went on to rate us from year to year, contrary to the royal act of indulgence, and the Province laws, * * * they stripped the pewter from the shelves of such as had it; and they took away skillets, kettles, pots, and warming-pans, from those who had it not. Others they deprived of the means by which they got their bread: namely, workmen's tools and spinning wheels. They drove away geese and swine from the doors of others. From some that had cows they took one or more of them; from some that had but one, they took that away. They took a yoke of oxen from one; and they thrust some into prison, where they suffered a long and tedious imprisonment. One brother was called from us, was ordained pastor of a Baptist church, and came for his family; at which time they seized and drew him away, and thrust him into prison, where he was kept in the cold winter, till somebody paid the money and let him out."

We add a few specifications condensed from the records of the church, kept by Henry Fisk, clerk. In 1750 a spinning wheel was taken from A. Bloice, five pewter plates from D. Fisk, a cow from J. Pike, a trammel, andirons, shovel and tongs, from John Blunt, a cradle from J. Perry, goods from John Streeter, household goods from Benjamin Robins, and also from H. Fisk, a cow from David Morse, goods from Phineas Collar, and from John Newell; and during the same year, John Corey, J. Barstow, Josiah Perry, Nathaniel Smith, and David Morse, were imprisoned for ministerial rates.

The next year, a steer was taken from J. Perry, goods from John Streeter, a cow from H. Fisk, a cow from Josiah Perry, a yoke of oxen from David Morse, goods from Phineas Collar, and also from John Newell, and carpenters' tools from Benj. Robins; and the same year A. Bloice and John Blunt were imprisoned.

In 1753, the town petitioned the General Court, by its agent, Col. Moses Marcy, that all the unimproved land in Sturbridge might be taxed to support the minister. This called forth an eloquent remonstrance from the Baptists; from which we copy the following sentences:

"The people called Baptists, may it please your Excellency and Honors, have no objection in the world against just taxes, operating from a legal origin, for the necessary and honorable support and defence of the civil government, or to paying our equal proportion of the Province, County, and Town taxes. [To do this] for the rational and virtuous purposes aforesaid is a part of our religion; as also, cheerfully to support His Majesty's government of this Province, with affluent hearts and ready hands, is part of our political creed. But on the contrary side, — to be harassed, insulted, impoverished, and imprisoned, as several of the people called Baptists have been since your Excellency's embarkation home to England, for their refusal to pay ministerial rates, we look upon and feel to be sorely galling and oppressive. No less than five of our brethren of the town of Sturbridge, have for the ministerial rate, been forced away from their respective families, and committed to Worcester jail, twenty miles distant from their habitations. Moreover and exclusive of these imprisonments, and the damages therefrom arising, the losses, costs, and damages, which the said people of the Baptist persuasion in said Sturbridge have sustained in and about four years past, amount to upwards of eight hundred and fifty pounds of the old tenor, so called; and all originating from the ministerial tax. These pressures, oppressions, and afflictions, bend and bow us down greatly, causing the oppressed to cry, as we now do, humbly and imploringly, that your Excellency and this Honorable Court would be pleased to take our distressed condition into due consideration, that so we may not be given up for a prey to our oppressors, and,— instead of having our lands subjected to a fresh, additional, ministerial tax, as prayed for by the said Moses Marcy, in his petition afore referred to, and of which we cannot in conscience pay one farthing,—that your complainants, the said people called Baptists, freeholders and residents in Sturbridge aforesaid, may have their heavy burdens unloosed, their grievances redressed, and that no ministerial rates or tax, in any shape whatever, may ever hereafter operate against them. And your Memorialists and Respondents will ever pray.

HENRY FISK,
JONATHAN PERRY," etc.

At the suggestion of a friend, we subjoin the names of the members of the several Councils at Titicut, described in chapter VIII. These Councils were all held by New-Light Churches.

FIRST COUNCIL AT TITICUT, OCT. 2, 1751.

From Canterbury — *Solomon Paine* and Joseph Cleaveland.
" Plainfield — *Thomas Stevens, Jr.*, and Peter Mellen.
" Norwich — *Jedediah Hide* and John Burchard.
" Providence — ———— Barzillai Richmond.
" Cambridge — *Nathaniel Draper* and James Perry.

SECOND COUNCIL AT TITICUT, MAY 27, 1752.

From Beech Woods — *James Mead* and Dea. Wm. Smith.
" Rehoboth — *Samuel Peck.*
" Coventry — *Samuel Drown.*

The separate churches in Canterbury, Plainfield, Providence, and Beech Woods, (Middleboro',) were invited to join in this Council; but messengers from the last church only appeared. Elders Peck and Drown were invited to sit and act with the Council, and did so.

THIRD COUNCIL AT TITICUT, NOV. 1, 1752.

From Canterbury — *Solomon Paine.*

" Plainfield — *Thomas Stevens, Jr.*, Joseph Warren, and Dea. Simon Spaulding.

From Providence — *Joseph Snow*, Benjamin Cushing, and Barzillai Richmond.

Alexander Miller, pastor of a church in Voluntown, was present, and was their scribe.

FOURTH COUNCIL IN TITICUT, JAN. 31, 1753.

From Exeter — *David Sprague.*
" Westerly — *Stephen Babcock.*
" Warwick — *Peter Werden.*
" Stonington — *Weight Palmer.*
" Providence — *Joseph Snow.*
" Norton — *William Carpenter.*
" Rehoboth — *Samuel Peck.*
" Coventry — *Samuel Drown.*
" Brookline — *Jonathan Hide.*
" Cambridge — *Nathaniel Draper.*
" Attleboro' — *Joshua Everett.*

The first four of these held to believers' baptism.

FIFTH COUNCIL IN TITICUT, JULY 11, 1753.

From Exeter — *David Sprague.*
" Rehoboth — *Samuel Peck* and John Pierce.
" Warwick — *Peter Werden.*
" Norton — *William Carpenter.*

We add the following citation of churches to the second meeting at Exeter:

" WESTERLY, KINGS COUNTY, COLONY OF R. I.

" Stephen Babcock, pastor of the church of Christ Jesus in Stonington and Westerly, in union: To the united churches scattered abroad in New England, grace, mercy, and peace be multiplied amongst you. Great and manifold are the favors of Almighty God to us, in these goings down of the sun, in reviving his ancient work of convicting and converting souls, and calling us from vain conversation and all false worship, to follow our ever glorious Lord and Master, Jesus Christ, in the regeneration; at whose command we have separated from carnal churches, etc. And amongst all the Divine favors and mercies we have been favored with, gospel fellowship is not the least; here the wolf and lamb lie down together; here the circumcised and uncircumcised meet together; here all denominations, that are sound in principles, may meet and commune together. In very deed all heaven is contained in divine fellowship. Amen.

At the request of fifteen of the united churches in the Exeter Association, I send forth this Citation that you meet together at Exeter, on the second Tuesday of September, 1754, by two or more of your representatives, to consult the affairs of Christ's kingdom, and to see what further may be done relating to the settlement between the two denominations, viz., Baptists and Congregationalists, and to consult all other matters that may be to God's glory, the advancement of his kingdom in the world, and the good of the united churches: Amen. Into whose hands this citation shall come, you are hereby desired to send a copy, signed by your elder or clerk, to all the neighboring churches, and also to all christian churches that have a desire to be enrolled in said Convention; farewell. Jerusalem is builded as a city that is compact together. Peace be within thy walls, and prosperity within thy palaces. For my brethren, my companions' sakes I will say, Peace be within thee, amen and amen.

Yours, but not my own,

STEPHEN BABCOCK."

March 25th day, 1754.

APPENDIX B.

THE CONFESSION OF FAITH AND COVENANT

PREPARED BY THE REV. ISAAC BACKUS, AND ADOPTED BY THE FIRST BAPTIST CHURCH IN MIDDLEBOROUGH, AT ITS ORGANIZATION, JANUARY 16, 1756.

ARTICLES OF FAITH.

PART I.

1. WE BELIEVE THAT THERE IS BUT ONE only, the living and true God, who is a Spirit, infinite, eternal and unchangeable in his Being, wisdom, power, holiness, justice, goodness and truth. Deut. 6: John 4: 24, Psal. 147: 5, and 90: 2, Jam. 1: 17, Isa. 40: 28, Jerem. 10: 10, Isa. 6: 3, Exod. 34: 6, 7.

2. That there are three persons in the Godhead, the Father, Son, and Holy Ghost, who are but one God, the same in substance, equal in power and glory, 1 John 5: 7, Phil. 2: 6, Acts 5: 3, 4.

3. That the Holy Scriptures of the Old and New Testaments, are the Word of God, which he hath given, as our only perfect rule of faith and practice. Acts 20: 32, 2 Tim. 3: 15, 16, 17.

4. That God who is infinite in knowledge, and perfectly views all things from the beginning to the end of time, hath fore-ordained that whatsoever comes to pass, either by his order or permission, shall work for the eternal glory of his great Name. Acts 15: 18, Rom. 9: 17—23, Acts 2: 23, Psal. 76: 10.

5. In the beginning, God created heaven and earth, and the sea, and all that in them is, — and he upholds and governs all things by the word of his power. Exod. 20: 11, Heb. 1: 3, Dan. 4: 35.

6. That God made man in his own image, in knowledge, righteousness and true holiness; and made with him a covenant of life, the condition whereof was perfect obedience. Gen. 1: 26, 27, and 2: 16, 17, Galat. 3: 10.

7. Man, being left to himself, soon fell from that happy and glorious estate in which he was made, by eating the forbidden fruit, whereby he brought himself and all his posterity into a state of death. Gen. 3: 6, Rom. 5: 12, 19.

8. Man being thus dead, his help and recovery is wholly in and from God. Hosea 13: 9, Ephe. 2: 8, John 6: 44.

9. God the Father, of his mere good pleasure from all eternity, hath chosen a number of poor lost men, in Christ Jesus, to eternal salvation. Rom. 8: 29, 30, Ephe. 1: 4, 5.

10. Jesus Christ, the eternal Son of God, hath come and taken on him human nature; and in that nature hath yielded a perfect obedience to the laws that we have broken, and suffered death for our sins, and hath brought in a complete and everlasting righteousness; and hath risen and ascended to the right hand of God, and ever liveth to make intercession for us. Heb. 10: 6—10, Dan. 9: 24, Heb. 7: 25.

11. The Holy Ghost, and he only, can and doth make a particular application of the redemption purchased by Christ, to every elect soul. John 3: 5 and 16: 7—15.

12. The Spirit of God applies this redemption by convincing us of our sinful, lost and miserable condition, and then discovering the glorious Saviour, as he is offered to us in the Gospel, in his suitableness and sufficiency, and enabling us to embrace him with our whole souls, whereby he is made unto us wisdom, righteousness, sanctification and redemption. John 16: 8 and 1: 12, 1 Cor. 1: 30.

13. The life of religion consists in the knowledge of God, and conformity to him in the inward man; which necessarily produceth an external conformity to his law; and brings us to live in obedience to his holy will, in all our ways, and in our several places and relations. John 17: 3, Mat. 23: 26, Ephe. 2: 10, Tit. 2d Chap.

14. True believers being united to Jesus Christ by faith, have communion with God; and by his Spirit they are united to each

other, and have communion one with another, whereby they are made partakers of each others' gifts and graces. 1 John, 1: 3, Rom. 1: 11, Phil. 1: 7.

15. We believe that the first day of the week, commonly called the Lord's day, is the Christian Sabbath. Mat. 28: 1—6, John 20: 19, 26, Rev. 1: 10, Heb. 4: 8, 9, 10.

16. That God hath appointed the ordinance of Civil Government for the defending of the poor as well as of the rich, in their civil rights and privileges; and the work of the civil magistrate is, to punish moral evils, and to encourage moral virtue, without touching upon anything that infringes upon the conscience, or pretending to dictate and govern in the worship of the Eternal God; which belongs only to Jesus Christ, the great law-giver and head of his Church. Rom. 13: 1—4, 1 Peter 2: 13, 14, 15, 1 Tim. 1: 8, 9, 10, Mat. 23: 8, 9, 10, Luke 22: 25, 26, Isa. 33: 20, 21, 22, Ephe. 1: 22.

17. We believe there will be a general resurrection both of the just and unjust; and that God hath appointed a day in which he will judge the world in righteousness by Jesus Christ; and will reward every man according to his works; when the wicked shall be sent into everlasting punishment, and the righteous be received into life eternal. John 5: 28, 29, Rom. 2: 16, Mat. 16: 27 and 25: 46.

PART II.

CONCERNING CHURCH AFFAIRS.

1. WE BELIEVE THAT A VISIBLE CHURCH OF CHRIST is a number of his saints and people, by mutual acquaintance and communion, voluntarily and understandingly, covenanting and embodying together for the carrying on the worship and service of God. 1 Pet. 2: 5, 1 Cor. 1: 2, Acts 2: 42—47.

2. That Baptism and the Lord's Supper are ordinances of Christ, to be continued until his second coming; and that the former is requisite to the latter, *that is to say*, that those are to be admitted into the communion of the Church, and to partake of all its ordinances,—who, upon profession of their faith, have been baptized by immer-

sion* in the name of the Father, and of the Son, and of the Holy Ghost. Mat. 28: 19, 20, 1 Cor. 11: 23, 26, Acts 2: 41 and 9: 18, 26 and 8: 12, 36—39, Mat. 3: 6, 16, Rom. 6: 4, John 3: 23.

3. Since none but saints can rightly partake of these ordinances, therefore the door of the Church should be carefully kept at all times against all such as cannot give scriptural evidences of their union to Christ by faith. 1 Cor. 11: 27, 29, Mat. 7: 6, 15—20, Ezek. 44: 7, 9, Isaiah 26: 2.

4. A church thus gathered, hath power to choose and ordain those officers that Christ hath appointed in his Church, namely: Bishops or Elders, and Deacons; and also to depose such officers as evidently appear to walk contrary to the gospel, and to discipline their members; though in some such cases it is convenient and profitable to request the advice of neighboring churches of Christ. Acts 1: 21—26 and 6: 3, Num. 8: 10, Mat. 18: 15—18, Acts 15th chap.

5. A Bishop or Elder hath no more power to decide any case or controversy in the Church, than any private brother; yet they having superior gifts for teaching and ruling ought to exercise and improve the same for the benefit of the church, and the church ought to be subject to the gifts bestowed on the minister from the Lord, while he is rightly acting in his place; — whose work is to lead in the actings of the church, and to administer the sacraments, and devote himself to the work of teaching, warning, rebuking and exhorting the people publicly, and from house to house. Mat. 20: 25—28, 1 Pet. 5: 3, Mat. 28: 19, Acts 20: 20, 28, 31.

6. The Deacon's office-work is, to take care of the poor, and to have the oversight of the temporal affairs of the Church, and to minister at the Lord's table. Acts 6: 1—4, 1 Tim. 3: 8—13.

7. Every saint is commanded to be faithful, to improve every gift and talent that is bestowed on them; in order to which, there ought

* "The place where Mr. Backus administered the ordinance of baptism when at home, was in a stream of water but a few rods from his dwelling. The stream has become so small and shallow, that a man who had nothing to judge from but its present size, might conclude that Mr. Backus could not have immersed there, but must have sprinkled the candidates while he stood on the margin, or must have led them into the water *ankle-deep*, and then sprinkled them."—REV. SILAS HALL.

to be such a gospel freedom that the church may know where every particular gift is, that it may be improved in its proper place, and to its right end; even the glory of God, and the good of his people. And the Church ought to be subject to such improvements. Rom. 13 : 5—8, 1 Peter 4: 10, 11, and 5: 5.

COVENANT.

We do now in the presence of the great all-seeing and most glorious God, and before angels and men, give ourselves up to the Lord Jehovah, Father, Son and Holy Ghost; and avouch Him this day, to be our God, our Father, our Saviour, and our Leader; and receive him as our portion forever. We give up ourselves unto the Lord Jesus Christ, and adhere to him as the Head of his people in the covenant of grace; and rely on him as our prophet, priest and king, to bring us to eternal blessedness. We acknowledge our everlasting and indispensable obligation to glorify our God, by living a holy, righteous and godly life, in this present world, in all our several places and relations. And we do engage, by the assistance of the Divine Spirit, to improve all our time and strength, talents and advantages, for his glory, and the good of our fellow men; promising by Divine help to walk in our house with a perfect heart; and to train up those under our care in the ways of God. And we also give up ourselves to one another in covenant, promising to act towards each other as brethren in Christ; watching over one another in the love of God; and to watch not only against those that are considered more gross evils, but also against all foolish talking and jesting which is not convenient; vain disputing about words and things which gender strife; disregarding promises, and not fulfilling engagements; tattling and backbiting; spending time idly at taverns or elsewhere; and vain and unnecessary worldly conversation on the Lord's days; and whatsoever else that is contrary to sound doctrine according to the glorious gospel of Christ; promising to hold communion together in the worship of God, and in the ordinances and discipline of his church, according as we are, or shall be, guided by the Spirit of God in his word; expecting that he will yet further and more gloriously open his word and the mysteries of his kingdom; flying to the blood of the everlasting covenant for the pardon of our many errors, and praying that the Lord would prepare and strengthen us for every good work, to do his will, working in us that which is well pleasing in his sight, through Jesus Christ, to whom be glory for ever and ever. Amen.

The following ministers of the Gospel have gone forth from the First Baptist Church in Middleboro', namely: James Mellen, Abner Lewis, Asa Hunt, Elijah Codding, Job Macomber, Samuel Nelson, David Leonard, Zenas Lockwood Leonard, Stephen Smith, Nelson Lewis Leonard, Silas Hall, Thomas Conant, George Leonard, William Harrison Alden. Another, David Weston, has, we believe, commenced a course of study with a view to entering the ministry.

APPENDIX C.

SANDEMANIANISM.

THE design of this work has not led us to exhibit in detail the various forms of error opposed by Mr. Backus. Indeed, most of them are but too well understood at the present time. But it has been suggested by a friend that the peculiar opinions of Mr. Sandeman are not generally known, and ought therefore to be briefly stated. Mr. Backus charges Sandeman, and we think justly, with endeavoring to explode the following scriptural distinctions, namely:

1. The distinction between *doctrinal* and *experimental* knowledge; between right *notions* of truth in the *head* and *knowing* them in the *heart*.

2. The distinction between a *slavish* and a *childlike* fear.

3. The distinction between believers and careless sinners; or rather the recognition of any difference in addressing them upon religious themes.

"The foundation of whatever is distinguishing in the system," says Andrew Fuller, "seems to relate to *the nature of justifying faith*. This Mr. S. constantly represents as *the bare belief of the bare truth;* by which definition he intends, as it would seem, to exclude from it everything pertaining to the will and the affections, except as effects produced by it. 'Every one,' says he, 'who obtains a just *notion* of the person and work of Christ, or whose *notion* corresponds to what is testified of him, is justified, and finds peace with God, simply by that *notion*.'" It may be noticed still further, as an indication of the radical difference between the views of Mr. Sandeman and of evangelical Christians generally, that the writings of such men as Flavel, Boston, Guthrie, Doddridge, the Erskines, etc., are represented by him as furnishing "a devout path to hell," and the writers themselves as Pharisees, "than whom no sinners were more hardened, and none greater destroyers of mankind."

For further information we must refer the reader to Mr. Sandeman's "Letters on Theron and Aspasia," and to the works of Andrew Fuller, II. p. 561 sq.

APPENDIX D.

EXTRACTS FROM MINUTES OF THE WARREN ASSOCIATION.

The minutes of the first three meetings of the Warren Association, have never, we believe, been published; but they still exist in manuscript among the papers of Mr. Backus. The Association will doubtless see to it that these minutes are printed in due time. Meanwhile we select from them two letters; the first sent by the Philadelphia to the Warren Association, and the second, a circular letter written by President Manning.

"The Elders and Messengers of the several Baptist churches, met in Association at Philadelphia, the 14th, 15th, and 16th days of October, A. D. 1766:—To the Elders and Messengers of the several Baptist churches of the same faith and order, to meet in Association at Warren, in the colony of Rhode Island, the 18th day of September, A. D. 1767; send greeting. Dearly Beloved Brethren: When we understood that you had concluded to meet at the time and place above mentioned, with a view to lay the foundation stone of an Associational building, it gave us peculiar joy, in that it opened to our view a prospect of much good being done. You will perhaps judge this our address to you premature, because as yet you have only an *ideal* being, as a body by appointment. But if you should call this our forwardness blind zeal, we are still in hopes you will not forget that our embracing the first opportunity of commencing christian fellowship and acquaintance with you, affords the strongest evidence of our approbation of your present meeting, and how fond we should be of mutual correspondence between us in this way.

"A long course of experience and observation has taught us to have the highest sense of the advantages which accrue from associations; nor indeed does the nature or thing speak any other language. For as particular members are collected together and united in one body, which we call a particular church, to answer those ends and purposes which could not be accomplished by any single member, so a collection and union of churches into one associational body, may easily be conceived capable of answering those still greater purposes, which any particular church could not be equal to. And by the same reason, a union of associations will still increase the body in weight and strength, and make it good, that a threefold cord is not easily broken.

"Great, dear brethren, is the design of your meeting; great is the work which lies before you. You will need the guidance and influence of the Divine Spirit, as well as the exertion of all prudence and wisdom. It is therefore our most ardent prayer, that you may meet in love, that peace and unanimity may subsist among you during your consultations, that you may be animated with zeal for the glory of God, and directed to advise and determine what may most conduce to promote the Redeemer's kingdom.

"From considering the divided state of our Baptist churches in your quarter, we foresee that difficulties may arise, such as may call for the exercise of the greatest tenderness and moderation, that if haply, through the blessing of God on your endeavors, those lesser differences may subside, and a more general union commence.

"As touching our consultations at this our meeting, the minutes of our proceedings (a printed copy whereof we shall herewith enclose) will inform you; and if in anything further you should be desirous of information with regard to us, we refer you to our reverend and beloved brethren, Morgan Edwards, John Sand, and Samuel Jones, who as our representative delegates will present you with this our letter, and whom we recommend to christian fellowship with you.

"And now, dear brethren, farewell. May the Lord bless and direct you in all things, and grant that we may all hereafter form one general assembly at his right hand, through infinite riches of free grace in Christ Jesus our Lord.

Signed by order and in behalf of the Association, by

BENJAMIN MILLER, Moderator.
SAMUEL JONES, Clerk."

CIRCULAR LETTER WRITTEN BY PRESIDENT MANNING.

"The Elders and Messengers of several churches belonging to the Association, met in Warren, in the colony of Rhode Island, etc. To the several churches they represent, — Greeting.

"Dear Brethren: We have had the pleasure of meeting your representatives at the Association, who in general have brought us good news from the churches. We rejoice to see that the Son of Man is pleased to walk in the midst of his golden candlesticks, the churches, to dispense his blessings to his people, and to attend the Word of the Kingdom with Divine power to the salvation of sinners. Come, help us to magnify the Lord for his unspeakable mercy and goodness. Yet we find that the enemies of truth are busily employed in endeavoring to subvert it, and in vexing and oppressing those who stand up as advocates for the cause of God. Brethren, we sympathize with you under your afflictions, while we call to mind the declaration of your ascended Head to his beloved flock whom he left behind: *In the world ye shall have tribulation.* Yet how refreshing is what follows: *But be of good cheer, I have overcome the world.* Those who live godly in Christ Jesus shall suffer persecution. Let not the powers of the world, who set themselves to oppose, discourage you. Search for the mind of Christ in his Word; which being discovered, pay a sacred regard thereto. Call no man master on earth; and remember that the followers of Christ carry their cross in imitation of their Divine Master. Brethren, suffer us, however, to beseech you to use all proper means to obtain relief from the burdens imposed upon you, by taking heed to the general plan which we as a body propose to pursue. But while you attend to human means, let your cries be incessant to Him who hears and will redress the cries of the oppressed. Pray for those who despitefully use you. Remember that love enters deeply into the spirit of our holy religion; and that the glorious Founder thereof has given us the most striking example of it, in loving and dying for his enemies. Walk soberly and inoffensively towards those without; and let your conduct prove that it is the power of truth, the force of conscience, that makes you Baptists, and not an affectation of singularity. And as you are persuaded that you have been taught by the Spirit of God, so let your light shine before others that you may win them to the truth. In the meantime, carefully guard against any designs to ensnare you, or to engage you in any combination with them that may eventually prove to the detriment of the cause.

"Finally, may the Lord Jesus afford you his presence, and bless you with abundant increase in all grace, to the glory of his great name."

APPENDIX E.

PETITIONS FROM ASHFIELD.

"To His Excellency, Francis Bernard, Esq., Captain General and Governor-in-Chief in and over His Majesty's Province of Massachusetts Bay, in New England, and Vice-Admiral of the same; and to His Honorable Council and House of Representatives: We whose names are underwritten present our humble Prayer to His Excellency and to your Honors, as follows:—

We would inform His Excellency and your Honors, that one half of us settled in this town before the last war, (which was then called Huntstown,) and built a fort and defended ourselves three years' time, before we had any help by soldiers from Authority; excepting ten men for ten days to gather our corn; in which time we could do little else in the summer, but guard ourselves and scout in the woods to see if we could make discovery of the enemy, and thereby were some guard to the towns below us. After the war was over, we being of the persuasion that is called Ana-Baptist, proceeded to settle ourselves in a church form, and to settle a minister, we then being by far the major part of the inhabitants of the town. He was ordained by the assistance of three neighboring ministers of the same constitution; and we were about building a meeting-house, but were forced to desist by means of there settling in town a number of men of a contrary persuasion; who, by the help of some few that were here before, and other proprietors, have by a major vote raised money to build another meeting-house which we have no privilege of, and settled another minister and given him a large settlement and salary, and compel us to pay our equal proportion with them; so that even our own minister is compelled to pay theirs, or we for him. By reason of which oppression, together with the distresses of the war aforesaid, we are brought under distressful circumstances, which, we think, cry aloud for some pity to be shown to us. For we have our own minister to provide for according to our ability, and have yearly our money taken away from us, or our land sold at an out-cry to support their worship, so that we have already suffered extremely. And they have also voted £4, lawful money upon each right, to finish their meeting-house and to support their minister, which if we are obliged to pay, we see nothing but that we, or many of us, must be turned out from our houses and lands. We pray therefore that His Excellency and your Honors would take our distressed case into your wise consideration, and free us and our lands from paying any more towards the maintenance of the minister, or finishing the meeting-house, of a society we do not belong unto; — we being willing to pay our Province taxes and all others, except the above mentioned. So pray your humble petitioners and loyal subjects.

N. B. There are upwards of ninety souls that attend our meeting on Lord's days.

Dated Ashfield, May 24, 1768."

Two years later they sent in another petition, in which, after narrating various futile attempts to obtain relief, they proceed as follows:

"Therefore our lands were set at public vendue and sold for a very small part of their value. They have sold mowing ground, winter grain, orcharding, one poor man's dwelling house, and our burying place. And all this for a rate which we cannot in conscience pay. So that we are not only deprived of liberty of conscience, which our most gracious Sovereign has granted us in common with others, his loyal subjects, (which we have a right to, in religion and reason,) but we are in a great measure disinherited, and are in a fair way to be turned naked into the wide world.

"We humbly beg leave to say, these things are hard, very hard.

For if we may not settle and support a minister agreeable to our own conscience, where is liberty of conscience?

"And if we may be allowed that liberty — which is most reasonable, by what law, or with what equity, are we forced to pay for the settlement of another, with whom we cannot in conscience join? or to build a meeting-house for a society that we do not belong to? * * * We plead for nothing but liberty of conscience and charter privilege. We humbly pray your Honors to take these things into your wise consideration, and show some pity to your distressed petitioners," etc.

APPENDIX F.

JOHN ADAMS'S ACCOUNT OF THE PHILADELPHIA CONFERENCE.

"GOVERNOR Hopkins and Governor Ward, of Rhode Island, came to our lodgings and said to us, that President Manning, of Rhode Island College, and Mr. Backus, of Massachusetts, were in town, and had conversed with some gentlemen in Philadelphia who wished to communicate to us a little business, and wished we would meet them at six in the evening at Carpenter's Hall. Whether they explained their affairs more particularly to any of my colleagues, I know not; but I had no idea of the design. We all went at the hour, and to my great surprise found the hall almost full of people, and a great number of Quakers seated at the long table with their broad brimmed beavers on their heads. We were invited to seats among them, and informed that they had received complaints from some Anabaptists and some Friends in Massachusetts, against certain laws of that province, restrictive of the liberty of conscience, and some instances were mentioned in the General Court, and in the courts of justice, in which Friends and Baptists had been grievously oppressed. I know not how my colleagues felt, but I own I was greatly surprised and somewhat indignant, being, like my friend Chase, of a temper naturally quick and warm, at seeing our State and her delegates thus summoned before a self-created tribunal, which was neither legal nor constitutional.

"Israel Pemberton, a Quaker of large property and more intrigue, began to speak, and said that Congress were here endeavoring to form a union of the Colonies; but there were difficulties in the way, and none of more importance than liberty of conscience. The laws of New England, and particularly of Massachusetts, were inconsistent with it, for they not only compelled men to pay to the building of churches and support of ministers, but to go to some known religious assembly on first days, etc., and that he and his friends were desirous of engaging us to assure them that our State would repeal all those laws, and place things as they were in Pennsylvania.

"A suspicion instantly arose in my mind, which I have ever believed to have been well founded, that this artful Jesuit, for I had been apprised before of his character, was endeavoring to avail himself of this opportunity to break up the Congress, or at least to withdraw the Quakers and the governing part of Pennsylvania from us; for, at that time, by means of a most unequal representation, the Quakers had a majority in their House of Assembly, and, by consequence, the whole power of the State in their hands. I arose and spoke in answer to him. The substance of what I said, was, that we had no authority to bind our constituents to any such proposals; that the laws of Massachusetts were the most mild and equitable establishment of religion that was known in the world; if indeed they could be called an establishment; that it would be in vain for us to enter into any conferences on such a subject, for we knew beforehand our constituents would disavow all we could do or say for the satisfaction of those who invited us to this meeting. That the people of Massachusetts were as religious and conscientious as the people of Pennsylvania; that their conscience dictated to them that it was their duty to support those laws, and therefore the very liberty of conscience, which Mr. Pemberton invoked, would demand indulgence for the tender consciences of the people of Massachusetts, and allow them to preserve their laws; that it might be depended on, this was a point that could not be carried; that I would not deceive them by insinuating the faintest hope, for I knew they might as well turn the heavenly bodies out of their annual and diurnal courses, as the people of Massachusetts at the present day from their meeting-house and Sunday laws. Pemberton made no reply but this: 'Oh! sir, pray don't urge liberty of conscience in favor of such laws!' If I had but known the particular complaints which were to be alleged, and if Pemberton had not broken irregularly into the midst of things, it might have been better, perhaps, to have postponed this declaration. However, the gentlemen proceeded and stated the particular cases of oppression, which were alleged in our general and executive courts. It happened that Mr. Cushing and Mr. Samuel Adams had been present in the General Court when the petitions had been under deliberation, and they explained the whole so clearly that every reasonable man must have been satisfied. Mr. Paine and I had been concerned at the bar in every action in the executive courts which was complained of, and we explained them all to the entire satisfaction of impartial men, and showed that there had been no oppression or injustice in any of them." In his diary Mr. Adams describes the affair thus: "In the evening we were invited to an interview, at Carpenter's Hall, with the Quakers and Anabaptists. Mr. Backus is come here from Middleborough with a design to apply to the Congress for a redress of grievances of the anti-pedobaptists in our Province. The cases from Chelmsford, the case of Mr. White of Haverhill, the case of Ashfield and Warwick were mentioned by Mr. Backus. Old Israel Pemberton was quite rude, and his rudeness was resented; but the conference, which held till eleven o'clock, I hope will produce good."

APPENDIX G.

DOCTRINAL CORRESPONDENCE WITH PRESIDENT MAXCY.

"MIDDLEBORO', March 17, 1797.

"DEAR SIR:—The near connection I have long had with the family from whence you sprang, my early acquaintance with your change of mind, the concern I had in introducing you into the ministry and into the office you now sustain in our College, have all laid me under strong obligations to seek your welfare and to watch against everything which may hurt your usefulness. But how to behave in these trying times, so as to be faithful and yet avoid all unnecessary controversy, hath been difficult for me to determine.

When you published your opinion about the first sin of Adam, in a funeral sermon for President Manning, my heart was grieved. Dr. Rogers soon wrote to me about it from Philadelphia; but he afterwards informed me that when you were there, you satisfied him about it. And after you published your sermon on the first of Romans, Dr. Rippon wrote to me from London of a report which had reached there, that you had published a sermon upon universal salvation; but I informed him to the contrary, though the discourse wanted some peculiarities of Christianity. Judge then, how it must have appeared to me, last September, to see not only a new edition of your first sermon but also a preface to it, in which you set up a Socinian and a Universalist as high or higher in virtue than President Edwards,—who is esteemed by Europe as well as America, one of the greatest Christians and divines which this age has produced. What may we next hear from England?

"I should have written to you long before now, if I had been in possession of said sermon and preface; but I have been almost confined for three months, and did not obtain them till last week. Before this I saw your late discourse on the Atonement of Christ, which gave me fresh encouragement concerning you. I can therefore open my mind to you with hopes of real benefit to us both. This I could not do to Mr. Winchester, after I had discovered the use of known deceit in him. For on July 25, 1780, I heard him preach in Dr. Stillman's pulpit; when he spoke expressly against the doctrine of universal salvation; though he was soon after forced to own that he was then inclined to think it true, and he has informed the world so in the preface to the Boston edition of his dialogues, 1795. * * * Had you known these things as I do, you would not have extolled his virtue as you have done in your late preface. But as I believe you to be a sincere friend, and as you own that you may be in an error about the death which was threatened to Adam if he ate the forbidden fruit, I shall give you my reasons against your opinion.

"You say 'the loss of life is the plain meaning of the word death.' (Preface, p. 4.). It is indeed so; and the loss of life to the soul is as much the literal meaning of the word, as is the loss of life to the body. Yea, after Adam had died spiritually, God said: "Dust thou art, and unto dust thou shalt return," Gen. 3 : 19. His soul died *in the day* that he sinned, but his body did not, until about nine hundred years after. The truth of God, therefore, could not be maintained by holding that it was only natural death which he intended, when He said: "In the day thou eatest thereof, thou shalt surely die." Darkness, guilt, and confusion, which are spiritual death, came upon him that very day. Jer. 17: 5, 6. Ro. 3 : 17. Is. 53 : 10. Matt. 26: 38 and 27, 46. 2 Cor 5: 21. Heb. 10 : 14. Though it was impossible for the Son of God to be made a *sinner*, yet he suffered more for us than any sinner can do in hell. He was made a curse for us, that we might receive the promise of the spirit through *faith*. Gal. 3 : 13, 14. * * * What you say in your sermon about the death that was threatened in the precept to Adam, was not a sudden thought, because you have published it a second time. Yet you hold that he died spiritually before God said, dust thou art, and unto dust thou shalt return, p. 16. Spiritual death was therefore threatened in the first precept, and natural death was the consequence which was declared afterwards.

"In the second place you suppose "losing existence" was the death that Adam was *afraid of;* and therefore, that this second declaration explains death as being the loss of natural life, and not of existence, p. 15; though this is only supposition and not a proof of the point.

"Thirdly, you argue that threatening spiritual death could neither reform the sinner, deter others from sinning, nor satisfy Divine justice — the great end of punishment, p. 17, 18.

"Fourthly, you say: "The implication of spiritual death in the threatening would have rendered the punishment perfectly agreeable to Adam, after his transgression," p. 18, and you quote an author in the margin to prove it. Upon all which I would observe:

"1. If the fear of spiritual death could not deter Adam from sinning, no more could the fear of natural death; since he knew no more what it was than he did of spiritual death.

"2. The law of God as given to man in innocency, was not designed to reform sinners, but to keep man from sinning, or to discover the justice of God in his condemnation. And no angel in heaven knew anything about the pardon and salvation of sinners, until God revealed it in the seed of the woman, whose heel was to be bruised. When Christ was born of a virgin, he was seen of angels, 1 Tim. 3: 16. They saw more of God then than they ever did before.

"3. Spiritual death was so far from being agreeable to Adam, after it was inflicted upon him, that he said to God, "I heard thy voice, and I was afraid, because I was naked, and I hid myself," Gen. 3: 10. And this was before God said, 'Dust thou art, and unto dust shalt thou return.' Darkness, guilt, confusion, and the fear of further punishment, were what Adam felt; and this was far from being agreeable to him or to his wife.

"But fifthly, you say: "Had spiritual death been implied in the punishment denounced against Adam, man's salvation on the present constitution of redemption could not have been effected," p. 19. This you argue from your opinion that spiritual death is being a sinner, which Christ never was nor can be. But you ought to know, that God never threatened to make man a sinner, but to make him miserable, should he dare to sin. And Christ suffered more misery for man in a short time, than man can suffer to eternity. He said, "My soul is exceeding sorrowful, even unto death." And when he hung upon the cross, and darkness was over all the land, he cried, "My God, my God, why hast thou forsaken me?" Thus he "made his soul an offering for sin." "He made him to be sin for us who knew no sin, that we might be made the righteousness of God in him." "For by one offering he hath perfected forever them that are sanctified." They who are sanctified are set apart for God from eternity, are effectually called in time, and are kept by the power of God through faith unto eternal salvation. For as by one man's disobedience, many were made sinners; so by the obedience of one, shall many be made righteous, Ro. 5 : 19. God did not make men sinners, but Adam made them so, by breaking the law of God; and we cannot make ourselves righteous, but that is done wholly by the merits of Christ and by the influences of his spirit in his people. All men who spring from Adam by natural generation, are made sinners; and all who are born again by the spirit of Christ, are made righteous in him.

"But you pass over this chapter, and fix on another, which speaks of the coming of natural death by Adam, and of the resurrection of the body by the power of Christ. There it is said, "As in Adam all die, even so in Christ shall all be made alive," 1 Cor. 15 : 22. Upon which you say: "These words make it evident that those made alive in Christ are as numerous as those subjected to death by Adam. Language cannot express this idea with more certainty. Those therefore, who believe that the death introduced by Adam was spiritual, temporal and eternal, if they would be consistent, ought to believe in universal salvation," p. 21, 22. But if the word *all* is not considered as it relates to the children of Adam and to Christ's children, then we must hold universal salvation. For the resurrection of damnation is not being made alive by Christ, but it is the second death, Rev. 20: 14. Then Christ will put all his enemies under his feet, 1 Cor. 15 : 25. In this chapter God speaks of the resurrection of his children, and not one word of the resurrection of the wicked. But Christ had said before: "The hour is coming, in the which all that are in their graves shall come forth, they that have done good, unto the resurrection of life; and they that have done evil, unto the resurrection of damnation," Jo. 5 : 28, 29. So here it is said: "As in Adam all die, even so in Christ shall all be made alive." And for all such it is said, the sting of death is sin, and the strength of sin is the law; but thanks unto God who giveth us the victory, through our Lord Jesus Christ," 1 Cor. 15 : 22, 56, 57. No other men will be made alive at the last day but those who are delivered from the guilt and power of sin before that day — the day when death and hell shall be cast into the lake of fire, which is the second death, Rev. 20 : 12, 14. Such were never made alive in Christ, as all men died in Adam. * * *

"The enmity which men have discovered against the sovereignty of the grace of God, as revealed in the Holy Scriptures, hath now prevailed so far, that every art is made use of to put other senses upon the words of revelation than God intended therein. He said to Moses: "I will have mercy on whom I will have mercy, and I will have compassion, on whom I will have compassion. So then it is not of him that willeth, nor of him that runneth, but of God that showeth mercy, Ro. 9 : 15, 16. This was the doctrine which God made use of in all the reformation, that was wrought in Germany, England, and Scotland, after the year 1517; and by the same doctrine he wrought all the reformation that has been in our day, both in Europe and America. Elect according to the foreknowledge of God the Father, through sanctification of the Spirit, unto obedience and sprinkling of the blood of Jesus Christ, is the only way of salvation which he hath revealed, 1 Pet. 1 : 2. And when any person is clearly convinced of sin by the power of the Spirit of God, and then has a revelation of the blood and righteousness of Christ as infinitely free and sufficient to relieve his guilty conscience, he hath a greater certainty of the truth of the Scriptures, than all the human learning on earth can give him. And though, as the raging sea dashes against the rocks, so men rage against this doctrine; yet it stands firmer than all the rocks and mountains upon earth.

"President Edwards had his imperfections; yet God honored him as much as any minister in our land. Dr. Hopkins published a book, the year after Edwards died, and many others since, which have filled our land with controversy and given the enemy an occasion to reproach the truth, especially, about the sovereignty of grace and the earnest and free calls of the gospel to all sinners, without any good in them. But to put either of these upon a level with Dr. Priestley, who in the most public manner has denied that Christ is truly God, and that he ever made an atonement for the sins of men, must be exceedingly hurtful to young minds and grievous to others. God will finally do him justice; and O! that he may bring him to repentance! But he never ought to be called a Christian as long as he denies the Divinity and merits of Jesus Christ. A gentleman, who was educated at Yale College, was fond of Priestley's writings for some time, but he confessed to a near friend of mine last year, that all his foundation was gone, and he knew not what would become of him after death. He also seriously gave it as his opinion that Dr. Priestley had done as much at least to promote infidelity, both in Europe and America, as any man in our day.

"God says: 'Faithful are the wounds of a friend, but the kisses of an enemy are deceitful.' Prov. 27: 6. And as far as I know my heart, these lines are from your hearty friend,

ISAAC BACKUS.

PRESIDENT MAXCY."

"R. I. COLLEGE, June 26, 1797.

"REV. AND DEAR SIR:— Some time since, I received a letter from you, assigning your reasons against my sentiments concerning the death threatened to Adam. These reasons I have read with attention, and shall let them have all that weight with me, which your age, experience and theological information deserve. I do not mean here to enter into an examination of the various points objected against; but only to observe that most of my friends appear to have misunderstood my leading ideas on the present subject. I never believed that spiritual death was not included in the penalty of the *moral* law; neither did I ever believe that the prohibition laid on Adam, was the moral law. I have considered it as a positive law, and natural death only its penalty. If this be not the case, I can give no account of the origin of natural death. I admit, and always have admitted, all the consequences of the fall, exactly in the manner that orthodox divines have admitted them. My object has been to keep up a distinction between the law, by the breach of which natural death was introduced, and the law by the breach of which spiritual death was introduced.

"My sentiments in general have been grossly misrepresented, particularly with regard to universalism, a doctrine which I believe contrary to the whole tenor of Scripture. Some things which I have published were rash and imprudent. I am particularly sorry for them, as they gave pain to those who were some of the first friends of the College. I shall be cautious in future. I am much obliged to you for the very frank and open manner in which you address me in your letter. I consider it as a mark of your real friendship for me and the College. Your advice to me will at all times be acceptable, and I shall feel myself under obligations for it. Believe me, Revd. Sir, to be your sincere friend and brother in the Gospel of Christ,

JONA. MAXCY."

"MIDDLEBORO', July 31, 1797.

"DEAR SIR:—Yours of June 26th gave me much satisfaction, both because you therein retract some publications which were grievous and also as you frankly give me your ideas of principles which I have long believed to be true. That you have been misunderstood in many things, even by your friends, as you observe, is doubtless true; and a great part of the controversies among Christians proceed from the same cause, which made me desirous to obtain your real ideas, if I could; and I thank you for giving them freely. I am as far as you are from a desire to enter into any controversy; and perhaps it will produce none for me to give you my ideas of the main point in which we still seem to differ.

"I will not say that the precept which forbade our parents eating the forbidden fruit, was a *moral* precept in the strict sense of the word; yet I believe they broke the moral law in violating that precept. For the moral law is, to love God with all our powers and our neighbors as ourselves. And nothing can be more contrary to pure love, than to believe the devil before him, so as to violate his plain command. By this the race of Adam was *made sinners*, which is spiritual death, Ro. 5: 19. And how any of them could be *made righteous*, as is then declared, the moral law never discovered. Neither Adam in a state of innocence, nor any angel in heaven, knew anything about pardon for sin or cleansing from iniquity, until God revealed them in the seed of the woman, whose blood was typified in Abel's offering a lamb by faith; and all the blood ever shed by God's command in sacrifice, pointed to the blood of Christ upon the cross. After the death of Christ, those who rejected him and continued those sacrifices, were no better than murderers and idolaters; as is declared in the last chapter of Isaiah, which the martyr Stephen applies to them in the seventh of the Acts. So that though the pure moral law did not make any difference between one tree and another; yet when God had done it by express command, Adam broke the moral law in breaking that command just as really as he could in any act of rebellion against his Creator. Yea, he therein rebelled against heaven and seized upon earth as his own. And the same disposition has ever appeared in all his posterity.

"In a word, the moral law requires us to believe all that God reveals and to obey all his commands to us, though human reason could discover nothing of the many of these commands without revelation. Reason should make us cautious that we are not imposed upon by false pretences to revelation; but where the Scripture speaks plainly, it should silence all disputes, Gal. 4: 30. It is a more sure word of prophecy than an audible voice from heaven, which, though true, was soon gone, while the written word remains, 2 Pet. 1: 17, 21. The angels desire to look into what God has revealed to men and learn much thereby, 1 Pet. 1 : 12, Eph. 3 : 9, 10. And how earnest should we be to imitate their example, when innumerable evils prevail by setting up reason above revelation. Some have strenuously asserted that saving faith in Christ is not required by the moral law, which is another mode of setting up reason above revelation. For he that believeth not God, hath made him a liar; and if that is not a moral evil, and setting to our seal that God is true, a moral virtue, what can be so? Jo. 5: 10, and 3: 33. Yours,

Isaac Backus."

INDEX.

C.

D.

E.

F.

G.

T.

U.

V.

W.

Y.

IMPORTANT

LITERARY AND SCIENTIFIC WORKS,

PUBLISHED BY

GOULD AND LINCOLN,

59 WASHINGTON STREET, BOSTON.

ANNUAL OF SCIENTIFIC DISCOVERY;

Or, Year Book of Facts in Science and Art. By DAVID A. WELLS, A. M. 12mo, cloth, $1.25.

This work, commenced in the year 1850, and issued in the month of January, annually, embraces an enumeration and description of every important Invention, Discovery, or Scientific Theory, reported during the year. Each volume is distinct in itself, and contains ENTIRELY NEW MATTER, with a fine portrait of some person distinguished for his attainments in science and art.

LAKE SUPERIOR;

Its Physical Character, Vegetation, and Animals. By L. AGASSIZ, and others. One volume, octavo, elegantly Illustrated. Cloth, $3.50.

THE PLURALITY OF WORLDS.

New Edition. With a SUPPLEMENTARY DIALOGUE, in which the author's reviewers are reviewed. 12mo, cloth, $1.00.

This masterly production, which has excited so much interest in this country and in Europe, will now have increased attraction in the SUPPLEMENT, in which the author's reviewers are triumphantly reviewed.

COMPARATIVE ANATOMY OF THE ANIMAL KINGDOM.

By Prof. C. TH. VON SIEBOLD and H. STANNIUS. Translated, with Notes, Additions, &c., By WALDO J. BURNETT, M. D. One vol., octavo, cloth, $3.00.

This is unquestionably the best and most complete work of its class ever yet published.

WORKS BY HUGH MILLER.

THE FOOTPRINTS OF THE CREATOR; or, The Asterolepis of Stromness. With Illustrations. Memoir of the Author by LOUIS AGASSIZ. 12mo, cloth, $1.00.

MY SCHOOLS and SCHOOLMASTERS; or, The Story of my Education. With an elegant Likeness. 12mo, cloth, $1.25.

This is a personal narrative of a deeply interesting and instructive character, concerning one of the most remarkable men of the age.

THE OLD RED SANDSTONE; or, New Walks in an Old Field. Illustrated with Plates and Geological Sections. 12mo, cloth, $1.00.

FIRST IMPRESSIONS OF ENGLAND AND ITS PEOPLE. With a fine Engraving of the Author. 12mo, cl., $1.00.

A thrillingly interesting, and very instructive book of travels; presenting the most perfectly life-like views of England and its people, to be found in the language.

DR. BUCKLAND said, "He would give his left hand to possess such powers of description as this man."

THE NATURAL HISTORY OF THE HUMAN SPECIES.

Its Typical Forms and Primeval Distribution. By CHARLES HAMILTON SMITH. With an Introduction, containing an Abstract of the Views of Blumenbach, Prichard, Bachman, Agassiz, and other writers of repute. By SAMUEL KNEELAND, Jr., M. D. With elegant Illustrations. 12mo, cloth, $1.25.

It is a book of learning, and full of interest, and may be regarded as among the comparatively few real contributions to science.—[Christian Witness.

CYCLOPÆDIA OF ANECDOTES OF LITERATURE AND THE FINE ARTS.

A choice selection of Anecdotes of the various forms of Literature, of the Arts, of Architecture, Engravings, Music, Poetry, Painting and Sculpture, and of the most celebrated Literary Characters and Artists of different Countries and Ages, &c. By KAZLITT ARVINE, A. M. With numerous Illustrations. 725 pages, octavo, cloth, $3.00.

This is unquestionably the choicest collection of ANECDOTES ever published. It contains THREE THOUSAND AND FORTY ANECDOTES, and more than ONE HUNDRED AND FIFTY ILLUSTRATIONS. It is admirably adapted to literary and scientific men, to artists, mechanics, and others, as a DICTIONARY FOR REFERENCE, in relation to facts on the numberless subjects and characters introduced.

KITTO'S POPULAR CYCLOPÆDIA OF BIBLICAL LITERATURE.

Condensed from the larger work, by the author, JOHN KITTO, D. D. Assisted by JAMES TAYLOR, D. D. With *over* 500 *Illustrations.* Octavo, 812 pp., cloth, $3.00.

This work answers the purpose of a commentary, while at the same time it furnishes a complete DICTIONARY OF THE BIBLE, embodying the products of the best and most recent researches in biblical literature, in which the scholars of Europe and America have been engaged. It is not only intended for ministers and theological students, but is also particularly adapted to parents, Sabbath-school teachers, and the great body of the religious public.

HISTORY OF PALESTINE.

With the Geography and Natural History of the Country, the Customs and Institutions of the Hebrews, etc. By JOHN KITTO, D. D. With upwards of 200 Illustrations. 12mo, cloth, $1.25.

Beyond all dispute this is the best historical compendium of the Holy Land, from the days of Abraham to those of the late Pasha of Egypt, Mehemet Ali. — [Edinburgh Review.

☞ In the numerous notices and reviews, the work has been strongly recommended, as not only admirably adapted to the FAMILY, but also as a text-book for SABBATH and WEEK DAY SCHOOLS.

CHAMBERS'S CYCLOPÆDIA OF ENGLISH LITERATURE.

Two large imperial octavo volumes of 1400 pages; with upwards of 300 elegant Illustrations. By ROBERT CHAMBERS. Embossed cloth, $5.00.

This work embraces about ONE THOUSAND AUTHORS, chronologically arranged and classed as Poets, Historians, Dramatists, Philosophers, Metaphysicians, Divines, etc., with choice selections from their writings, connected by a Biographical, Historical, and Critical Narrative; thus presenting a complete view of English literature from the earliest to the present time. Let the reader open where he will, he cannot fail to find matter for profit and delight. The selections are gems — infinite riches in a little room; in the language of another, "A WHOLE ENGLISH LIBRARY FUSED DOWN INTO ONE CHEAP BOOK!"

CHAMBERS'S MISCELLANY OF USEFUL AND ENTERTAINING KNOWLEDGE.

By WILLIAM CHAMBERS. With Illustrations. Ten vols., 16mo, cloth, $7.00.

CHAMBERS'S HOME BOOK AND POCKET MISCELLANY.

A choice Selection of Interesting and Instructive Reading for the Old and the Young. Six vols. 16mo, cloth, $3.00.

This work is fully equal, if not superior, to either of the Chambers's other works in interest, containing a vast fund of valuable information, furnishing ample variety for every class of readers.

CHAMBERS'S REPOSITORY OF INSTRUCTIVE AND AMUSING PAPERS.

With Illustrations. 16mo, cloth, bound. 4 vols. in two, $1.75; and 4 vols. in one, $1.50.

SACRED RHETORIC;

Or, Composition and Delivery of Sermons. By HENRY J. RIPLEY, Professor in Newton Theological Institution. Including Professor Ware's Hints on Extemporaneous Preaching. 12mo, 75 cts.

THE PREACHER AND THE KING;

Or, Bourdaloue in the Court of Louis XIV. An Account of that distinguished Era, Translated from the French of L. F. BUNGENER. With an Introduction by the Rev. GEORGE POTTS, D. D. New edition, with a fine Likeness, and a Sketch of the Author's Life. 12mo, cloth, $1.25.

It combines substantial history with the highest charm of romance. Its attractions are so various that it can hardly fail to find readers of almost every description. — [Puritan Recorder.

THE PRIEST AND THE HUGUENOT;

Or, Persecution in the Age of Louis XV. Translated from the French of L. F. BUNGENER. 2 vols., 12mo, cloth, $2.25.

☞ This is truly a masterly production, full of interest, and may be set down as one of the greatest Protestant works of the age.

FOOTSTEPS OF OUR FOREFATHERS.

What they Suffered and what they Sought. Describing Localities and portraying Personages and Events conspicuous in the Struggles for Religious Liberty. By JAMES G. MIALL. Thirty-six fine Illustrations. 12mo, $1.00.

An exceedingly entertaining work. The reader soon becomes so deeply entertained that he finds it difficult to lay aside the book till finished. — [Ch. Parlor Mag.

A work absorbingly interesting, and very instructive. — [Western Lit. Magazine.

MEMORIALS OF EARLY CHRISTIANITY.

Presenting, in a graphic, compact, and popular form, Memorable Events of Early Ecclesiastical History, etc. By JAMES G. MIALL. With numerous elegant Illustrations. 12mo, cloth, $1.00.

☞ This, like the "Footsteps of our Forefathers," will be found a work of uncommon interest

WORKS BY JOHN HARRIS, D. D.

THE PRE-ADAMITE EARTH. Contributions to Theological Science. 12mo, cloth, $1.00.

MAN PRIMEVAL; or, the Constitution and Primitive Condition of the Human Being. With a fine Portrait of the Author. 12mo, cloth, $1.25.

PATRIARCHY; or, THE FAMILY. Its Constitution and Probation; being the *third* volume of "Contributions to Theological Science." $1.25.

THE GREAT TEACHER; or, Characteristics of our Lord's Ministry. With an Introductory Essay. By H. HUMPHREY, D. D. 12mo, cloth, 85 cts.

THE GREAT COMMISSION; or, the Christian Church constituted and charged to convey the Gospel to the World. Introductory Essay by W. R. WILLIAMS, D. D. 12mo, cloth, $1.00.

ZEBULON; Or, the Moral Claims of Seamen. 18mo, cloth, 25 cts.

PHILIP DODDRIDGE.

His Life and Labors. By JOHN STOUGHTON, D. D., with beautiful Illuminated Title-page and Frontispiece. 16mo, cloth, 60 cents.

THE EVIDENCES OF CHRISTIANITY,

: exhibited in the writings of its apologists, down to Augustine. By W. J. BOLTON, of Gonville and Caius College, Cambridge. 12mo, cloth, 80 cents.

WORKS BY DR. TWEEDIE.

GLAD TIDINGS; or, The Gospel of Peace. A series of Daily Meditations for Christian Disciples. By Rev. W. K. TWEEDIE, D. D. With elegant Illustrated Title-page. 16mo, cloth, 63 cts.

THE MORN OF LIFE; or, Examples of Female Excellence. A Book for Young Ladies. 16mo, cloth. *In press.*

A LAMP TO THE PATH; or, the Bible in the Heart, the Home, and the Market Place. With an elegant Illustrated Title-page. 16mo, cloth, 63 cts.

SEED TIME AND HARVEST; or, Sow Well and Reap Well. A Book for the Young. With an elegant Illustrated Title-page. 16mo, cloth, 63 cts.

☞ The above works, by Dr. Tweedie, are of uniform size and style. They are most charming, pious, and instructive works, beautifully gotten up, and well adapted for "gift-books."

WORKS BY JOHN ANGELL JAMES.

THE CHURCH MEMBER'S GUIDE; Edited by J. O. CHOULES, D D. New edition. With an Introductory Essay by Rev. HUBBARD WINSLOW. Cloth, 33c.

CHRISTIAN PROGRESS. A Sequel to the Anxious Inquirer. 18mo, cloth, 31c.

☞ one of the best and most useful works of this popular author.

THE CHURCH IN EARNEST. Seventh thousand. 18mo, cloth, 40 cents

MOTHERS OF THE WISE AND GOOD.

By JABEZ BURNS, D. D. 16mo, cloth, 75 cents.

We wish it were in every family, and read by every mother in the land.—[Lutheran Observer.

MY MOTHER;

Or, Recollections of Maternal Influence. By a New England Clergyman. With a beautiful Frontispiece. 12mo, cloth, 75 cents.

This is one of the most charming books that have issued from the press for a long period. "It is," says a distinguished author, "one of those rare pictures painted from life with the exquisite skill of one of the 'Old Masters,' which so seldom present themselves to the amateur."

THE EXCELLENT WOMAN.

With an Introduction by Rev. W. B. SPRAGUE, D.D. Containing twenty-four splendid Illustrations. 12mo, cloth, $1.00; cloth, gilt, $1.75; extra Turkey, $2.50.

☞ This elegant volume is an appropriate and valuable "gift book" for the husband to present the wife, or the child the mother.

MEMORIES OF A GRANDMOTHER.

By a Lady of Massachusetts. 16mo, cloth, 50 cents,

THE MARRIAGE RING;

Or, How to make Home Happy. By JOHN ANGELL JAMES. Beautiful illustrated edition 16mo, cloth, gilt, 75 cents.

A beautiful volume, and a very suitable present to a newly-married couple.—[N. Y. Christian Intelligencer.

WORKS BY WILLIAM R. WILLIAMS, D. D.

RELIGIOUS PROGRESS; Discourses on the Development of the Christian Character. 12mo, cloth, 85 cts.

This work is from the pen of one of the brightest lights of the American pulpit. We scarcely know of any living writer who has a finer command of powerful thought and glowing, impressive language than he.—[DR. SPRAGUE, Alb. Atl.

LECTURES ON THE LORD'S PRAYER Third edition. 12mo, cloth, 85 cts.

Their breadth of view, strength of logic, and stirring eloquence place them among the very best homilitical efforts of the age. Every page is full of suggestions as well as eloquence.—Ch. Parlor Mag.

MISCELLANIES. New improved edition. *Price reduced.* 12mo, $1 25.

IMPORTANT WORK.

KITTO'S POPULAR CYCLOPÆDIA OF BIBLICAL LITERATURE. Condensed from the larger work. By the Author, JOHN KITTO, D. D., Author of "Pictorial Bible," "History of Palestine," "Scripture Daily Readings," &c. Assisted by JAMES TAYLOR, D. D., of Glasgow. With *over five hundred Illustrations*. One volume octavo, 812 pp., cloth, 3,00.

THE POPULAR BIBLICAL CYCLOPÆDIA OF LITERATURE is designed to furnish a DICTIONARY OF THE BIBLE, embodying the products of the best and most recent researches in biblical literature, in which the scholars of Europe and America have been engaged. The work, the result of immense labor and research, and enriched by the contributions of writers of distinguished eminence in the various departments of sacred literature, has been, by universal consent, pronounced the best work of its class extant, and the one best suited to the advanced knowledge of the present day in all the studies connected with theological science. It is not only intended for *ministers* and *theological students*, but is also particularly adapted to *parents, Sabbath school teachers, and the great body of the religious public*. The *illustrations*, amounting to *more than three hundred*, are of the very highest order.

A condensed view of the various branches of Biblical Science comprehended in the work.

1. BIBLICAL CRITICISM, — Embracing the History of the Bible Languages; Canon of Scripture; Literary History and Peculiarities of the Sacred Books; Formation and History of Scripture Texts.
2. HISTORY, — Proper Names of Persons; Biographical Sketches of prominent Characters; Detailed Accounts of important Events recorded in Scripture; Chronology and Genealogy of Scripture.
3. GEOGRAPHY, — Names of Places; Description of Scenery; Boundaries and Mutual Relations of the Countries mentioned in Scripture, so far as necessary to illustrate the Sacred Text.
4. ARCHÆOLOGY, — Manners and Customs of the Jews and other nations mentioned in Scripture; their Sacred Institutions, Military Affairs, Political Arrangements, Literary and Scientific Pursuits.
5. PHYSICAL SCIENCE, — Scripture Cosmogony and Astronomy, Zoology, Mineralogy, Botany, Meteorology.

In addition to numerous flattering notices and reviews, personal letters from *more than fifty of the most distinguished Ministers and Laymen of different religious denominations in the country* have been received, highly commending this work as admirably adapted to ministers, Sabbath school teachers, heads of families, and *all* Bible students.

The following extract of a letter is a fair specimen of individual letters received from *each* of the gentlemen whose names are given below: —

"I have examined it with special and unalloyed satisfaction. It has the rare merit of being all that it professes to be, and very few, I am sure, who may consult it will deny that, in richness and fulness of detail, it surpasses their expectation. Many ministers will find it a valuable auxiliary; but its chief excellence is, that it furnishes just the facilities which are needed by the thousands in families and Sabbath schools, who are engaged in the important business of biblical education. It is in itself a library of reliable information."

W. B. Sprague, D. D., Pastor of Second Presbyterian Church, Albany, N. Y.
J. J. Carruthers, D. D., Pastor of Second Parish Congregational Church, Portland, Me.
Joel Hawes, D. D., Pastor of First Congregational Church, Hartford, Ct.
Daniel Sharp, D. D., late Pastor of Third Baptist Church, Boston.
N. L. Frothingham, D. D., late Pastor of First Congregational Church, (Unitarian,) Boston.
Ephraim Peabody, D. D., Pastor of Stone Chapel Congregational Church, (Unitarian,) Boston.
A. L. Stone, Pastor of Park Street Congregational Church, Boston.
John S. Stone, D. D., Rector of Christ Church, (Episcopal,) Brooklyn, N. Y.
J. B. Waterbury, D. D., Pastor of Bowdoin Street Church, (Congregational,) Boston.
Baron Stow, D. D., Pastor of Rowe Street Baptist Church, Boston.
Thomas H. Skinner, D. D., Pastor of Carmine Presbyterian Church, New York.
Samuel W. Worcester, D. D., Pastor of the Tabernacle Church, (Congregational,) Salem.
Horace Bushnell, D. D., Pastor of Third Congregational Church, Hartford, Ct.
Right Reverend J. M. Wainwright, D. D., Trinity Church, (Episcopal,) New York.
Gardner Spring, D. D., Pastor of the Brick Church Chapel Presbyterian Church, New York.
W. T. Dwight, D. D., Pastor of Third Congregational Church, Portland, Me.
E. N. Kirk, Pastor of Mount Vernon Congregational Church, Boston.
Prof. George Bush, author of "Notes on the Scriptures," New York.
Howard Malcom, D. D., author of "Bible Dictionary," and Pres. of Lewisburg University.
Henry J. Ripley, D. D., author of "Notes on the Scriptures," and Prof. in Newton Theol. Ins.
N. Porter, Prof. in Yale College, New Haven, Ct.
Jared Sparks, Edward Everett, Theodore Frelinghuysen, Robert C. Winthrop, John McLean, Simon Greenleaf, Thomas S. Williams, — and a large number of others of like character and standing of the above, whose names cannot here appear.

H

MODERN ATHEISM.

MODERN ATHEISM, under its Forms of Pantheism, Materialism, Secularism, Development, and Natural Laws. By JAMES BUCHANAN, D.D., LL.D. 12mo, cloth, $1.25.

The Author of this work is the successor of Dr. Chalmers in the Chair of Divinity in the New College, Edinburgh, and the intellectual leader of the Scottish Free Church.

FROM HUGH MILLER, AUTHOR OF "OLD RED SANDSTONE," &c., &c. — The work before us is one of at once the most readable and solid which we have ever perused.

FROM THE "NEWS OF THE CHURCHES." — It is a work of which nothing less can be said, than that, both in spirit and substance, style and argument, it fixes irreversibly the name of the author as a leading classic in the Christian literature of Britain.

FROM HOWARD MALCOM, D. D., PRESIDENT OF LEWISBURG UNIVERSITY. — No work has come into my hands, for a long time, so helpful to me as a teacher of metaphysics and morals. I know of nothing which will answer for a substitute. The public specially needs such a book at this time, when the covert atheism of Fichte, Wolfe, Hegel, Kant, Schelling, D'Holbach, Comte, Crousse, Atkinson, Martineau, Leroux, Mackay, Holyoake, and others, is being spread abroad with all earnestness, supported, at least in some places, both by church influence and university honors. I cannot but hope that a work so timely, scholarly, and complete, will do much good.

It is one of the most solid and remarkable books in its department of literature; one of the most scholarly and profound productions of modern Christian literature. — WORCESTER TRANSCRIPT.

Dr. Buchanan has earned a high and well-deserved reputation as a classical writer and close logical reasoner. He deals heavy, deadly blows on atheism in all its various forms; and wherever the work is read it cannot fail to do good. — CHRISTIAN SECRETARY.

It is a work which places its author at once in the highest rank of modern religious authors. His analyses of the doctrines held by the various schools of modern atheism are admirable, and his criticism original and profound; while his arguments in defence of the Christian faith are powerful and convincing. It is an attractive as well as a solid book; and he who peruses a few of its pages is, as it were, irresistibly drawn on to a thorough reading of the book. — BOSTON PORTFOLIO.

The style is very felicitous, and the reasoning clear and cogent. The opposing theories are fairly stated and combated with remarkable ease and skill. Even when the argument falls within the range of science, it is so happily stated that no intelligent reader can fail to understand it. Such a profound, dispassionate work is particularly called for at the present time. — BOSTON JOURNAL.

It is justly described as "a great argument," "magnificent in its strength, order, and beauty," in defence of truth, and against the variant theories of atheism. It reviews the doctrines of the different schools of modern Atheism, gives a fair statement of their theories, answers and refutes them, never evading, but meeting and crushing their arguments. — PHILA. CHRISTIAN OBSERVER.

Dr. Buchanan is candid and impartial, too, as so strong a man can afford to be, evades no argument, undertakes no opposing view, but meets his antagonists with the quiet and unswerving confidence of a locomotive on iron tracks, pretty sure to crush them. — CHRISTIAN REGISTER.

We hail this production of a master mind as a lucid, vigorous, discriminating, and satisfactory refutation of the various false philosophies which have appeared in modern times to allure ingenuous youth to their destruction. Dr. Buchanan has studied them thoroughly, weighed them dispassionately, and exposed their falsity and emptiness. His refutation is a clear stream of light from beginning to end. — PHILA. PRESBYTERIAN.

We recommend "Modern Atheism" as a book for the times, and as having special claims on theological students. — UNIVERSALIST QUARTERLY.

It is remarkable for the clearness with which it apprehends and the fairness with which it states, not less than for the ability with which it replies to, the schemes of unbelief in its various modern forms. It will be found easy to read—though not light reading — and very quickening to thought, while it clears away, one by one, the mists which the Devil has conjured around the great doctrines of our Faith, by the help of some of his ingenious modern coadjutors, and leaves the truth of God standing in its serene and pristine majesty, as if the breath of hatred never had been breathed forth against it. — CONGREGATIONALIST.

Dr. Buchanan has here gone into the enemy's camp, and defeated him on his own ground. The work is a masterly defence of faith against dogmatic unbelief on the one hand, and that universal skepticism on the other, which neither affirms nor denies, on the ground of an assumed deficiency of evidence as to the reality of God and religion. — N. Y. CHRISTIAN CHRONICLE.

It is a clearly and vigorously written book. It is particularly valuable for its clear statement and masterly refutation of the Pantheism of Spinoza and his School. — CHRISTIAN HERALD.

WORKS RECENTLY PUBLISHED AND IN PRESS

THE LIFE AND POSTHUMOUS WORKS OF
THE REV. JOHN HARRIS, D. D.

Late Principal of New College, London, and formerly Theological Tutor of Cheshunt College.

Edited by the Rev. PHILIP SMITH, B. A.,
Formerly a colleague of Dr. Harris in Cheshunt and New Colleges.

This series of the Remains of their late lamented author will contain the

SERMONS AND CHARGES delivered by him in various parts of the country, during the height of his reputation as a preacher.

A TREATISE ON NATURAL AND REVEALED RELIGION, exhibiting, in one view, the latest results of his Theological Studies; and a Fragment, complete in itself, of the work which was interrupted by his death, on

THE DIVINE GOVERNMENT OF NATIONS. Besides other Minor Writings and Fragments.

The works will not extend beyond four elegant royal 12mo volumes. The MEMOIR will be in one volume, uniform with the works. The first volume, consisting of Sermons, has just been published, and the second volume will shortly be issued.

The Sermons of Dr. Harris will probably prove to be among his most popular productions. They are quite unlike other writings of the same class. Many of them are master-pieces of originality and eloquence. Some of them will compare favorably with the most celebrated pieces of pulpit oratory. The pulpit was Dr. Harris's favorite theatre of action, and it is well known that he bestowed immense labor in preparation for it. In consequence, he acquired the highest reputation as a preacher, and his services were in constant request on important occasions. Thus it happened that most of the Sermons here presented were preached twenty times or more. But impressive as they must have been when uttered by the living voice, they are scarcely less so when read from the printed page. They stir the soul like strains of martial music.

THE POOR BOY AND MERCHANT PRINCE; or, ELEMENTS OF SUCCESS DRAWN FROM THE LIFE AND CHARACTER OF THE LATE AMOS LAWRENCE. A Book for Youth. By WILLIAM M. THAYER, author of "The Morning Star," "Life at the Fireside," etc. etc. 16mo, cloth. 75 cents.

The publishers feel that the character of this little work warrants them in styling it ONE OF THE BEST BOOKS FOR BOYS THAT HAS EVER BEEN ISSUED. Its basis is the life and character of AMOS LAWRENCE, and its design is to do for boys what the "DIARY AND CORRESPONDENCE" of Lawrence is fitted to do for men, young and old. Lawrence is the model man to whom the eye of the boy is directed in every chapter, and his sayings and doings, so far as they have a bearing on the subject in hand, are produced and commented upon. But Lawrence is not the only character presented; numerous anecdotes of other distinguished persons are introduced, all going to show that Lawrence, and such men, possessed certain elements of character essential to success, in common. The work is thus rendered extremely entertaining, while it is all the while highly instructive.

HARMONY QUESTIONS ON THE FOUR GOSPELS, for the use of Sabbath Schools. By Rev. S. B. SWAIN, D. D. VOL. I. 18mo. 12½ cts.

This is the first of a new series of Question Books, which will be completed in three volumes. The plan differs from all others in this, that it is based upon a HARMONY of the gospels. Instead of taking one of the gospels, — that of Mathew, for instance, — and going through with it, the author takes from ALL of the gospels those parts relating to the same event, and brings them together in the same Lesson. In this way the pupil gets a view of events in THE ORDER OF TIME, and also a view, at one glance, of all the connected circumstances. The questions are so framed as to avoid two extremes; that of multiplying difficulties on the one hand, and that of making everything easy on the other. But few of the questions can be answered by YES OR NO. A PRACTICAL bearing is given to the subject of every lesson.

THE EPISTLE OF PAUL TO THE ROMANS. With NOTES, chiefly Explanatory. Designed for Teachers in Sabbath Schools and Bible Classes, and as an Aid to Family Instruction. By HENRY J. RIPLEY, Prof. in Newton Theological Inst. 12mo, cloth, 67 cts. *just published.*

PROGRESS OF BAPTIST PRINCIPLES.

A. C. Kendrick, D. D., Prof. Rochester University, N. Y.

It is a book of genuine and solid merit. It is a clear, scholarly, and candid statement of the leading distinctive principles of our denomination, with their grounds and their progress. It is pervaded also by an excellent spirt. The author has done the church a service in preparing the work, and you in publishing it.

Francis Wayland, D. D. Providence, R. I.

If any one desires to see this whole subject treated with great fullness of research, and with singular fairness and ability, I would refer him to Professor Curtis's work on the "Progress of Baptist Principles."

Pharcellus Church, D. D., New York.

I have found it logical in arrangement, lucid in statement, forcible in argumentation, catholic in spirit, and triumphant in its vindication of INDIVIDUALISM, that cardinal idea of Baptists in the formation of civil and ecclesiastical society, the personal and voluntary character of all preparation for Christian ordinances and privileges, and altogether a faithful sketch of the wonderful progress of those principles in modifying Christian life and conviction, and in founding the institutions of Church and State, for the past hundred years. A subject more instructive could not have been selected, none more cardinal to our common Christianity none better fitted to explode false dogmatisms, and pernicious ecclesiasticisms; and it is commendation enough of the book that its treatment of it is equal to the transcendant theme.

Horatio B. Hackett, D. D., Prof. in Newton Theol. Inst.

I regard the work of Prof. Curtis as a well written, well digested, and reliable treatise. I would sooner place it in the hands of any one wishing to understand the principles of the Baptists, or to defend them, than any work that I know of.

Baron Stow, D. D., Boston.

It supplies a want in our Christian literature, and does it in a form and a spirit of which no Baptist can be ashamed. While it embodies a large amount of information, evidently the product of thorough, discriminating research, its style is distinguished for purity, clearness and vigor. It is every way creditable to the author, and to the denomination whose principles he candidly and courteously developes.

Rev. Henry C. Fish, Newark, N. J.

I have greeted no work of recent date with a warmer welcome than that of Professor Curtis. That it fills a place not before filled, and meets a real want in the literature of our country, and especially of our denomination, no one can doubt. Could I reach the ear of every Baptist minister and laymember in the land, I would say, "Buy the PROGRESS OF BAPTIST PRINCIPLES, and read it, and lend it to your neighbor; it will deepen the conviction of the truthfulness and immence importance of the sentiments which you hold; and while it will cherish no unkind or uncharitable feelings towards any other denomination, it will make you more firmly and intelligently attached to your own.

Rev. George W. Samson, Washington, D. C.

This treatise is the completest ever published; and its brevity united with its completeness makes it a book "for the people" in this reading age. It would be diffiult to conceive a more perfect handbook of history and criticism upon those points increasing in interest, not only among Baptists, but among other Christian denominations, than this work.

Prof. Milo P. Jewett, author of "Mode and Subjects of Baptism."

I have read it with great attention and with deep interest. Lucid in arrangement, simple and perspicuous in style, cogent in argument, redolent of heavenly charity in spirit, it contains MULTUM IN PARVO, the quintessence of all that has been said on the Baptismal controversy, from Apostolic times to the present day. It needs only to be known to be obtained by all our ministers, and by many intelligent private members of our churches. Indeed, I know of no book, more suggestive, none more instructive, to the mind of any serious, intelligent Pedobaptist.

Adam Wilson, D. D., Paris, Me.

I know of no other book that contains so many statistics on the subject. The book is written in an excellent spirit, and I do not see why it would not be 'nteresting to all lovers of historical truth, whatever may be their religious sentiments.

M. B. Anderson, D. D., LL.D., Pres. Rochester University.

It is learned, clear and candid, and while it will be indispensable to the library of the intelligent Baptist, it will be found of hardly less value to Christians of other denominations who desire to form clear views of the internal and external organization of the church, and the points at issue between the supporters of different theories on this subject. As a vindication of the character and principles of the Baptists, and a proof of the extent to which they have affected the thinking and acting of the Christian world, it is particularly able, and must continue to have a standard and permanent value.

NEW WORKS

THE TEACHER'S LAST LESSON. A MEMOIR OF MARTHA WHITING, late of the Charlestown Female Seminary, consisting chiefly of Extracts from her Journal, interspersed with Reminisences and Suggestive Reflections. By CATHARINE N. BADGER, an Associate Teacher. With a Portrait, and an Engraving of the Seminary. 12mo. Cloth. $1.00. Second Edition.

THE subject of this Memoir was, for a quarter of a century, at the head of one of the most celebrated Female Seminaries in the country. During that period she educated more than *three thousand* young ladies. She was a kindred spirit to Mary Lyon, the celebrated founder of Mount Holyoke Seminary, with whom, for strength of character, eminent piety, devotion to her calling, and extraordinary success therein, she well deserves to be ranked.

MY MOTHER: or Recollections of Maternal Influence. By a NEW ENGLAND CLERGYMAN. 12mo. Cloth. 75 Cents.

THIS is a new and enlarged edition of a work that was first published in 1849. It passed rapidly through three editions, when the sale was arrested by the embarrassment of the publisher. The author has now revised it, and added another chapter, so that it comes before the public with the essential claims of a new work. . . .
It is the picture of a quiet New England family, so drawn and colored as to subserve the ends of *domestic education*. The central figure is the author's mother, around whom are grouped the various members of the family. Biographical sketches and lessons of practical wisdom are so intermingled, that while the former relieve the latter, these in turn give force and significance to the sketches. . . . . . . The author has already distinguished himself in various walks of literature, but from motives of delicacy towards the still surviving characters of the book, he chooses for the present to conceal his name. . . . . . A writer of wide celebrity says of the book, in a note to the publisher — "It is one of those rare pictures, painted from life, with the exquisite skill of one of the *old masters*, which so seldom present themselves to the amateur."

THE IMITATION OF CHRIST. By THOMAS A'KEMPIS. With an Introductory Essay, by Dr. CHALMERS. Edited by HOWARD MALCOLM, D. D. A NEW EDITION, with a LIFE OF THOMAS A'KEMPIS. By Dr. C. ULLMAN, author of "Reformers before the Reformation." 12mo, cloth. 85 cents.

⁂ This work has, for three hundred years, been esteemed one of the best practical books in existence, and has gone through a vast number of editions, not only in the original Latin, but in every language of Europe.

This may safely be pronounced the best Protestant edition extant. It is reprinted from Payne's edition, collated with an ancient Latin copy. The peculiar feature of this *new edition* is the improved page, the elegant, large, clear type, and the NEW LIFE of A'KEMPIS, by Ullmann. Born nearly five hundred years ago, Thomas A'Kempis is almost unknown. While the Memoir prefixed to former American editions, and purporting to give all the facts, is contained in a few paragraphs, this life extends to more than fifty pages.

Dr. Payson, in conversing with a young minister, once said, "If you have not seen '*Thomas A'Kempis*,' I beg you to procure it. For spirituality and weanedness from the world, *I know of nothing equal to it*."

EXCLUSIVENESS OF THE BAPTISTS. A Review of the Rev. ALBERT BARNES' Pamphlet on "Exclusivism." By HENRY J. RIPLEY, Newton Theological Institution. 12mo, printed cover, 13 cents.

A thorough, candid, yet searching Review of Dr. Barnes' unfounded charges against the Baptists. It contains much important information on controverted subjects between Baptists and Pedo-Baptists, especially that usually termed "Close Communion." No better work can be placed in the hands of any one desiring light on this subject. The manner of treatment, the size, and the price, all render it admirably adapted to general circulation.

www.ingramcontent.com/pod-product-compliance
Lightning Source LLC
LaVergne TN
LVHW020126110826
845151LV00001B/290

* 9 7 8 1 4 2 5 5 4 1 3 2 3 *